Unlocking the Employment Potential in the Middle East and North Africa

Unlocking the Employment Potential in the Middle East and North Africa

Toward a New Social Contract

THE WORLD BANK
Washington, D.C.

1 2 3 4 07 06 05 04

ISBN 0-8213-5678-X

Cover photo: © Royalty-Free/CORBIS

Library of Congress Cataloging-in-Publication Data

Unlocking the employment potential in the Middle East and North Africa : toward a new
  social contract.
      p. cm. — (Orientations in development series)
  Includes bibliographical references.
  ISBN 0-8213-5678-X
    1. Labor market—Middle East. 2. Labor market—Africa, North. 3. Employment—
Middle East. 4. Employment—Africa, North. I. World Bank. II. Orientations in
 development

HD5811.9.A6U55 2004
331.12'042'0956—dc22

                                        2004040700

Contents

Figures

Tables

Foreword

This book is about the future prosperity of the Middle East and North Africa (MENA). Together with the other companion volumes—on trade and investment, governance, and gender—prepared on the occasion of the Annual Meetings of the World Bank and the International Monetary Fund in Dubai, the book is a contribution by the World Bank to ongoing debates and dialogues about development in the region. These books address the core development challenges facing MENA in the early 21st century that would allow it to unlock its rich potential for prosperity.

The Bank's role in this region is not only, or even mostly, about lending. We are fundamentally about ideas, bringing together the best knowledge, expertise, and experience and putting them at the service of the world. Like the companion volumes, this book synthesizes existing as well as new knowledge and research. It establishes priorities and directions for a comprehensive and structured policy reform agenda that are cognizant of the specific economic and social circumstances of our clients, in this case the governments and peoples of MENA.

Few challenges confronting the economies and societies of the MENA region are as pressing as those emanating from their labor markets. Almost every country in the region suffers from high unemployment, which mostly affects the young, the educated, and women. This book describes the origins of MENA's poor labor market trends in the 1990s as the outcome of the long-term processes through which the region's political economies became organized around a redistributive–interventionist social contract.

Although MENA's labor market dysfunctions share structural features with other regions of the world, its labor market dynamics are nonetheless unique in the extent to which deeply embedded rigidities coexist with a rapidly expanding labor force—indeed, the fastest-growing labor force of any region in the world. This combination poses especially daunting challenges and places a singular burden on MENA governments to respond. Thus far, however, regional responses have been inadequate.

Drawing on the companion volumes in this series, this book points to key areas in which MENA governments will need to focus their attention in the immediate future. These areas include removing barriers to private sector activity, integrating local economies into global markets, and enhancing the management of natural resources. Although none of these specific recommendations are entirely new, the book integrates them into a comprehensive framework that rests on a foundation of better governance.

Current conditions, the book argues, require a shift from top-down, selective strategies of reform to ones that are comprehensive, inclusive, and accountable. A vision of progress in the future demands a more tightly coupled relationship between economic reform and political reform. These interdependencies must be addressed if MENA is to make meaningful progress toward a social contract that protects workers, promotes employment, and creates the conditions for sustained economic growth and broadly shared improvements in standards of living.

Over the past decade, MENA governments have helped to lay the foundations for reform. Now they must build on these foundations and make comprehensive reform strategies a reality. We at the Bank stand ready to assist the governments and citizens of MENA in their quest for a more prosperous future. This report is a modest contribution toward the goal.

JEAN-LOUIS SARBIB
VICE PRESIDENT
MIDDLE EAST AND NORTH AFRICA REGION
THE WORLD BANK

Acknowledgments

The MENA Development Reports are coordinated by the Office of the Chief Economist for the Middle East and North Africa Region of the World Bank, which is led by Mustapha Kamel Nabli, who has provided overall guidance and supervision.

The main author of this volume is Tarik Yousef. The core team of authors includes Pedro Alba, Ragui Assaad, Paul Dyer, Steven Heydemann, and Jennifer Keller. Other contributors include Fatma El-Hamidi, Michael Robbins, Elizabeth Ruppert Bulmer, Mona Said, and Jackline Wahba. The production team consists of Isabelle Chaal, Paul Dyer, Manuel Felix, Krisztina Mazo, and Michael Robbins.

Background papers were provided by As'ad AbuKhalil, Richard Adams, Pierre-Richard Agénor, Nabila Assaf, Joel Beinin, Najy Benhassine, Adama Coulibaly, Raj Desai, Maurice Girgis, Faris Hadad-Zervos, Sara Johansson, Anders Olofsgård, Carlos Silva-Jauregui, Thirumalai Srinivasan, Dirk Vandewalle, and Marie-Ange Véganzonès.

This volume was reviewed externally by Yousef Al-Ebraheem, Philippe Fargues, Samir Radwan, and Mohamed Redjeb and internally by Ibrahim Elbadawi, Aart Kraay, and William Maloney. It is also based on inputs and comments from Petros Aklilu, Hamid Alavi, Zoubida Allaoua, Mohamed Al-Magarief, Claus Astrup, Ahmet Aysan, Don Babai, Hazem Beblawi, Mehdi Benyagoub, Sue Berryman, Gordon Betcherman, Nadereh Chamlou, Dipak Dasgupta, Guilio de Tommaso, Sebastien Dessus, Karim El-Aynaoui, Sherine El-Shawarby, Habib Fetini, Emmanuel Forestier, Clement Henry, Charles Humphreys, Farrukh Iqbal, Omer Karasapan, Jennie Litvack, Karim M'chich, Nadir Mohammed, Paul Moreno Lopez, Jennifer Olmsted, Gaobo Pang, Marsha Posusney, Gudivada Rao, Setareh Razmara, Susan Razzaz, Alan Richards, Stefano Scarpetta, Masakazu Someya, David Steel, Denis Sullivan, Hasan Tuluy, Insan Tunali, Aristomene Varoudakis, Paolo Zacchia, and Leila Zlaoui.

The background papers and main themes of this volume were discussed at sessions of the Economic Research Forum (ERF) meetings in Sharjah in 2002, the Arab Monetary Fund–Arab Fund for Economic and Social Development seminar on Labor Markets and Unemployment in the Arab Countries in Abu Dhabi in 2002, and the American Economic Association meetings in Washington, D.C., in 2003. The team is grateful for the many comments and suggestions provided by the participants at these meetings.

The book was edited by Bruce Ross-Larson and Communications Development International and by Publications Professionals LLC. The World Bank's Office of the Publisher managed editorial and print production, including book design.

The team would like to thank all of those who contributed and participated in the various stages of production of this book, including those whose names may have been inadvertently omitted.

Acronyms and Abbreviations

CD	Cobb-Douglass
CDD	Contrats à durée déterminée
CES	Constant elasticity of substitution
EU	European Union
FDI	Foreign direct investment
GATT	General Agreement on Tariffs and Trade
GCC	Gulf Cooperation Council
GDP	Gross domestic product
GNI	Gross national income
ICT	Information and communication technology
MENA	Middle East and North Africa
NGO	Nongovernmental organization
OECD	Organisation for Economic Co-operation and Development
SOE	State-owned enterprise
TFP	Total factor productivity
TIMSS	Trends in International Mathematics and Science Study
UAE	United Arab Emirates
UGTT	Union Générale Tunisienne du Travail
UNIDO	United Nations Industrial Development Organization
WTO	World Trade Organization

Creating 100 Million Jobs for a Fast-Growing Work Force

Over the next two decades, the Middle East and North Africa (MENA) region faces an unprecedented challenge. In 2000, the labor forces of the region totaled some 104 million workers, a figure expected to reach 146 million by 2010 and 185 million by 2020. Given this expansion, the economies of the region will need to create some 80 million new jobs in the next two decades. With unemployment now at about 15 percent, the more ambitious goal of absorbing unemployed workers in addition to the new entrants implies the need to create close to 100 million jobs by 2020, a doubling of the current level of employment in the first two decades of the 21st century.

In no small measure, MENA's economic future will be determined by the fate of its labor markets. The problems to be overcome are enormous; their complexity is daunting. Yet the costs of inaction and the benefits of dynamic labor markets underscore the imperative of acting quickly and decisively. If current trends continue, economic performance and the well-being of workers will be undermined by rising unemployment and low productivity. If labor market outcomes improve, however, MENA's growth will accelerate, raising the living standards of the population across the region.

This report argues that meeting this employment challenge will require the transformation of MENA's societies and economic structures. MENA needs a new development model that is based on a reinvigorated private sector, greater integration into the world economy, and better management of oil resources. These drivers of future growth and job creation require a foundation of better governance. Moreover, this transformation necessitates a new social contract.

Evolution of MENA's Social Contract

The social contracts established in the postindependence era have given rise to enduring institutions, interests, norms, and practices—structuring the constraints and incentives governments now face as they contend with demands for and against policy reform. The contracts have defined state–labor relations across the region and have established expectations and obligations that have proved deeply resilient. They remain a powerful presence in debates about social and economic policy reform, even as their effect on employment, wages, working conditions, foreign investment, trade, and overall macroeconomic performance has become deleterious. Understanding what the social contract in MENA embodies—its origins, its developmental consequences, its effects on labor markets—is crucial to any assessment of labor market prospects and possibilities.

From the 1940s to the 1970s, the MENA social contract acquired distinctive features, institutional arrangements, public policies, legitimating discourses, and modes of state–society relations, with several core attributes:

- A preference for redistribution and equity in economic and social policy

- A preference for states over markets in managing national economies

- The adoption of import-substitution industrialization and the protection of local markets from global competition

- A reliance on state planning in determining economic priorities

- An encompassing vision of the role of the state in the provision of welfare and social services

- A vision of the political arena as an expression of the organic unity of the nation, rather than as a site of political contest or the aggregation of conflicting preferences.

Social Contract Delivers Early Dividends

Despite the turmoil that accompanied the emergence and consolidation of social contracts in MENA countries, subsequent decades were marked by unprecedented levels of economic growth and social development. Between 1965 and 1985, MENA's economic growth rates were among the highest in the world, averaging 3.7 percent per capita a year. The social contract also meant low levels of poverty and income inequality. The social payoffs from these policies have been enormous, with dramatic reductions in mortality and increases in life expectancy, school enrollment rates, and literacy levels.

These results had important political consequences. They reinforced redistributive mechanisms that sustained the well-being of large segments of MENA populations, deepening the popularity of these mechanisms among social groups that governments identified as core constituencies. From the 1960s through the 1980s, these social groups emerged as prominent winners in the political economies created by the interventionist–redistributive social contract. The welfare gains also helped to cement an "authoritarian bargain," with citizens trading restrictions on political participation in exchange for economic security and the public provision of social services, welfare, and other benefits.

Social Contract Is under Strain: 1980s and 1990s

But over time, gaps widened between (a) the embedded set of institutional arrangements and expectations and (b) the diminished capacity of governments to sustain redistributive commitments. By the early 1980s, the inability of the MENA social contract to sustain the economic gains of previous decades became clear—and by the late 1980s, the strains had grown into a major economic crisis. The triggers of the crisis were declining oil prices, shrinking demand for migrant labor, and reduced remittance flows.

In response to the growing economic difficulties, most governments in MENA adopted some form of economic stabilization program. Policy shifts were marked by caution and gradualism, but across the region, governments cut subsidies, reduced public expenditure, and reformed exchange rate regimes. By the early 1990s, these reforms began to have beneficial effects. Debt levels declined, inflation was brought under control, and macroeconomic performance was on average positive.

MENA governments also began a gradual and selective transition from economic stabilization to structural adjustment—a move strongly supported by international financial institutions. Reforms included many that are now familiar markers of economic restructuring: privatization of state-owned enterprises (SOEs), fiscal reform and trade liberalization, deregulation, and strengthening the institutional foundations for a market-led economy.

However, implementation of these reform measures has been uneven, hesitant, and incomplete. Partly as a result, MENA's economic recovery in the 1990s was generally weak. In the past 15 years, gross domestic product (GDP) per capita growth has averaged 1.0 percent a year, labor productivity has remained low, and unemployment rates have increased.

Emergence of Poor Labor Market Outcomes

Although the rate of population growth has declined, the pressure of population flows in MENA remains high. Between 1990 and 2000, with annual growth rates averaging 2.2 percent, MENA's population increased by 6.1 million people a year compared with 4.6 million in the 1970s and 6.7 million in the 1980s. In the current decade, with population growing at an even slower rate of 2.0 percent, the region is still adding more than 6 million people every year. It is safe to assume, however, that the era of high population growth is over. Evidence increasingly suggests that MENA is on a trajectory of declining population growth rates for the foreseeable future.

Demographic Burden Becomes a Demographic Gift

The maturing of MENA's age structure has placed the region in a unique position at the beginning of the 21st century. Between 1990 and 2020, the growth of the economically active population (ages 15–64) will exceed that of the economically dependent population by a much greater amount than in any other region. As East Asia's experience has shown, this differential—the so-called demographic gift—provides MENA with an opportunity to accelerate economic growth through faster accumulation of factors of production.

Lower dependency ratios imply a potential for higher savings and investment. Rapid labor force growth, especially with increased education and longer life expectancy, provides economies with a larger pool of productive workers. As a result, policymakers in MENA are facing new challenges. These demographic changes are shifting the policy focus from providing health and education for a young population to facilitating employment and output growth.

Labor Market Pressures Have Accelerated Since the 1980s

While creating the potential for employment and growth, the dynamics of demography in MENA have created some of the most intense pressures on labor markets observed anywhere in the world in the post–World War II period. High population growth rates between the 1950s and the 1980s have led to the rapid expansion of the working-age population. With rising labor force participation rates since 1980, the labor supply has grown and the absolute number of new labor market entrants has increased over time.

The pressure of young workers on labor force growth has been persistently high in MENA. The period 1990–2010 will witness the greatest labor force pressures from young male and female workers. Rising female labor participation since the 1980s, in particular, constitutes one of the most important developments affecting the size and gender composition of the region's labor supply. Not only are young men and women entering labor markets in greater numbers, but also they are increasingly more educated, a consequence of the considerable resources devoted by governments to human capital accumulation.

Unemployment Rose and Real Wages Were Stagnant in the 1990s

The growing supplies of workers constitute one of the fundamental forces driving labor market outcomes in MENA. But since employment outcomes are determined by the interaction of supply and demand, no complete account of labor markets can be made without an assessment of labor demand, as determined by economic conditions and policies internal and external to the region. From this perspective, the strong economic performance of MENA before the mid-1980s and its weaker performance in the subsequent period have been fully reflected in labor market outcomes.

By definition, if labor supply exceeds the level of employment, the unemployment rate rises. Over the past decade, the growth in the labor force has exceeded employment growth in most countries in the region. As a result, unemployment in MENA is among the highest in the world. A conservative estimate puts unemployment at about 15 percent of the work force. The problem affects almost every country in the region. Recently, even the oil-exporting countries that traditionally imported expatriate labor to supplement the national work force have witnessed rising rates of unemployment.

Unemployment in MENA is concentrated among youths, whose unemployment rates range from 37 percent of total unemployment in Morocco to 73 percent of total unemployment in Syria, with a simple average of 53 percent for all countries for which data are available. There is a gender dimension to the profile of unemployment as well. Unemployment rates for the region as a whole are nearly 50 percent higher for women than for men.

MENA's weak labor market outcomes in the 1990s have characterized not only unemployment but also real wages. Real wages have increased marginally in some countries, but they have either stagnated or declined in most, thus extending a trend that began in the 1980s. Worker productivity, which is the basis for real wages, increased in the 1990s by less in MENA than in any other region except Europe and Central Asia, which had been undergoing significant economic restructuring.

Unemployment and Output Trends Are Linked

Lower labor demand accounts for the slow pace of job creation in the 1990s, hence contributing to high unemployment. The most important indicator of trends in labor demand is output growth. Strong output growth both reflects and leads to employment growth and lower unemployment, because the work force is an essential factor of production that contributes directly to the expansion of output.

In MENA, as elsewhere, faster output growth has generally gone hand in hand with lower unemployment, whereas slower growth has invariably implied higher levels of unemployment. Thus, the story of MENA in the 1990s is of weak output performance in the face of rapid labor force growth, with the result that output per laborer barely improved—if at all.

Despite stabilization efforts, the declines in capital accumulation that marked the 1980s continued into the 1990s, with nearly every country in MENA realizing lower rates of physical capital accumulation than it did in the previous decade. The lack of a strong response from the private sector stemmed primarily from the slow and protracted pace of policy reforms. Although the early macroeconomic and structural reforms improved economic outlooks, most countries failed to follow through on reforms.

Government Continues to Dominate Labor Markets

At the microeconomic level, poor labor market outcomes are driven largely by reduced demand from the public sector and by slow growth of the private sector. Unemployment rates are highest for young new entrants into the labor market who have intermediate and higher education. Thus, the unemployed are essentially those who would have had a chance at a formal job in government after years of guaranteed public sector employment. Unemployment rates are low for those who have no formal education and who are not eligible for employment in the public sector.

The structure of unemployment also suggests that a significant part of unemployment results from high job expectations by workers with some formal education, as well as from a low valuation of these credentials by the private sector, because education systems have concentrated on making public sector jobs accessible rather than on building skills. Although government hiring has been curtailed in recent years, the structure of the labor market remains segmented. Educated new entrants continue to queue for government jobs, despite falling civil service wages, because of such nonwage benefits as allowances and job security.

Although real wage levels appear to be flexible, moving downward in times of slow growth, the dominant role of government as employer introduces rigidities in the wage structure that distort labor market incentives. Higher returns to formal education in the public sector encourage the accumulation of such credentials even if they do not add to worker productivity and are undervalued by the private sector. The resulting concentration of educated workers in unproductive public sector employment goes a long way toward explaining the low contribution of human capital to economic growth in the region.

MENA has fared well relative to other regions in income inequality and poverty levels, thanks in large measure to the redistribution of oil rents through labor remittances or increased government employment. Although fairly effective in reducing poverty, government employment is an inefficient safety net, because most of the benefits go to educated workers who are underrepresented among the poor. Moreover, the costs of excessive government employment are reduced economic and total factor productivity growth, which can limit poverty reduction over the long run.

Unlocking the Potential for Job Creation

The challenge of job creation requires a comprehensive approach to reform, although the priorities and sequencing of policy reforms will vary across countries by specific initial conditions, including resource endowments, reform progress to date, and quality of institutions. The need for a comprehensive approach does not diminish the value of incrementalism in advancing reform agendas. Nor does it underestimate the importance of sequencing reforms in ways that maximize prospects for success.

It does, however, shape the view of what is needed to restore economic opportunity and to secure the well-being of MENA's populations. MENA requires a broad-based transformation of its economies to strengthen the core drivers of economic growth and to create viable prospects for job creation to absorb the tens of millions of men and women entering the work force over the coming two decades.

Scope and Limitations of Labor Market Intervention

Reforming the institutional and regulatory framework is integral to better functioning labor markets. Policy proposals that aim to alleviate current pressures and to generate better outcomes must address structural rigidities, including the state's role as both employer and labor market regulator. To be effective and sustainable in the long run, the realignment of incentives toward work in the private sector should rely on both push and pull factors. The menu of policies ranges from natural attrition and hiring freezes, to accelerated attrition through substantial wage adjustments or benefit cuts, to explicit retrenchment through layoffs.

More flexible hiring and dismissal procedures are the most relevant policy issues in the reform of labor regulations affecting the private sector in MENA. These regulations limit job creation and reduce flexibility in the work force. As a result, workers endure long unemployment spells, which lead to skill degradation and lack of work experience. Unemployment of women and youths also rises, which may limit the opportunities of disadvantaged groups to emerge from poverty. With few job opportunities in the formal economy, workers are pushed into the informal sector, where social protection is lacking.

Empirical simulations indicate that direct policy interventions would lead to positive labor and macroeconomic effects, in most cases contributing to higher employment, private investment, and output growth in the long run. Reflecting complementarities between policies, the simulations suggest that a comprehensive rather than a piecemeal approach delivers the biggest effect. However, the employment and growth payoffs associated with even the most comprehensive package of interventions are modest considering the magnitude of job creation needed in MENA.

Thus, labor market reforms are a necessary component of policy reforms, but they are not sufficient for addressing the scope of the employment challenge facing the region now and over the next two decades. Although certain priorities for reform are common to all countries in the region, such as reducing the role of the public sector in labor markets, the importance and likely effect of other reforms will vary across countries. Economic and political conditions and a careful understanding of labor market issues in each country must determine the priority areas of reform.

Limitations of Active Labor Market Policies

Active labor market policies are another type of intervention used widely in both developing and industrial countries. From wage and employment subsidies, to training and retraining for the unemployed, to direct job-creation programs and job-search and assistance services, these policies are designed to create employment opportunities and to manage labor market risks. In MENA, as in other regions that lack functioning national unemployment insurance systems, active labor market programs constitute a relevant instrument for tackling labor market dislocations.

Despite the political appeal and contribution to poverty alleviation of active labor market policies, evidence from industrial and developing countries suggests that such policies do little to remedy structural problems in labor markets or to reduce high unemployment. Even with spending on these programs in MENA already high and projected to grow, only a small share of the labor force is likely to be covered by these programs. Furthermore, to be effective, active labor market policies need to be carefully targeted and monitored. If inappropriately designed, such programs may have high fiscal costs and negative economic effects.

Traditional Engines of Job Creation

Government may continue to be a source of employment for a minority of new job seekers. But it is highly unlikely and even undesirable for the public sector to remain a leading sector of job creation in the future. Fiscal constraints and low worker productivity imply that any expansion in public sector employment will come at an increasing fiscal cost and may not be sufficient to absorb the unemployed and new graduates queuing for government employment. Barring an acceleration of employment growth in the formal private sector, the rising numbers of new entrants would be pushed into the informal economy.

The prospects for labor migration are equally limited in the near future. Although intraregional migration provided an important outlet for workers in the labor-exporting countries during the oil boom in the 1970s and 1980s, the past decade has seen a rapid deceleration in the net inflows of MENA workers in the receiving countries. Today's unemployment and the projected rapid expansion of the national labor force in the receiving countries in the Gulf Cooperation Council provide further incentives to reduce the inflows of migrant workers in general. Meanwhile, migration to Europe is constrained by policy and would provide only a partial solution to the employment challenge.

MENA's Need for New Development Policies

This volume and the accompanying volumes on trade and investment and on governance argue that, for MENA countries to accelerate job creation and growth, they must address a set of long-standing policy and institutional challenges to complete three fundamental and interrelated realignments in their economies:

1. *From public sector dominated to private sector dominated,* by reducing the barriers to private activity while creating regulatory frameworks to ensure that private and social interests are mutually reinforcing

2. *From closed to more open,* by facilitating the integration into global goods, services, and factor markets while putting in place safeguards for financial stability and social protection

3. *From oil dominated and volatile to more stable and diversified,* by making fundamental changes in institutions managing oil resources and their intermediation to economic agents.

The growth and employment effects of such an integrated package of policy realignments are potentially very large. On the basis of the experience of comparable countries, the companion trade study estimates that output per worker could increase by some 2 to 3 percent a year. The companion governance study, using similar international evidence, estimates that a commitment to improving the institutions of accountability in public administration could raise output growth per capita by between 0.8 percent and 1.3 percent a year. Together, these studies suggest that output-per-worker growth could be raised by at least 3.5 percentage points.

The positive implications of such performance for future job creation are profound. For instance, bridging only half the gap between the current 6 percent share of nonoil merchandise exports in total exports and its potential of 20 percent, with the associated increases in domestic and foreign private investment, would cut the unemployment rate in the region by 4 percentage points. The broader reform agenda would bring even larger benefits.

Transition 1: Reinvigorating the Private Sector

Since the late 1980s, most MENA countries have tried, with varying intensity and success, to expand private sector activity. At the same time, the importance of the public sector has declined, as seen in steps taken to privatize and to reduce subsidies to SOEs. But governments still represent a large share of value added in MENA. As a result, the contribution of the private sector to value added increased only marginally in the 1990s. The same pattern has characterized the share of the private sector in total investment, which did not increase enough to compensate for the decline in public investment.

These disappointing trends reflect not only macroeconomic policy outcomes but also weaknesses in the business environment that discourage entrepreneurship and firm creation. New firms face significant barriers to entry, in terms of both the time and cost of administrative approvals. New firms also face significant difficulties securing start-up and operating capital with public banks. Regulations do not facilitate the restructuring of businesses that are still viable, whereas nonviable firms are not permitted to close operations expeditiously, thereby raising the social and economic costs of bankruptcy.

In addition, MENA compares poorly with other regions in the complexity of filing a legal claim and in the time needed to initiate and to complete such a claim. Even where the legal processes are defined, the unpredictability of enforcement creates problems for entrepreneurs. Businesses also suffer from weaknesses in the financial system and in the administration of licensing, regulations, taxes, and import duties. Furthermore, weaknesses in infrastructure, such as telecommunications and transport, greatly impede business activity and investment.

Transition 2: Integrating with the World Economy

MENA remains one of the least-integrated regions, having failed to take advantage of the expansion in world trade and foreign direct investment (FDI) in the past two decades. Since the mid-1980s, global trade has expanded more than output has, to the advantage of middle-income countries. In MENA, despite large hydrocarbon exports, trade declined from about 100 percent of GDP in the mid-1970s to 60 percent in the mid-1980s and has stagnated since. These negative trends were accompanied by high and increasing product concentration, loss of export dynamism in nonfuel exports, and little participation in global production sharing.

Integration with global private capital flows has also been sluggish, in sharp contrast to the experience of comparable country groupings. Excluding the Persian Gulf countries, MENA received about US$2.2 billion in net inflows of FDI in 2000, or slightly more than 1 percent of the US$158 billion that flowed to developing countries worldwide. These inflows averaged less than half a percentage point of GDP for most of 1985–2000. The Arab Republic of Egypt accounted for half the MENA total (US$1.2 billion), and Jordan (US$750 million) and Tunisia (US$560 million) for about a quarter each.

MENA's weak integration with world markets reflects unfavorable incentives, compounded by large behind-the-border constraints. Exchange rates in the region have been persistently overvalued, by as much as 22 percent on average during 1985–2000. Trade regimes in MENA are among the most protective in the world. Transport, logistics, and communications costs are high across most of the region, thus adding a third layer. Those transaction costs, combined with the weaknesses in the business climate and constraints on the participation of foreign capital, have discouraged FDI.

Transition 3: Managing Oil Resources Better

Many MENA countries need to undergo a final transition to become more stable and diversified economies. This transition requires better management of oil resources and a broadening of the productive base of economic activities. Such improvements imply setting up institutions and fiscal rules that insulate public expenditures from oil price volatility and that save oil revenues so they can continue to benefit citizens when oil resources decline. These changes also mean improving the efficiency of public expenditures through better systems of budgeting that emphasize performance and accountability.

Diversifying productive activities is a growing priority, not only for countries whose known oil reserves will soon be depleted, but also for all other oil producers. Per capita exports of hydrocarbon products have been declining across the region, with falling real prices, rising domestic demand for energy, and rapid population growth. Governments will need to develop new sources of revenue to ensure the efficiency of public expenditures.

Central Role of Better Governance to the Transition

The government's role in the economy needs to be redefined. If states no longer serve as employers of first resort, they can be more engaged as partners in creating and sustaining opportunities for employment. A vigorous state role in improving social services—especially health, education, and social security—is essential to establishing the conditions that will permit workers to thrive and economies to grow at competitive rates. State support will be needed to transform existing institutions of labor representation into a true system of collective bargaining. New state capacities are required for the effective administration of social programs aimed at overcoming dysfunctions in labor markets and at protecting workers during economic transition.

Efforts to reform MENA's economies hinge on the credibility of government and on the capacity of state institutions to manage a complex, long-term process of change. MENA governments are handicapped by the limits of institutional structures organized to support redistributive and interventionist policies and by the difficulties such institutions confront in adapting to new tasks, new policy demands, and new regulatory environments. Governments need the institutional and regulatory instruments to manage the difficult process of economic transition under conditions of economic volatility and social vulnerability.

Accordingly, governance reforms are essential to permit MENA governments to credibly articulate and realize a new vision of state–society relations. The tasks associated with this aim demand a degree of government initiative, creativity, and competence that must be cultivated aggressively throughout the region. To move forward, governments themselves must link economic performance to the quality of governance. They must create rule-of-law mechanisms to ensure their own accountability and transparency—including in budgeting and fiscal policy—to enable citizens to scrutinize government performance and to hold officials accountable for their actions.

MENA's Need for a New Social Contract

Reform of the MENA social contract is crucial for the future of the region's labor markets. The redistributive–interventionist social contract jeopardizes the well-being of workers. It shifts economic activity to the informal sector and leaves too many workers unprotected. It constrains investment and growth, thereby undermining the capacity of governments to deliver on their commitments to economic and social justice. Under conditions of high unemployment, resistance to reform deepens among those whom the social contract protects.

MENA's social contract offers a minority of workers security of employment, but at the expense of declining wages and standards of living. The social contract is important in preserving programs that benefit the working poor, but safety nets are stretched beyond their capacity. Declining state revenues and the worst projected employment gap in the world render the existing social contract unsustainable.

The rigid, exclusionary, and inefficient aspects of the social contract need to be restructured. Yet reforms will not be credible unless they take into account the social needs of workers and unless they ensure that economic outcomes are socially acceptable among MENA's citizens. Doing so requires a renewed political commitment to widely valued social policies—a new social contract that links reform to the principles of poverty reduction, income equality, and income security that have guided MENA's political economies for almost 50 years.

A new social contract will have long-term benefits for MENA. It will balance the need for labor market flexibility with the rights of workers, helping to avoid social dislocation and conflicts by offering a positive role to labor in the transition to and in the coordination of more flexible systems of production. Furthermore, it will create mechanisms for supporting workers as they respond to changes in the structure of employment associated with privatization and with the shift to more open economies with different skill requirements and greater dependence on new information technologies.

Securing those gains demands a clear vision of how tomorrow's labor markets should be organized. The desired outcome is not an unregulated labor market that exposes workers to harsh working conditions, employment volatility, and income insecurity. Nor is it a labor market in which growth is achieved through a race to the bottom, accompanied by declining living standards for workers and by worsening income inequality. New development policies are needed that support a race to the top and that ensure that workers participate in the benefits of economic growth.

The challenge of restructuring the social contract in MENA does not arise from a lack of information about what needs to be done. Pathways to reform are much better mapped today than they were only two decades ago, including the need to tailor reforms to country-specific conditions and to link them to socially desirable outcomes. Past decades have produced extensive knowledge about what works in development strategies and policy reform, as well as what does not work.

Understanding the Obstacles to Reform Is Critical

Why, despite economic stagnation, the exhaustion of selective reform strategies, and a worsening employment crisis, have MENA governments been reluctant to change course? This reluctance is often explained as the rational response of incumbent leaders to circumstances in which the costs of reform are immediate, while its benefits are both delayed and, to some extent, uncertain.

Yet aversion to political risk is at best a partial explanation for the trajectory of economic reform in MENA. Certainly, periods of economic transition entail adjustment costs that are not evenly distributed across social groups. Also, powerful social actors have a vested interest in sustaining the status quo.

Political caution and attention to the effects of reform on workers and the poor are warranted. But there are also political, economic, and social costs associated with maintaining a nonviable status quo. In MENA, those costs are becoming more severe, thus confirming the belief that slow and selective reform lacks credibility and exacerbates social polarization.

Inadequate responses to sustained economic stagnation have become a serious drain on the political resources of MENA governments, and those who benefit from the status quo find their positions increasingly insecure. The erosion of living standards for segments of the population intensifies popular disaffection, even as new communications technologies make citizens more aware of the gaps between their economic conditions and those in other parts of the world.

Soft Budget Constraints and Political Challengers Have Impeded Reform

Soft budget constraints shaped the structure and limits of reform processes in MENA during the 1980s and 1990s. Revenues generated outside the domestic economy and flowing directly to the state through foreign aid, oil exports, and strategic rents cushioned the impact of economic stagnation and permitted governments to adopt limited reforms, while postponing difficult decisions about structural adjustment and reorganization of the social contract.

Another factor that impeded the reform process was the challenge of radical movements. Economic and political reforms became loosely coupled—or were decoupled entirely—as governments responded to the appeal of opposition movements and, in some cases, to the violence of extremist groups by reviving strategies of political control and reinvigorating the national security concerns that impeded the reform of governance in MENA.

As a result, top-down management of reform by decree replaced earlier efforts to generate support for economic reform by opening the political arena. Engagement with reform remained selective and limited. Efforts to advance structural adjustment programs coincided with the erosion of political inclusiveness and accountability.

The combination of reform by decree and the compression of political space constrained the development of precisely the forms of state capacity that are needed to sustain the long-term transition toward market-oriented political economies in MENA. Not least, possibilities for establishing a consensus around a renewed social contract became more remote.

Economic and Political Reform Must Be Linked

These strategies have run their course. They have weakened the capacity of governments to address severe employment imbalances, to resolve labor market dysfunctions, and to advance a new vision of the MENA social contract as the basis for more productive relations among the state, labor, and the private sector. Under these conditions, the reluctance to implement economic reforms is at odds with the strong preference of MENA governments for political and social stability.

To move the reform process beyond its current limits, governments will need to revive national conversations about reforming the labor market, restructuring redistributive programs, and redefining the terms of the social contract. With the existence of large middle classes in MENA societies, the revival of political life—once again a prerequisite for economic growth—is certainly possible. At the same time, a selective, top-down approach to economic reform that sidesteps the need for political change to secure the legitimacy of reform and the credibility of government commitments is no longer adequate.

Support from External Partners Is Critical

As the region steps up to unlock the promise of a better future, external partners, as vigorous proponents of reform, have an important role to play in supporting MENA's transition. Although Europe is MENA's most important trade partner, other partners also need to support faster and deeper integration of MENA into the world economy by facilitating the accession of more MENA countries to the World Trade Organization (WTO), by encouraging more intraregional trade and investment, and by lifting economic sanctions. A more liberal policy toward agricultural exports and labor migration from MENA would reinforce the foundations of a strong Euro–Mediterranean partnership.

Although external financial and economic support would be welcome, MENA's prosperity depends heavily on establishing regional security and stability. There is strong evidence that violence and conflict have severely impeded the pace of reform and of trade and investment integration, at times rivaling the detrimental influence of poor domestic policies. Persistent conflict has also had large neighborhood effects throughout the region, spilling from conflict-ridden countries to neighboring countries. Greater commitment is required on the part of MENA governments to contain internal and regional sources of instability. And the international community needs to rethink its response to persistent conflict in the region. Multilateral efforts are urgently needed to resolve the Israeli–Palestinian conflict and to return Iraq to a state of normalcy.

Main Responsibility Rests with MENA

Almost a decade ago, a World Bank report asked MENA to "Claim the Future" and take the steps needed to secure the economic well-being of their citizens (World Bank 1995a). Since that earlier study, some progress has been made, but far more remains to be done. Images of well-educated but unemployed youths now define MENA for much of the world. Because of earlier inaction, MENA's leaders face more difficult choices and a more urgent need to act. The old social contract no longer provides a viable starting point for reform. A new social contract is needed, one that integrates market-based strategies of growth and inclusiveness and accountability with long-standing commitments to social equity.

CHAPTER 1

Introduction

Labor Market Outcomes in the Post–World War II Period

During the era of state-led industrialization in the 1960s and the oil boom in the 1970s, unemployment in the Middle East and North Africa (MENA) countries was on a steady decline. Open unemployment in the largest economies of the region was present on a modest scale and hardly different in nature from what was observed in the advanced industrial economies. Reflecting those conditions, wage growth was steady, as was the expansion in household income.

As late as the early 1980s, some labor-abundant countries were reporting shortages of workers in the face of rapid labor force growth, and rural areas were being depopulated by rural–urban and international migration. The oil-exporting economies had become increasingly reliant on millions of foreign workers, especially from other MENA countries, to augment acute national labor shortages and rising demand for workers. Europe, as well, became an important destination for migrant workers from the region.

It is not surprising that, under those conditions, earlier predictions of rising labor supplies because of population dynamics elicited little concern on the part of policymakers in the region. The vitality in MENA's labor markets between the 1960s and early 1980s was amply reflected in the region's impressive per capita growth record and in its rapid advances in education and life expectancy.

By the early 1990s, however, labor market outcomes in MENA displayed little of their previous dynamism. The once-vibrant regional economy had come to a sudden halt following the oil bust in the mid-1980s. Demand for expatriate workers in the receiving countries was scaled back, causing remittance income in the sending countries to fall rapidly.

In the face of continued rapid labor growth, the collapse of oil prices, and the emergence of serious macroeconomic imbalances, unemployment rates rose to levels unseen in generations, while real wages stagnated and productivity collapsed. Open unemployment was on the rise, especially among educated young workers.

As a result, lower unemployment and rapid job creation have been transformed into the most pressing challenges facing the economies of the region. And the fact that in most countries unemployment rates remained high or continued to climb in the course of the 1990s has amplified the sense of urgency among policymakers and citizens on the need to tackle this challenge head on.

Scope and Methodology of the Report

This report provides a comprehensive account of contemporary labor markets in MENA.

It integrates questions about how to build vibrant labor markets and how to restore the region's growth performance into a document that also addresses questions about population dynamics, socioeconomic trends, employment regulations, the quality of governance, opportunities in the world economy, and the effect of a redistributive social contract on prospects for reform.

Readers will note at the outset that the report goes beyond a technical discussion of labor market outcomes to include attention to the broader political–economic aspects of state–society relations. The attention to the social, institutional, and political factors that shape labor market outcomes is well founded in the academic tradition and policy arena. Labor markets, perhaps more so than any other factor market, are socially and politically constructed.

In MENA, as elsewhere, labor markets are the product of historical processes of state, social, and economic formation that result in tight linkages between them and other dimensions of an economy, society, and polity. They are inherently influenced by demographic profiles, by levels of educational attainment, and by the social policies that determine, in part, the economic risks and opportunities citizens face.

Although MENA falls within a larger universe of countries that are struggling to overcome high unemployment, this volume underscores the conditions that distinguish MENA's labor market problems from those in other regions. Not only does MENA face labor force pressures of an unprecedented scale, but also, more importantly, it has a tradition of state intervention that has been resistant to change.

Thus, in MENA's case in particular, it is these broader political–economic considerations that underscore both the dire need for policy reform and the urgency with which it must be carried out. Across the region, intellectuals and commentators are engaged in debates on the future of labor markets that motivate and echo precisely the concerns addressed in this volume and the approaches chosen to examine them.

This understanding of labor markets is a necessary starting point in organizing reform programs that are capable of overcoming political obstacles and that deliver benefits to the societies that urgently need such reforms to work. In that sense, this volume is an attempt to assess and understand the full range of conditions that must be taken into account if reforms in MENA are to move forward.

Structure and Organization of the Report

The report begins with an analysis of labor markets in MENA as the outcome of the long-term processes through which the region's political economies became organized in the decades following World War II around a redistributive–interventionist social contract (chapter 2). It emphasizes the norms, expectations, and practices that followed from the broad understandings formed in this period concerning the role of the state in the economy, the organization of labor markets, and the orientation of governance.

Although the social contract delivered early dividends, the strains on its capacity became clear over time with the deteriorating outcomes in MENA's labor markets since the mid-1980s. Chapter 2 singles out the crucial role that demographic changes have played in unraveling the sustainability of MENA's social contract for citizens and for the region's economic performance.

Chapter 3 provides a long-term perspective on demographic and socioeconomic trends driving rapid labor force growth in MENA. It emphasizes the large potential for rapid economic growth on account of MENA's demographic transition, especially in view of the region's impressive record in raising educational achievement.

While noting the intensity of past and future labor force pressures in MENA relative to other regions in the world, the chapter stresses the importance of trends in labor demand in assessing employment trends and in identifying the sources of high unemployment at present. The analysis of labor market outcomes in the 1990s is linked to the region's growth performance, as well as to trends in factor accumulation and productivity. These findings, in turn, provide the necessary benchmark for assessing the effect of policy reforms to date on labor market outcomes.

Chapter 4 examines the structure of employment and wages at a more disaggregated level. It assesses the effect of explicit and implicit public sector employment guarantees on the age, gender, and educational profiles of the unemployed. A detailed analysis of the returns to education in the 1990s sheds further light on the institutional underpinnings of high unemployment and labor market segmentation.

In addition, the chapter highlights growing trends in informalization and, in some cases, defeminization of employment in MENA and relates these trends, in turn, to lower demand for labor in the public sector and other sources of labor market rigidity. Finally, the chapter examines the relationship between poverty and labor market outcomes as well as trends in income and wage inequality.

Thus, chapters 2–4 constitute the diagnostic part of the report, setting the stage for exploring the menu of future reforms that can address the employment challenge in MENA. Chapters 5–7 comprise the analysis of future options and policy recommendations.

Chapter 5 begins with an examination of direct interventions in labor markets through the reform of public sector hiring and wage-setting practices. It also examines the regulatory framework governing employment in the private sector. The scope and limitations of these interventions are assessed using detailed empirical simulations. The chapter also considers the role of active labor market policies.

The chapter argues that, while necessary and politically appealing, labor market reforms are not sufficient to address the employment challenge facing the region now and over the next two decades. This conclusion lays the foundation for considering a comprehensive approach to reform that extends beyond labor markets to the orientation of MENA's development policies.

Chapter 6 begins with an assessment of the likely contribution of traditional engines of employment growth toward future job creation. After concluding that the prospects for alleviating labor market pressures through public sector employment and migration are limited, it identifies a set of needed transitions to advance the goals of job creation and growth.

The chapter elaborates on the pillars of a new development model by drawing on the companion volumes in this series. It underscores the need to promote private sector expansion as a driver of employment, to deepen the integration of MENA's markets into the global economy, and to improve the management of natural resources. Furthermore, it argues that the success of these transitions requires better governance.

The need for a comprehensive approach to reform in the future is the starting point for chapter 7, which argues that transformation of MENA's labor markets cannot be detached from broader processes of economic and political change. The chapter links economic reform to progress in the reorganization of the social contract that structured state–society relations for more than 40 years.

After identifying political–economic obstacles to past reform efforts, the chapter calls for a vision of reform that demands a more tightly coupled relationship between economic and political reform and that links the future of MENA's labor markets to a new social contract.

Findings in Comparative Perspective

The findings presented throughout this volume reinforce the lessons of an expanding literature on the political economy of reform. They confirm the importance of good governance for successful reform and the need for accountable and participatory reform strategies. This volume also confirms the value of reform strategies that treat equity and efficiency as complementary rather than competing outcomes and that achieve labor market flexibility while preserving essential social guarantees.

Thus, the messages here are consistent with an emerging consensus about how to create socially equitable strategies of economic growth—strategies that advance the interests of workers while improving overall economic performance.

CHAPTER 2

Evolution of State–Labor Relations in the Middle East and North Africa

Across the Middle East and North Africa (MENA) region during the 1940s and 1950s, societies developed social contracts with a distinctively interventionist and redistributive character. These contracts were expressed and institutionalized through explicit commitments from MENA governments that were articulated in constitutions, basic laws, and other documents that established the state as an instrument of social transformation, mass political mobilization, and economic redistribution. Although the form and content of the contracts varied, they reflected a widely held understanding of the policies for economic and social development.

Legacy of the Social Contract

In some cases, the social contract asserted a commitment to radical populism, with intensive regulation, if not outright expropriation, of private assets and with control of organized labor through state corporatist systems of interest representation. In others, it reflected a paternalistic rationale for statism, with interventionist policies directed in support of emergent private sectors. The differences are not trivial, for they help to account for the significant variation in the developmental experiences of MENA countries. Nonetheless, the overall direction of economic and social policies in MENA during these formative decades exhibited a measure of convergence around an interventionist–redistributive form of social contract.

Accordingly, throughout MENA, there has been a consistent pattern of similarities in styles of regulation, forms of state intervention, and modes of interest representation. There also have been similarities in the nationalist and redistributive policies through which state elites sought to legitimize their developmental projects, if not their political authority more generally, despite differences in the intensity with which populist versus paternalistic rhetoric accompanied shifts in economic and social policy (Salamé 1987). Similar patterns also existed in how the boundaries of political inclusion and exclusion were transformed through the politics of mass incorporation, with private sectors becoming increasingly marginal to political life in Algeria, Egypt, Iraq, Libya, Yemen, Syria, and—to a lesser extent—Tunisia. In these cases, workers and peasants were privileged over the owners of capital in the consideration of whose interests needed to be taken into account in making economic and social policy and of which actors had a legitimate claim to state resources.

The social contracts established during the independence era have given rise to enduring institutions, interests, norms, and practices that now structure the constraints and incentives governments face as they contend with demands for policy reform and resistance to that reform. The contracts have defined patterns of state–labor relations across the region and established expectations and obligations that have proved deeply resilient. They remain a powerful presence in debates about social and economic policy reform, even as their effect on employment, wages, working conditions, foreign investment, trade, and overall macroeconomic performance has become deleterious. Understanding what the social contract in MENA embodies—its origins, its developmental consequences, its effects on labor markets—is crucial to any assessment of labor market prospects and possibilities.

Definition of the Social Contract

The social contract refers generally to an agreement between the members of a society—or between the governed and the government—defining and limiting the rights and duties of each. In the modern European context, the term *social contract* generally refers to a collective agreement that regulates employment and wages and that is secured through bargaining among representatives of the state, labor, and capital. Such compacts provide wage stability to employers and address the interests of organized labor in distributive equity and secure employment, with the state providing the institutionalized channels for conflict resolution and the guarantees to stabilize agreements.

In MENA countries, the social contract encompasses a wider array of factors than is commonly held in Europe. Conceptualized not solely as an institutionalized bargain among collective actors, it encompasses norms and shared expectations for the overall organization of a polity. These norms and expectations shape the perceptions of actors whose interests must be taken into account in making economic and social policy. They also determine which social groups have a legitimate claim on state resources and what demands state actors may legitimately make on society. Accordingly, these norms and expectations have significant institutional consequences. They define the boundaries of acceptable policy choice, and they affect the organization of interests in society by helping to determine who wins and who loses in a given political economy. Furthermore, they influence the institutional forms that become accepted as legitimate mechanisms for organized interest representation—as well as the strategies for state and social actors to resolve conflicts.

Characteristics of the Social Contract

From the 1940s to the 1970s, the MENA social contract acquired a number of distinctive features, including institutional arrangements, public policies, legitimating discourses, and modes of state–society relations. Core attributes of the social contract are

- A preference for redistribution and equity in economic and social policy

- A preference for states over markets in managing national economies

- The adoption of import-substitution industrialization and the protection of local markets from global competition

- A reliance on state planning in determining economic priorities

- An encompassing vision of the role of the state in the provision of welfare and social services

- A vision of the political arena as an expression of the organic unity of the nation, rather than as a site of political contestation or the aggregation of conflicting preferences.

Another key marker in the rise of the interventionist–redistributive social contract was the emergence of centralized, hierarchical, and tightly regulated corporatist structures of interest representation in the first decade after independence. These arrangements provided the blueprint not just for the organization of state–labor relations, but also for relations between the state and a wide range of other social groups, including peasants, students, and women, as well as various professional associations. And although these arrangements reflect the intent of governments to control workers, corporatism created possibilities for agency, bargaining, and negotiation for the groups it was designed to contain (Beinin 2003, Bianchi 1989, Posusney 1997).

Institutionally and in terms of economic and social policies, these elements were consolidated through broadly similar strategies in a number of MENA states, including Algeria, Egypt, Iraq, Syria, and—to a lesser degree—Jordan, Morocco, Yemen, and Tunisia. These strategies included

- The rise of dominant single-party or ruling-party governments

- New, postindependence constitutions that enshrined interventionist and redistributive principles in the basic laws

- A wave of agrarian reform programs to redress inequalities in the rural economy

- Sweeping nationalizations of industry, banking, insurance, and trade in the late 1950s and early 1960s, producing a dramatic expansion in the scale of public sectors

- The centralization of trade unions and professional associations

- The consolidation of import-substitution industrialization as a strategy for establishing domestic industrial sectors

- Programs for state provision of social services, including education, housing, health care, food subsidies, and other benefits.

Context That Produced the Social Contract

Before 1950, the standard of living for the vast majority of the population in MENA was extremely low (Issawi 1982). For example, it is estimated in Egypt that per capita income stagnated for much of the first half of the 20th century. During that time, health indicators were among the worst in the world, and epidemics and malnutrition plagued the region. These conditions caused the crude death rate to remain high until 1950 (Omran 1980). Education levels were also low by international standards. In Egypt, adult illiteracy was estimated at 99.5 percent in 1939, and only 23.3 percent of children ages 5–19 were enrolled in school. Likewise, in Morocco, enrollment was even lower, with the number of foreign children in schools almost equal to the total of Moroccan children (Cowan 1958).

In addition to those weaknesses, MENA exhibited high levels of income and land inequality (figure 2.1). As was noted at the time, "the wealth of [MENA] is concentrated in the hands of relatively few individuals" (United Nations 1949). Before the land reforms of 1952, it is estimated that three-quarters of the population of agricultural Egypt owned no land or less than one acre. Other examples include Syria, where over half of the cultivated land consisted of large estates, and Lebanon, where fewer than 200 individuals owned approximately half of all the surveyed land (Grunwald and Ronall 1960).

FIGURE 2.1

Income and Land Inequality in Egypt, 1900–45

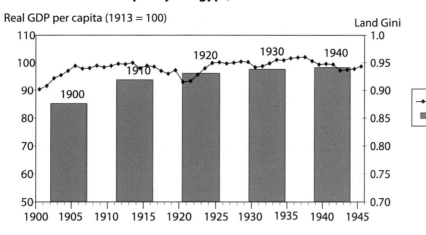

Note: The Land Gini coefficient measures the degree of inequality in land distribution. It ranges from 0 to 1, with higher levels indicating greater inequality in the distribution of land.
Sources: Gross domestic product (GDP), Yousef 2002; Land Gini, Egypt, various years.

It was in this context that the social contract in MENA was conceived in the period between 1930 and 1950. Domestic factors, combined with the region's earlier experience with globalization—the global diffusion of trends toward state expansion, intervention, import substitution, planning, and deepening of welfare that occurred in the mid-20th century—generated a complex regime of institutions, policies, norms, expectations, and practices that would become the social contract.

The first elements of the social contract began to appear during the period between the two World Wars, as states in MENA and in other developing regions responded to the collapse of international economic order during the Great Depression by moving toward import substitution and a new conception of the state as the primary provider of welfare (Thompson 2000). Its emergence is also linked to the circulation into the region in the years before and during World War II of then-novel economic theories, ranging from Keynesian demand management to development strategies that stressed the value of central planning and the need to protect infant industries from the pressure of global competition. Populist regimes in Latin America led the way in demonstrating the ability of these new policies to bring about economic benefits.

External Factors That Contribute to the Social Contract

During World War II, the Middle East Supply Centre, a regionwide Anglo-American organization, promoted import substitution to compensate for a wartime decline in exports into the region of food and other critical goods (Vitalis and Heydemann 2000). In the postwar period, international financial institutions, including the World Bank, recommended an expanded economic role for government in response to the presumed weakness of private sectors (World Bank 1952, 1955) and made access to loans conditional on the preparation of economic plans by governments. Cold War considerations led Western powers to view favorably the efforts of MENA governments to impose control over organized labor in order to contain Communist influences. The expansion of welfare systems in postwar Europe offered models for the provision of social services that were received positively by the political elite of newly independent MENA states.

Domestic Factors That Influenced the Social Contract

In addition to the foreign influences, much of the impetus for the consolidation of interventionist–redistributive social contracts came from within the region. The resilience of these social contracts as frameworks for the management of MENA political economies reflects the local conditions in which they arose. Specifically, it reflects the timing and sequencing of four processes: the rise of nationalist movements, the emergence of mass politics, the incorporation of labor into the political arena, and the introduction of electoral institutions as a by-product of the colonial presence in MENA states.

As the product of a historical context in which those processes were tightly interconnected, the MENA social contract took shape as a distinct variant of postwar welfare and redistributive arrangements that emerged as a more general model both in developing regions and in the welfare states of postwar Europe. Although many other states in the postwar period also adopted redistributive social policies and corporatist structures for the organization of labor, MENA states were distinctive among countries outside the Communist Bloc in the scope of state regulation of the economy and society and in the extent to which social policies became the vehicle for implementing radically redistributive social programs. Those distinctions have had important implications for current efforts to reform and reorganize MENA political economies.

Rise of Mass Politics

Throughout the MENA region, the emergence of mass politics occurred in association with (and was powerfully influenced by) colonial projects of state building—and with the rise of anticolonial independence movements. Central to this transition was the introduction of electoral systems of mass-based political representation across the states of the post–Ottoman Middle East, including the monarchies of Egypt, Iraq, and Jordan. The rise of mass politics, in turn, promoted the emergence of modern conceptions of citizenship and reinforced perceptions of the state as an agent of public welfare. It established new domains of rights, new strategies for claiming those rights, and new forms of political competition for control over the mechanisms of mass mobilization, including political parties, trade unions, and professional associations.

Those processes transformed nationalist struggles from activity dominated by elites into movements of mass political incorporation. They provided incentives for politicians to create inclusive social coalitions and valorized discourses of egalitarianism and mass participation—all of which were subsequently institutionalized through the formation of social contracts. They also reinforced the privileged position of organized labor, giving legitimacy to the claims of labor leaders to the resources and attention of the state. In this sense, the colonial construction (or broadening) of republican institutions throughout the Middle East during moments of nationalist mobilization was critical for the later emergence of interventionist–redistributive social contracts across the MENA region (Anderson 1986).

Moreover, workers in the Middle East were establishing their own claims for representation in the design of policies regulating working conditions, wages, and labor–management relations. Beginning in the 1930s, trade union membership grew rapidly in many MENA states (table 2.1 and figure 2.2). This expansion was accompanied by a growing political assertiveness of trade unions and by a notable increase in strikes and other actions intended both to incline the content of social policy toward workers and to support the goal of national independence.

Mass Politics and the Nationalist Movement

As in other regions, the institutions that resulted from this transformation simultaneously promoted the formation of collective identities and

TABLE 2.1

Trade Union Membership in Selected MENA Countries before 1960

Country	Date	Union membership	Share of workers in union (percent)
Egypt	1947	480,000	37.6
Tunisia	1956	155,000	30.5
Algeria	1954	375,000	28.8
Morocco	1952	670,000	72.0

Source: International Labour Office 1960.

FIGURE 2.2

Trade Union Membership in Egypt, 1950–60

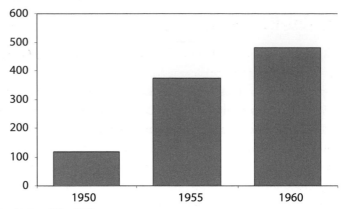

Thousands of members

Source: International Labour Office 1960.

the mobilization of organized interests. These institutions included not only labor unions, but also peasant unions, political parties, chambers of commerce, and other institutions that helped to construct social class as a legitimate basis for political mobilization. At the same time, the escalation of anticolonial movements within the republican frameworks promoted by Western powers created incentives among nationalist elites to support mass incorporation into the political arena. The political realm, previously reserved for elites, came to include the popular classes. For example, in Tunisia, a powerful trade union movement, the UGTT (Union Générale Tunisienne du Travail) was closely linked to the leading nationalist political party, the Neo-Destour, which negotiated Tunisia's independence from France. Egyptian nationalists viewed organized labor as an extension of the nationalist movement. Similarly, the Aden Trades Union Congress, created in 1956, supported nationalists seeking independence from the United Kingdom—in what became the People's Democratic Republic of Yemen in 1967.

Controlled mass incorporation also served the nationalist cause by establishing the legitimacy, "organic" integrity, and coherence of the "nations" on whose behalf local politicians articulated demands for independence. At the same time, mass mobilization, along with competition among established elites and new political entrepreneurs to control newly mobilized social groups, helped to create a more diffuse capacity for collective action across MENA societies. In a number of cases, these groups—labor unions in particular—acquired new leverage for collective bargaining. In Egypt, Lebanon, and Syria, they secured basic systems of work place regulation. These systems became the prototypes for the broader social contracts in subsequent years. By 1960, Egypt had ratified 30 international labor conventions, Algeria 31, and Morocco 24—all above the average of 17.3 for non-European states.

The Changing Political Arena

The political incorporation of workers and peasants transforms the strategic calculus of political actors (Collier and Collier 1991; Przeworski and Sprague 1986; Rueschemeyer, Stephens, and Stephens 1992; Waldner 1999). It upsets established alliances and makes new coalitions possible. In MENA, this politically potent combination of state-centered welfare republicanism and organic-nationalist approaches to mass mobilization—as well as the new institutions and capacities for the organization and management of collective interests—provided the essential ingredients for postindependence strategies of economic and social development.

Statist preferences and mass-based modes of popular mobilization quickly spilled over from social and economic policies to the domain of national security, a trend reinforced by the prevailing sense of instability and vulnerability among newly established governments. Across the region, threats to state security helped to consolidate the privileged position of militaries within MENA polities. These threats included the creation of the state of Israel and the subsequent escalation of the Arab–Israeli conflict. They also included ongoing instances of covert and overt foreign military intervention in the region, such as in Iran, Syria, and Egypt, as well as the Arab Cold War (Kerr 1971): the use of pan-Arab ideologies by politicians to justify intervening in the political affairs of neighboring states.

Oil revenues that flowed directly into state treasuries underwrote programs of military expansion in oil exporters and subsidized militaries elsewhere in the region. Within the first decade of independence, most states in MENA had constructed the foundations for what would grow to become massive national security regimes. Levels of military expenditure in MENA outpaced those of regions at similar levels of economic development. Growth in military spending was matched by the dramatic expansion of internal security apparatuses. These conditions, along with the global trends described above, represented the starting points—if not the necessary preconditions—for what would soon become a regionwide move to consolidate interventionist–redistributive social contracts (Ayubi 1995).

Codification of the Social Contract

The preferences articulated by the social contract were expressed explicitly in postindependence constitutions, basic laws, and public policies. In

Algeria, Egypt, Iraq, Syria, and elsewhere, constitutions refer to the re-distributive mission of the state, the privileged position of workers, and the need for states to assume responsibility for social welfare (table 2.2). Syria's 1950 constitution, for example, includes prominent references to the social functions of property, with calls for state control over agricultural production and marketing, state sponsorship of economic development, state control over trade unions, state responsibility for the delivery of social services, and state control of the educational system.

The emergence and consolidation of the interventionist–redistributive social contract were far from linear, and the contract was nowhere near uniform in the details of its design. Jordan, Morocco, and Lebanon, as well as the oil-producing states of the Arabian Peninsula, did not embrace populist and redistributive policies to the same degree as the secular, single-party republican governments. Yet even in these cases, governments pursued interventionist strategies of industrialization (including the Moroccan nationalization of private assets in 1972), agrarian reform, social service provision, and state control over labor. The spread and consolidation of the social contract, however, should not be seen as overdetermined. In a large number of newly independent

TABLE 2.2

Right to Work and State Responsibility Are Intertwined: Excerpts from the Constitutions of MENA Countries

Country	Excerpt from constitution
Algeria (1963)	*Article 10:* "The fundamental objectives of the democratic and popular Algerian Republic are: … the guarantee of the right to work."
Bahrain (1973)	*Article 13(b):* "The state guarantees the provision of job opportunities for its citizens and the fairness of work conditions."
Egypt, Arab Rep. of (1971)	*Article 13:* "Work is a right, a duty, and an honor ensured by the State."
Iran, Islamic Rep. of (1979)	*Article 28(2):* "The government has the duty, with due consideration of the need of society for different kinds of work, to provide every citizen with the opportunity to work and to create equal conditions for obtaining it."
Jordan (1952)	*Article 23(i):* "Work is the right of every citizen, and the State shall provide opportunities for work to all citizens by directing the national economy and raising its standards."
Kuwait (1963)	*Article 41(2):* "Work is a duty of every citizen, necessitated by personal dignity and public good. The State shall endeavor to make it available to citizens and to make its terms equitable."
Libya (1969)	*Article 4:* "Work in the Libyan Arab Republic is a right, a duty, and an honor for every able-bodied citizen."
Saudi Arabia (1993)	*Article 28:* "The State provides job opportunities for whoever is capable of working."
Syrian Arab Rep. (1973)	*Article 13(1):* "The state economy is a planned socialist economy which seeks to end all forms of exploitation."
Yemen, Rep. of (1991)	*Article 21:* "Work is a right, an honor, and a necessary tool for the advancement of society."

Source: OEFRE 2003.

states—including Egypt, Iraq, Lebanon, Morocco, Syria, and Tunisia—postcolonial politics initially took the form of intense struggles to determine whether the attributes mentioned here would provide basic frameworks for the management of local political economies.

The Social Contract and Labor Markets

Within the interventionist–redistributive social contract, the management of labor markets is achieved through a variety of mechanisms, which extend beyond the corporatist regulation of labor unions. Across MENA, government ministries and state agencies created after independence subjected labor–management relations to increasing regulation. In several countries, employers in industries with the highest levels of union participation experienced erosions in their authority to set wages and working hours and to hire, fire, and discipline workers. State-supervised arbitration procedures were established to resolve workplace disputes. In some cases, state regulation even mandated worker representation on corporate boards and set guidelines establishing the right of workers to a share of corporate profits.

State Regulation and Intervention Were Extensive

Work force regulations expanded under state ownership, mandating job security guarantees, social security programs, relatively high public sector wages with generous nonwage compensation benefits (such as family allowances), and prohibitions or sharp restrictions on the dismissal of workers. Such policies were intended to provide economic stability and security to organized labor and to serve as means of redistributing collective wealth. However, along with those protections came restrictions on the political activity of labor, including limits on the right to strike. Moreover, within those regulatory regimes, powerful incentives developed for rent-seeking, "cronyism," and state capture.

The general orientation of economic and social policy also affected labor markets. During the late 1950s and 1960s, governments moved from regulating private sectors to direct control of production through nationalization of private assets. In response, public sectors grew to become the dominant employers in many MENA states (figure 2.3). Import-substitution strategies also created constraints and incentives that influenced investment and production, with implications for labor demand and job creation. Regulation of agrarian sectors, land reform, and an urban bias in social policy had significant effects on rural labor markets, augmenting the rapid urbanization and, for the most part, elimi-

FIGURE 2.3

General Government Employment as a Share of Total Population

Percent

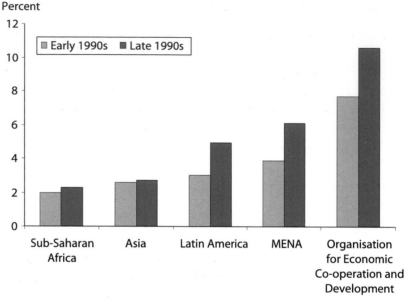

Source: Schiavo-Campo, de Tommaso, and Mukherjee 2003.

nating large landowners, who previously constituted the most powerful class in many MENA states (Beinin 2003).

Wide-scale public provision of social services rapidly expanded state bureaucracies, absorbing many new entrants into the public sector. In a number of states, public commitments to the development of human capital took the form of populist education policies that provided free, universal access to higher education and guaranteed public sector employment to secondary and university graduates (box 2.1). In the short term, these policies yielded net benefits, but over time the supply of job seekers outpaced rates of economic growth. States continued to honor employment guarantees, but the impact on productivity per worker over time was predictably negative.

Government preferences for redistribution had additional effects on labor markets. Strict systems of rent control, highly progressive tax codes, and subsidy regimes affected the broader economic environment in which workers in MENA made employment choices. Such policies did not directly target labor and were available to citizens without regard to employment status. Nonetheless, they constituted features of a political economy in which redistributive commitments of many kinds increased the resource endowment of workers and shaped the attitudes of labor in support of existing economic policies. These interventions re-

BOX 2.1

Egypt's Employment Guarantee

As part of the "Socialist Laws" of 1961–62, the Egyptian government initiated a policy that guaranteed employment to all university graduates. In 1964, Law 14 extended this policy to include graduates of any vocational secondary school or technical institute. Law 85 of 1973 expanded the guarantee to include all demobilized military conscripts of all educational levels. To oversee these new laws and to ensure a job for each graduate, the government created the General Administration for Graduates within the Ministry of Manpower and Migration.

As the number of graduates rose it became difficult for the government to maintain those guarantees. Between 1963 and 1983, the number of graduates increased at about 12 percent a year, compared with an overall labor force growth rate of 2 percent. Although the rate for graduates has since fallen, they still make up the bulk of new entrants in the labor market.

To reduce the burden of providing employment, the state limited enrollment in universities and technical and vocational institutes. The number of graduates peaked in 1986 and has since declined. The state also increased the waiting period for a government job (up to 13 years) to increase the opportunity cost of public employment. This change caused some graduates to pursue careers in the private sector, but the government's announcement in 1992 that graduates employed in the private sector would no longer be eligible for government jobs sparked mass resignations.

Although Egypt officially abandoned the socialist development path in 1973, public sector employment continued to grow and has remained a major burden on state finances. Guaranteeing government employment for all graduates is unsustainable in the long run, but because it is a crucial element of the social contract, the state has been unable to abrogate the laws associated with the guarantee.

Public Sector Employment as a Share of Total Employment in Egypt, 1973–98

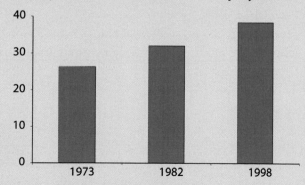

Sources: Arab Republic of Egypt, CAPMAS 1986, 1998.

Source: Assaad 1997.

flect the extent of state preferences for redistribution and how these preferences were expressed in the form of public policy. They also highlight the degree to which efforts to manage labor markets extended beyond direct state intervention into the workplace and beyond state constraints on the political activities of workers.

Economic Growth Marks the 1960s and 1970s

Despite the social and economic turmoil that accompanied the emergence and consolidation of social contracts in MENA countries, subsequent decades were marked by unprecedented levels of economic growth and social development. Between 1965 and 1985, MENA's economic growth rates were among the highest in the world, averaging 3.7 percent per capita a year (figure 2.4). Many factors contributed to these gains: rapid progress in early-stage industrialization, high levels of public spending, initial benefits from trade protection for domestic producers, rising public sector employment, and rising oil prices.

Oil Helps Sustain the Social Contract

Oil revenues played a pivotal role in sustaining the social contract in both exporting and nonexporting states (Beblawi and Luciani 1987; Chaudhry 1997). For oil producers, oil revenues permitted the creation of vast wel-

FIGURE 2.4

Average Annual Change in Real Gross Domestic Product Per Capita, by Region

Percent

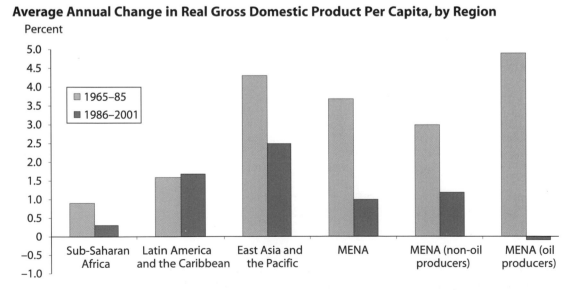

Note: Non-oil producers are Egypt, Jordan, Morocco, Syria, and Tunisia; oil producers are Algeria, Kuwait, Oman, and Saudi Arabia.
Source: World Bank 2003h.

BOX 2.2

Effect of Oil on Labor Markets in the Gulf Cooperation Council

The increase in oil production in the 1960s and the price boom of the 1970s provided the Gulf Cooperation Council (GCC) countries with the resources necessary to initiate elaborate programs for modernization. Massive infrastructure projects were launched to upgrade roads, communications, and public utilities. Governments also created programs to accelerate modernization through free education and health care. At the time, GCC countries suffered from a national labor shortage, which led to an increased reliance on imported labor. The size of the government bureaucracy began to expand with the hiring of nationals. Oil revenues were high enough that nationals entering the labor force could be hired almost exclusively by the public sector. Public sector employment facilitated the distribution of oil wealth and encouraged higher educational attainment by nationals. Over time, these trends have become entrenched, resulting in a highly skewed breakdown of nationals by sector of employment (see figure).

Share of National Labor Force Employed in Government in the GCC Countries

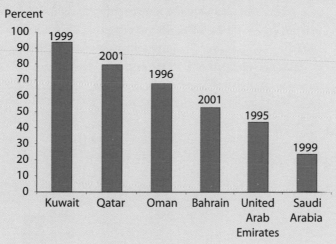

Source: Girgis, Hadad-Zervos, and Coulibaly 2003.

Source: Birks and Sinclair 1980.

fare systems that served as key mechanisms for the distribution of oil wealth to citizens, though not to noncitizen migrant workers (box 2.2). For non-oil producers, remittance income boosted household consumption, especially in rural areas. Loans, grants, and other forms of assistance from oil-producing states to non-oil producers boosted government revenues and sustained redistributive commitments. At the peak of the oil boom in the early 1980s, some 3.5 million Arab migrant workers were employed in Saudi Arabia and the Gulf states. Official remittances of migrant labor in the period from 1973 to 1984 totaled almost US$22 billion for Egypt, US$6.5 billion for Jordan, and US$8.2 billion for Morocco.

The Social Contract Addresses MENA's Deficiencies

The influence of the social contract also meant that the period of rapid growth in MENA was accompanied by low levels of income inequality and dramatic gains in a number of social indicators. According to a 1995 World Bank study, "the social payoffs" associated with the policies of the 1960s, 1970s, and 1980s "have been enormous." By the early 1990s, the region witnessed dramatic reductions in infant mortality, increases in life expectancy, school enrollment levels approaching 100 percent, and literacy levels that increased from an average of some 40 percent of the adult population to almost 60 percent (figure 2.5). Moreover, "the region's governments were effective in reducing poverty" (World Bank 1995a). As a result of income transfers and high overall growth rates, "by 1990, only 5.6 percent of the population in MENA lived on less than US$1 a day—the global benchmark for absolute poverty—compared with 14.7 percent in East Asia and 28.8 percent in Latin America" (World Bank 1995a).

These results had important political consequences. They reinforced the role of redistributive mechanisms in sustaining the well-being of

FIGURE 2.5

Average Years of Schooling, by Region

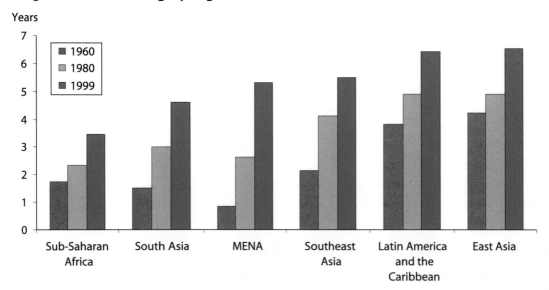

Source: Barro and Lee 2000.

large segments of MENA populations, deepening their popularity among social groups that governments identified as core constituencies. From the 1960s through the 1980s, these groups emerged as prominent winners in the political economies created by the interventionist–redistributive social contract. The welfare gains also helped to cement an "authoritarian bargain," with citizens trading restrictions on political participation for economic security and the public provision of social services, welfare, and other benefits (Vandewalle 2003).

The Social Contract Is under Strain: The 1980s and 1990s

Over time, gaps widened between a deeply embedded set of institutional arrangements, norms, expectations, and practices on the one hand and the diminished capacity of governments to sustain redistributive commitments on the other. As early as the 1970s, Egypt and Tunisia had begun to reevaluate some policies associated with the contract, taking tentative steps toward economic liberalization. The inability of the MENA social contract to sustain the economic gains of previous decades became increasingly clear by the early 1980s. By the end of the decade, the strains in the social contract had grown into a major economic crisis.

Oil Prices Collapse and Economic Crisis Occurs

The roots of this crisis were declining oil prices (figure 2.6), shrinking demand for migrant labor, reduced remittance flows, declining productivity, and a more competitive international environment. Political economies formed by the interventionist–redistributive social contract began to experience significant economic lags. With declining public revenues, redistributive commitments contributed to alarming increases in public debt in many MENA states as governments struggled to meet public sector wage bills ranging from 6 percent of gross domestic product (GDP) to almost 20 percent. Regulatory environments discouraged private investment, reduced opportunities for trade, and impeded the development of export-oriented industrial sectors, thus creating significant obstacles to the integration of MENA economies into global markets. In the 1980s and 1990s, labor productivity in MENA experienced a sustained decline. Unemployment levels increased, and governments faced growing pressure—both domestic and international—for economic reform.

Governments Respond to Economic Difficulties

By the 1990s, most governments in MENA—including Algeria, Egypt, Jordan, Morocco, Syria, Tunisia, and the oil exporters of the Arabian

FIGURE 2.6

Real Oil Price, 1976–2003

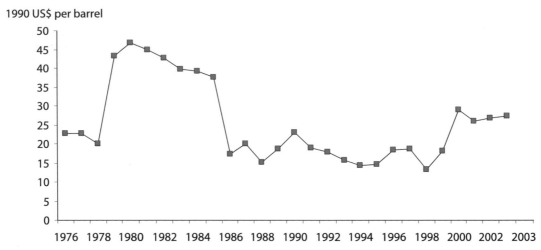

1990 US$ per barrel

Source: World Bank 2003f.

Peninsula—had adopted some form of economic stabilization program. Policy shifts were marked by caution and gradualism, but across the region, governments cut subsidies, reduced public expenditure, and reformed exchange rate regimes. Many governments entered international economic institutions, such as the General Agreement on Tariffs and Trade (GATT), later the World Trade Organization (WTO), and signed bilateral and multilateral trade agreements. These reforms began to have beneficial effects. Debt levels declined, inflation was brought under control, and macroeconomic performance was on average positive (figure 2.7).

MENA governments also began a gradual and selective transition from economic stabilization to structural adjustment—a move strongly supported by international financial institutions and Western governments. Reforms included many that are now familiar markers of economic restructuring: privatization of state-owned enterprises, fiscal reform and trade liberalization, deregulation, and strengthening of the institutional foundations for a market-led economy. However, implementation of these measures has been uneven, hesitant, and incomplete (Richards and Waterbury 1998) (figure 2.8). Partly as a result, MENA's economic recovery in the 1990s was generally weak. In the past 15 years, GDP per capita growth has averaged 1.0 percent a year (figure 2.4). Labor productivity has remained low, and unemployment rates have continued to increase.

FIGURE 2.7

Economic Stabilization in the 1990s, by Region

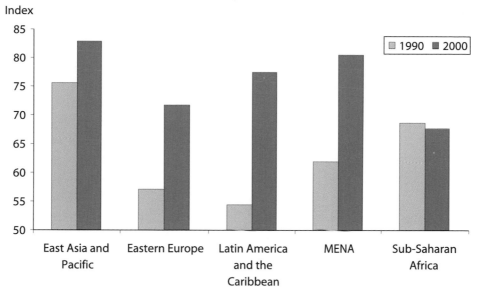

Note: A composite index of stabilization based on fiscal balance, current account balance, inflation, and black market premium.
Source: Dasgupta, Keller, and Srinivasan 2002.

FIGURE 2.8

Structural Reform in the 1990s, by Region

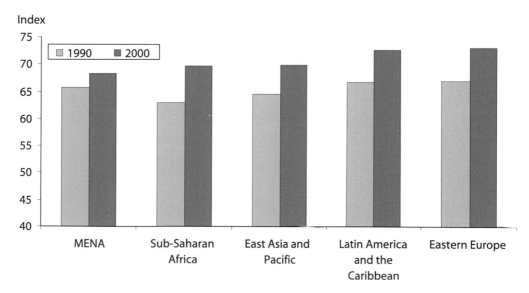

Note: A composite index of structural reform based on trade policy, tax policy, real exchange rate overvaluation, and privatization.
Source: Dasgupta, Keller, and Srinivasan 2002.

Vulnerability to External Shocks Increases

The lack of economic diversification and dependence on commodity exports left the region more vulnerable to trade shocks, oil price volatility, the Asian economic crisis, and the post-1998 decline in global economic growth. MENA was also highly vulnerable to the political shocks that accompanied the resurgence of Israeli–Palestinian violence; the terrorist attacks of September 11, 2001; and the U.S.-led military interventions in Afghanistan and Iraq. These events have hurt tourism, which is a critical source of foreign exchange, and have dampened both investment and trade. Furthermore, an extended drought in the late 1990s that affected much of MENA caused a sharp drop in agricultural production. Migration opportunities also receded as economic stagnation reduced labor demand within MENA and as Europe adopted more restrictive immigration policies. Current indicators suggest that the recovery of the 1990s has already peaked and that the region may again experience economic decline.

Some of these factors were beyond the control of MENA governments. Yet the uneven quality of economic policy reform—more progress on exchange rate stabilization, less on privatization; more progress on fiscal policy reform, less on the liberalization of labor markets—must, in large measure, be understood as a product of the embedded nature of the interventionist–redistributive social contract in MENA. Institutional arrangements created to link organized labor and the state became mechanisms for the expression of labor resistance to privatization (Posusney 1997). Governments faced political and social constraints in their attempts to reduce welfare expenditures. Often, austerity measures were greeted by significant and occasionally violent mass protests, such as those that took place in Tunisia in 1984, in Morocco in 1981, and in Egypt in 1977 (Harik and Sullivan 1992). Moreover, the economic gains generated by selective policy reforms often were captured by business elites with established ties to governments, thereby undermining the legitimacy of those reforms among MENA populations.

Adjustment Challenges the Social Contract

It would not be entirely accurate to attribute the limited economic policy reform in MENA to failures of political will, cronyism, or the political power of those whose interests are threatened by reform. Economic crisis has eroded—but not eliminated—preferences for redistribution, equity, and economic security that have marked economic and social policy in MENA since independence. In preserving important elements of the interventionist–redistributive social contract—and in seeking to avoid imposing adjustment costs of policy reforms on the least well off—MENA governments are responding to widely held understandings about the legitimate purposes of the state and the appropriate aims of economic policy (Waterbury 1998). No less than their European, Anglo-American, or Asian counterparts, Arab modes of capitalism reflect the legacies of long-standing social preferences that are not easily transformed. Even so, reforming the social contract in MENA has become an urgent priority.

Costs of the Redistributive Preference Are Rising

MENA is not the only region facing this challenge. Europe has been confronting a similar dilemma in recent years. In Europe, the policies intended to provide economic security for organized labor, to enhance human capital, and to promote socially just strategies of economic development have become, over time, a source of economic insecurity to growing numbers of citizens, most importantly workers (figure 2.9). Moreover, many of the obstacles to reform in MENA are also found in Europe. Both face broad-based opposition to the liberalization of labor markets and to the reduction in social expenditures, despite high, sus-

FIGURE 2.9

International Comparison of Unemployment Rates, 2002

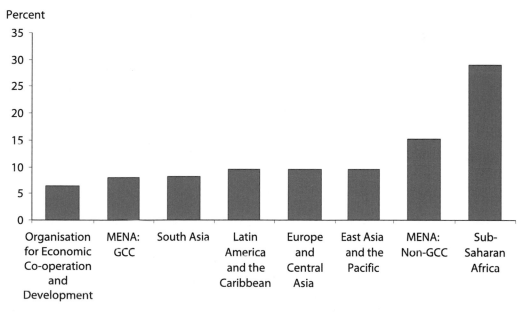

Note: Rates for the Gulf Cooperation Council (GCC) include nationals only.
Source: World Bank staff estimates from ILO 2002 and country sources.

tained unemployment and low levels of economic growth. Thus, in both industrial and developing regions, social contracts that favor redistribution, equity, and security over growth have taken an increasing toll on precisely the social sectors they are intended to protect.

Despite these commonalities, the process will be more difficult for MENA. The region has a tradition of greater state intervention. More importantly, the labor market pressures it will face in the future will dwarf the projections for Europe. In fact, as the next chapter underscores, the demographic transition in MENA has created the most intense labor market pressures observed anywhere in the world in the post–World War II period.

CHAPTER 3

Demography, Labor Growth, and Employment Outcomes

The Middle East and North Africa (MENA) population of nearly 330 million is the legacy of high population growth rates in the post–World War II period. Between 1950 and 1990, MENA's population grew faster than that of any region, averaging 2.8 percent growth a year. Population growth peaked in 1985 at 3.4 percent (figure 3.1). Although the rate of expansion has declined, the pressure of population flows remains high. Between 1990 and 2000, with annual growth rates averaging 2.2 percent, MENA's population increased by 6.1 million people a year compared with 4.6 million in the 1970s and 6.7 million in the 1980s. In the current decade, with population growing at an even slower rate of 2 percent, the region is still adding more than 6 million people every year. It is safe to assume, however, that the era of high population growth is over. Evidence increasingly suggests that MENA is on a trajectory of declining population growth rates for the foreseeable future (Courbage 1999; Rashad and Khadr 2002). These trends must be viewed within a context of long-term demographic change.

MENA's Demographic Transition

Like other regions, MENA has been undergoing a demographic transition, moving from an initial equilibrium of high birth and death rates, which is typical of agricultural or preindustrial societies, to a new equilibrium of low birth and death rates, as is found in the industrial economies of North America and Europe (Bongaarts and Bulatao 1999). During the transition, population growth rates initially expand as mortality rates fall and fertility rates remain high. With modernization, fertility declines, bringing about a steady fall in population growth. Much of the world has conformed to this pattern of long-term demographic change. The speed of the process, however, has varied widely across and within regions. In this regard, the countries in MENA exhibit both unique patterns and considerable diversity.

FIGURE 3.1

Population Trends and Projections in MENA, 1950–2025

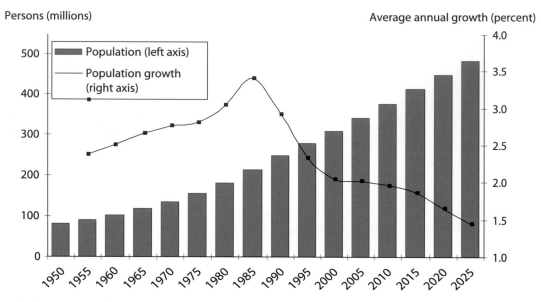

Source: United Nations Population Prospects 2002.

Mortality Rates Have Declined Rapidly

Beginning in the 1950s, MENA experienced the significant declines in mortality that signal the onset of the demographic transition. Countries launched impressive development programs, investing heavily in health care programs and participating in sanitation and disease control programs sponsored by the World Health Organization. The increasing availability of antibiotics, vaccinations, and insecticides after World War II had a profound effect on the spread of parasites and communicable diseases (Omran 1980). Mortality rates dropped steadily, from 24 deaths per 1,000 people in the early 1950s to 13 per 1,000 in 1980. Infant mortality rates dropped from 186 deaths per 1,000 births to 102 per 1,000 in the same period. These outcomes are striking when benchmarked against those of other developing regions. Although the region started out in the 1950s with some of the highest infant mortality rates in the world, by the 1990s, MENA was on par with two leaders in the developing world: East Asia and Latin America (figure 3.2).

Fertility Transition Was Slow

Mortality rates have continued to decline, but the pace has slowed as MENA converges with the industrial countries. Thus, the region's fer-

FIGURE 3.2

Infant Mortality Rates in Developing Regions, 1955–2025

Deaths per
1,000 infants

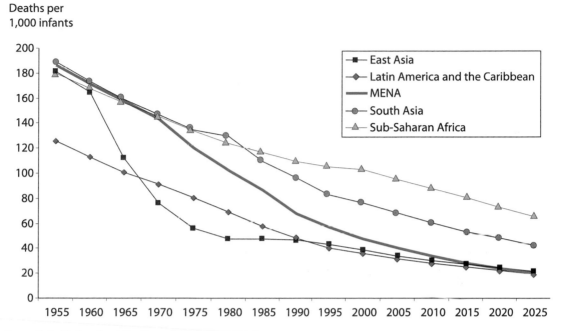

Source: United Nations Population Prospects 2002.

tility rates have become the driving force behind the demographic transition. In 1950, MENA had the highest fertility rate in the world at 7.0 children per woman, a position it maintained through 1970 (figure 3.3). And although the regional fertility rate has declined since 1970, the initial pace of the decline was slow. Between 1970 and 1990, fertility declined by 2.2 children per woman in Latin America and 3.1 in East Asia, but only 1.6 in MENA, a small change given the region's high initial levels. Since 1985, however, the fertility decline has accelerated dramatically, thereby narrowing the gap between MENA and other developing regions (Fargues 2003). Across much of MENA, evidence suggests that the fertility transition has gained momentum, thus setting the region on a path of low fertility in the 21st century.

Differences within MENA Are Significant

Within this regionwide trend, the timing and magnitude of the fertility decline in individual countries have varied (figure 3.4). Tunisia and Lebanon stand out as early leaders. Fertility rates peaked in both countries in the 1960s, with Tunisia at 7.3 and Lebanon at 6.4, but their rates had dropped to 2.3 by 2000. Several countries followed close behind.

FIGURE 3.3

Total Fertility Rates in Developing Regions, 1955–2025

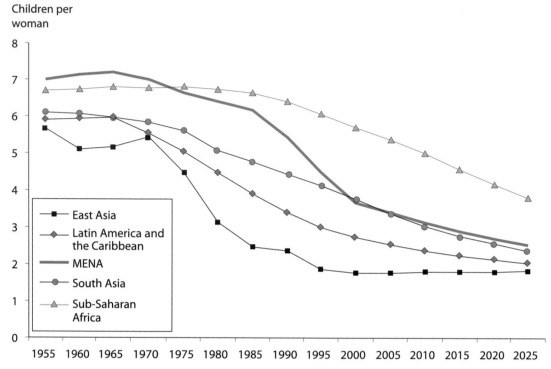

Children per woman

Source: United Nations Population Prospects 2002.

Bahrain, the Arab Republic of Egypt, Kuwait, Morocco, and the United Arab Emirates saw gradual but significant fertility declines in the 1970s, and rates are now at or below 3.5. Algeria and the Islamic Republic of Iran had fertility rates of nearly 6.5 as late as 1985 but have since registered significant declines, with fertility rates now lower than in Egypt. Jordan, Libya, Qatar, and the Syrian Arab Republic maintain relatively high fertility rates, ranging from 3.5 to 5.3, although all have seen the rates drop over time. In Iraq, despite early initial declines, fertility remains around 5.3. Although most Gulf countries have fertility rates below 3.0, the rate is 5.4 in Oman and 5.1 in Saudi Arabia. The Republic of Yemen has seen the smallest change in fertility, currently at 7.3 children per woman.

Determinants of Fertility Must Be Understood

Several factors explain the bulk of cross-country variations in fertility rates over time, the most important of which are health status and female education levels. Advances in health directly affect desired fertility and demand for children (Pritchett 1994). As infant and child mortality rates

FIGURE 3.4

Total Fertility Rates in MENA (Selected Countries), 1970 and 2000

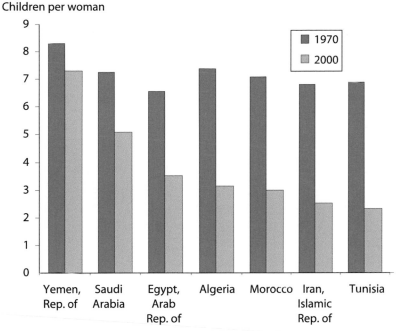

Children per woman

Source: United Nations Population Prospects 2002.

decline, couples expect more children to reach adulthood and, therefore, choose to have fewer children.

Female education influences fertility both directly and indirectly. Female education facilitates greater access to information about modern contraception and the benefits of family planning. Education also affects fertility by increasing the potential participation of women in the labor market. For women who participate in the labor force, the opportunity costs of having children are higher, and they may delay decisions about marriage and fertility.

Long-term increases in income levels and urbanization lower fertility by reducing the benefits of having children while raising the costs. In urban, industrializing economies, children no longer provide potential labor as they do in agricultural societies. Also, as income rises, so do the costs associated with rearing children, and parents may see the benefits of investing more in the quality of fewer children.

MENA Conforms to Global Patterns

The factors driving fertility trends in other regions appear to be playing the same role in MENA (Al-Qudsi 1998, Olmsted 2003). Although many MENA countries managed to reduce fertility by as much as other developing regions over the entire 1960–95 period, most of the reductions came only in the past decade. Low levels of female education before the 1980s are primarily responsible for this delay. Within MENA, differences in health conditions account for most of the variations in fertility reductions (box 3.1).

Orientation of Government Policies Has Changed

A significant portion of the decline in fertility, in MENA and elsewhere, comes from factors other than those discussed above. Slower rates of family formation among young adults because of unemployment, housing shortages, and marriage costs are at work (Kawar 2000, Singerman and Ibrahim 2001). Age at first marriage for both men and women in MENA is among the highest in developing countries. Furthermore, the acceleration in the fertility decline in the past decade may result, in part, from government population policies, which changed orientation in the late 1980s (Roudi-Fahimi 2001). Under the pressure of rapid population growth, governments began to realize the costs of high dependency burdens in expenditures on education, health, and infrastructure, as well as the socioeconomic effects of urban crowding and high youth unemployment. And countries that launched population programs early have generally secured the fastest fertility declines in the past decade, whereas those that have maintained pro-natal policies have the highest fertility rates in MENA (table 3.1, box 3.2).

Age Structure Is Changing Rapidly

The slow pace of the fertility decline in MENA before the 1990s not only delayed the transition from high to low population growth rates but also

TABLE 3.1

Government Policies on Fertility and Access to Modern Contraceptives, 2000

Policy on access to contraceptives	Policy on fertility level			
	Raise fertility	Maintain fertility	Lower fertility	No intervention
Direct support	n.a.	Bahrain, Islamic Rep. of Iran, Jordan, Lebanon, and Rep. of Yemen	Algeria, Arab Rep. of Egypt, Morocco, Tunisia, and Qatar	Djibouti, Iraq, and Syrian Arab Rep.
Indirect support	n.a.	n.a.	n.a.	Kuwait
No support	Saudi Arabia	Oman	n.a.	Libya and the United Arab Emirates

n.a. Not applicable.
Source: United Nations 2003.

BOX 3.1

Measuring Fertility Determinants

Isolating the effect of various factors on fertility is challenging given the multiple endogenous relationships between the fertility rate and its determinants. With this caveat in mind, a decomposition is presented here of the role of several determinants (health conditions, female education, male education, income, and urbanization) using panel regression analysis (Behrman, Duryea, and Székely 1999).

Nearly 38 percent of the fertility decline in MENA is due to improvements in health conditions, as measured by life expectancy after childhood, and nearly 20 percent is from advancements in female education. Changes in male education, urbanization, and gross domestic product per capita have a smaller role, accounting for less than 5 percent of the change in fertility. Also included are factors unexplained by the model, which account for 38 percent of the fertility decline. Other regions differ only slightly from MENA in the share of the fertility decline associated with these variables. In all regions, income, male education, and urbanization play small but significant roles, whereas health and female education play larger roles.

The experience of individual countries within MENA varies considerably, however. In Egypt, health explains 60 percent of the change in fertility rates, and female education explains nearly 29 percent. In Bahrain, health accounts for only 18 percent of the fertility decline, and female education explains 22 percent. In the Islamic Republic of Iran, 51 percent of the fertility decline is accounted for by health improvements, and 21 percent by female education. In Syria, 21 percent of the fertility decline is accounted for by female education, and 34 percent by health conditions.

Decomposition of Change in Fertility Rate between 1960 and 1995

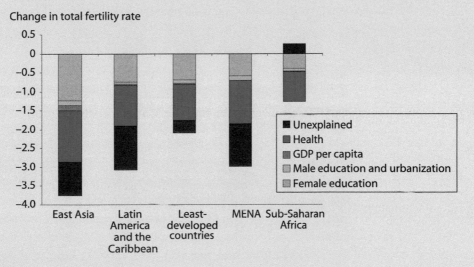

Change in total fertility rate

Source: Dyer and Yousef 2003.

BOX 3.2

Family Planning in the Islamic Republic of Iran

Following the 1979 revolution, the Iranian government implemented a number of pro-natal policies, including reducing the minimum age of marriage, removing contraceptives from the public health system, and providing subsidies for large families. After the Iran–Iraq War, however, policymakers became concerned about the costs associated with a population growth rate of 3.2 percent a year and a fertility rate of up to 6.6 children per woman during the Iran–Iraq War (see figure).

Actual and Projected Dependency Ratio and Fertility Rates in the Islamic Republic of Iran, 1950–2025

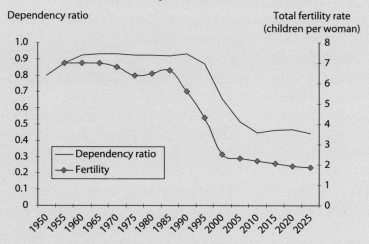

Source: United Nations Population Prospects 2002.

In 1989, the government launched a program to encourage couples to delay the first pregnancy and to spread out subsequent births, to discourage pregnancy for women younger than 18 and older than 35, and to limit family size to three children. Free family planning services and contraceptives were provided for married couples, and the government required both men and women to attend a course in modern contraception in order to secure a marriage license. More government attention was also given to lowering infant mortality, to promoting women's education and employment, and to extending social security benefits to all parents. In 1993, the Iranian *Majlis* introduced legislation to remove subsidies and other economic benefits for families with more than three children.

This inclusive and comprehensive family planning program has been highly successful. Although other factors have played a role, the demographic realities facing the Islamic Republic of Iran have undergone dynamic changes since the program's inception. Fertility rates have fallen precipitously (from 6.6 in 1985 to 2.5 in 2000), and population growth rates are now lower than 1.3 percent a year.

Source: Roudi-Fahimi 2002.

ensured that the young and economically dependent population (ages 0–14 and 65 and older) would dominate the region's age structure for some time to come. The dependency ratio—the ratio of the economically dependent to the working-age population (15–64 years old)—climbed from 0.81 in 1950 to a peak of 0.95 in 1970 and remained as high as 0.91 until 1980 (figure 3.5). The dependency ratio averaged 0.90 between 1950 and 1980, meaning that the region had 90 dependents for every 100 adults of working age. By comparison, East Asia's dependency ratio peaked at a much lower level of 0.76 and at an earlier date of 1965, and averaged 0.71 between 1950 and 1980. The dependency ratio was 0.83 in Latin America for the same period. By 1990, however, the dependency ratio in MENA had fallen to 0.86, and it continued to fall to 0.69 in 2000. It is forecast to fall for the next few decades, reaching 0.50 after 2025.

Fertility differences between the countries in MENA have been reflected in the trajectory of their dependency ratios (figure 3.6). Tunisia and Lebanon, which have led the region in fertility decline, saw their dependency ratios fall to 0.56 and 0.58, respectively, in 2000. Egypt and the Islamic Republic of Iran represent the norm in the region, with dependency ratios of 0.69 and 0.66, respectively. Not surprisingly, the slow

FIGURE 3.5

Actual and Projected Dependency Ratios in Developing Regions, 1950–2025

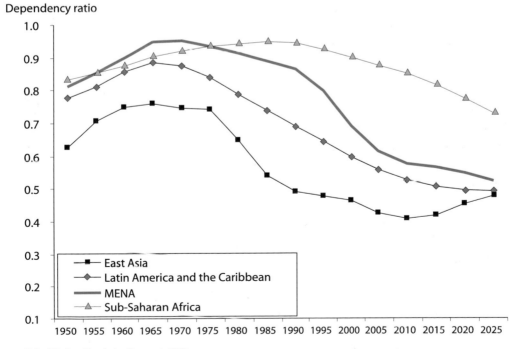

Source: United Nations Population Prospects 2002.

movers along the fertility transition remain burdened by high dependency rates. Saudi Arabia, despite the presence of large working-age migrant communities, currently maintains a ratio of 0.73. The Republic of Yemen has maintained the highest dependency ratio in the region since 1980 and is currently at 1.06.

Demographic Burden Becomes a Demographic Gift

The changing age structure of MENA's population has placed the region in a unique position at the beginning of the 21st century (Williamson and Yousef 2003). Between 1990 and 2020, the growth of the economically active population (ages 15–64) will exceed that of the economically dependent population by a much greater magnitude than in any other region. As East Asia's experience has shown, this differential, the so-called demographic gift, provides MENA with an opportunity to accelerate economic growth through faster accumulation of factors of production (Bloom and Williamson 1998) (figure 3.7). Lower dependency

FIGURE 3.6

Dependency Ratios in MENA (Selected Countries), 1980–2000

Dependency ratio

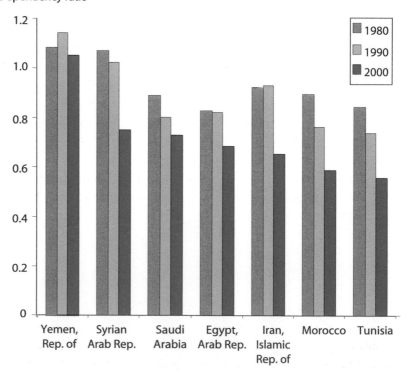

Source: United Nations Population Prospects 2002.

FIGURE 3.7

Gross Domestic Product Per Capita Growth and the Demographic Gift, 1965–90

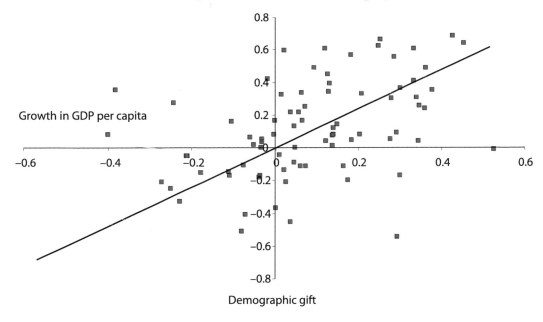

Demographic gift

Note: The figure shows the relationship between the demographic gift, defined as the difference between the growth of the economically active population and the total population, and gross domestic product (GDP) per capita growth conditional on a set of geographic, economic, and policy variables. Data are averages of the period 1965–90.
Source: Sachs and Warner 1997.

ratios imply a potential for higher savings and investment. Savings will increase more than investment, thus narrowing the domestic resource gap and reducing dependence on foreign capital. Rapid labor force growth, especially in the context of increased education and longer life expectancy, provides economies with a bigger pool of productive workers. As a result, policymakers in MENA are facing different challenges from those of the past. Ongoing demographic changes are shifting the policy focus from providing health and education for a young population toward facilitating employment and capital accumulation for maturing young adults.

Effect of Delayed Transition on Labor Force Growth

The timing and pattern of MENA's demographic transition have had an enormous effect on the dynamics of labor supply in the region. High population growth rates between the 1950s and the 1990s led to the rapid expansion of the working-age population. With rising labor force participation rates since 1980, the growth of labor supply and the increase in the absolute number of new labor market entrants have accelerated over time. Moreover, rapid population growth, in conjunction with the delayed fertility decline, has meant that pressures on labor markets have been sustained for a far longer period in MENA than in other regions. Labor force growth rates have averaged more than 3 percent a year between 1970 and 2010. No other developing region has experienced the magnitude and persistence of labor market pressures observed in MENA (figure 3.8). Consequently, the dynamics and determinants of labor supply in MENA are central to understanding the employment challenges and opportunities facing the region.

Demographic Transition Drives Labor Force Growth

The growth of the working-age population in MENA has risen steadily from 2 percent a year in the 1950s to more than 3 percent a year in the 1970s, where it remained until the 1990s. Rates of growth of the potential labor force began to decline in the past decade, but even today they remain high at 2.7 percent a year. East Asia, with its compressed demographic transition during the 1960s and 1970s, did not in that period exceed the average growth of the working-age population witnessed in MENA over the entire past half century. Despite a projected decline between now and 2020, growth in MENA's working-age population will be

FIGURE 3.8

Actual and Projected Labor Force Growth in Developing Regions, 1970–2010

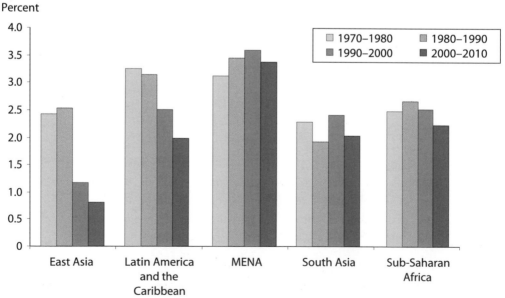

Percent

Sources: ILO 1996; United Nations Population Prospects 2002.

more than double that of East Asia today, one and a half times that of Latin America, and slightly above that of Sub-Saharan Africa.

Labor Force Participation Rates Have Been Rising

A general rise in participation rates among the working-age population has accompanied the growth in the working-age population in MENA (figure 3.9). After remaining stable at about 54.5 percent between 1970 and 1990, participation rates rose to 57.0 percent in 2000 and are projected to reach 61.0 percent by 2010. This increase has magnified the effect of labor market pressures resulting from the growth in the working-age population. As a result of these two factors, labor force growth accelerated from 2.1 percent a year in the 1960s to 3.1 percent in the 1970s, 3.4 percent in the 1980s, and 3.6 percent during the 1990s. The forecasted labor force growth rate between 2000 and 2010 is 3.5 percent a year, and not until 2020 will pressure on labor markets fall to more moderate rates last witnessed in the 1960s.

Although the absolute size of labor force flows in MENA relative to flows in other developing regions are small, the magnitudes are staggering from the perspective of the region. Between 1950 and 1990, 47 mil-

FIGURE 3.9

Dynamics of Labor Supply in MENA Countries, 1950s–2010s
(percent)

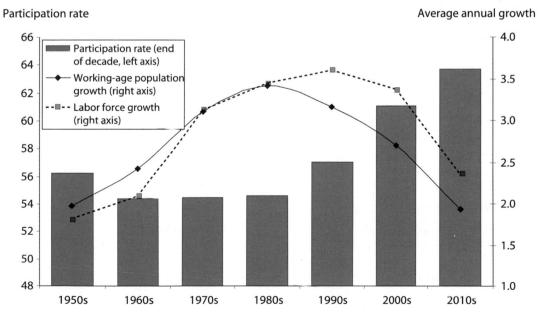

Sources: ILO 1996; United Nations Population Prospects 2002.

lion workers were added to the labor force, or 1.1 million workers a year. In the past decade alone, the labor force increased by some 32 million. Another 42 million will be added in this decade, and nearly 39 million in the next. Hence, in the first two decades of the 21st century, MENA's labor force will expand by as much as it did over the span of the previous half-century.

Migration Fuels the Expansion of Labor Supply in Oil-Exporting Countries

While demography and labor force participation trends have shaped growth in labor supply in the labor-abundant countries, migration has been the driving force behind labor force growth in the oil-exporting (labor-importing) countries. Expatriate workers responded to the sharp increase in labor demand following oil price increases in the 1970s. In the mid-1980s, 4.1 million foreign nationals were working in the oil-exporting countries of the Gulf Cooperation Council (GCC), representing some 67 percent of the total work force and almost 26 percent of the population (box 3.3). By some estimates, close to 10 percent of Egypt's labor force and almost 15 percent of the Republic of Yemen's were employed abroad in the region in the 1980s.

BOX 3.3

Evolution of the Labor Force in the Gulf Cooperation Council

From 1975 to 1985, the peak years of oil-led growth in the region, the GCC countries experienced unprecedented labor force growth of 7.7 percent a year, with growth in Bahrain reaching 10.5 percent and growth in Saudi Arabia reaching 8.1 percent. This growth was driven primarily by the large number of immigrants seeking work in the rapidly expanding, population-deficient economies of the Gulf. During this period, the nonnational labor force grew at an average annual rate of nearly 13 percent, reaching 15 percent in Bahrain and 17 percent in Saudi Arabia. For the GCC as a whole, nonnationals made up more than 67 percent of the labor force in 1985, up from 39 percent 10 years earlier.

As oil prices fell in the mid-1980s, however, growth in the region declined, and with it the demand for labor. Labor force growth in the GCC fell to 4.4 percent between 1985 and 1995, reflecting a drop to 4.4 percent in the labor force growth rate for nonnationals and an increase from 1.6 percent to 4.5 percent in the labor force growth rate for nationals. The total share of nonnationals within the GCC continued to increase through 1995, when the trend began to fade as demographic pressures in the GCC states led to larger numbers of nationals seeking work.

BOX 3.3 (continued)

Nonnationals as a Share of Total Labor Force, 1975–2000

Percent

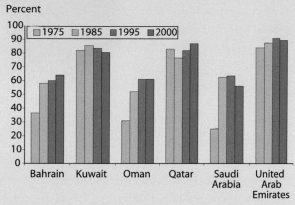

Source: Girgis, Hadad-Zervos, and Coulibaly 2003.

The fall in oil prices happened as the majority of Gulf countries began witnessing an increase in the share of their populations over the age of 15. Domestic labor market supply pressures have increased since the late 1990s. Thus, growth rates increased to 4.9 percent a year among nationals in the GCC labor force, while decreasing among nonnationals in all GCC countries, falling to 2.8 percent a year between 1995 and 2000. The share of nonnational workers in the total labor force has leveled off or declined in nearly all the GCC countries, falling from an average of 67 percent in 1995 to 64 percent in 2000. The decline has been largest in Saudi Arabia, where the share of nonnationals in the labor force has fallen from 64.2 percent to 55.8 percent.

Labor Force Growth in the GCC Countries, 1975–2000

Percent

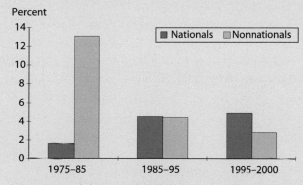

Source: Girgis, Hadad-Zervos, and Coulibaly 2003.

Source: Girgis, Hadad-Zervos, and Coulibaly 2003.

Since labor force participation rates are high among expatriate workers, the labor-importing countries have exhibited higher participation rates than have the rest of MENA. Between 1970 and 1990, the labor force in the oil-exporting countries grew at an average of 6.4 percent a year compared with 3.0 percent in the rest of MENA. Beginning in the 1990s, lower migration rates led to a marked deceleration in the growth of the labor force in these countries. Labor force growth remains high, but now it is driven, as in the rest of MENA, by rising participation rates and an expansion of the national working-age population.

Patterns of Demographic Transition Determine Country Profiles

In the labor-abundant (labor-exporting) countries of MENA, differences in the onset of the fertility decline and in labor force participation rates account for the diversity in labor force pressures faced by individual countries. By and large, countries that witnessed the earliest and fastest declines in fertility have experienced smaller and shorter strains on their labor markets than those undergoing later and slower fertility declines. In Morocco and Tunisia, two leading countries in the fertility decline, labor force growth rates peaked in the 1970s at 3.4 percent a year and 4.0 percent a year, respectively, and have since declined steadily to about 2.5 percent a year. In contrast, in Egypt, where fertility decline has been slow, labor market pressures have been persistent and have even increased in the current decade as female participation rates have risen. Labor force growth in Egypt has risen from 2.5 percent in 1980 to the current 3.1 percent.

In the Islamic Republic of Iran, the growth of the labor supply has risen from 3.6 percent in the 1980s to 3.9 percent in the current decade, which corresponds to its late but accelerated fertility decline. Syria experienced a similar pattern, with fertility rates high until the 1990s and falling quickly thereafter. Labor force growth rates in Syria will be at their highest between 1990 and 2010, averaging 4.2 percent a year (figure 3.10). The Republic of Yemen has the highest rates of labor force growth, along with the highest rates of fertility in the region. Its labor force growth will have averaged nearly 4.3 percent a year between 1990 and 2010.

Rural Migration Contributes to Urbanization

Across much of the region, rural-to-urban migration has intensified the growth of labor supply in urban centers. Reflecting the acceleration of migration because of higher wages and better health and education services in urban centers, urban populations in most countries continue to

FIGURE 3.10

Actual and Projected Average Annual Growth in the Labor Force of MENA Countries, 1970–2010

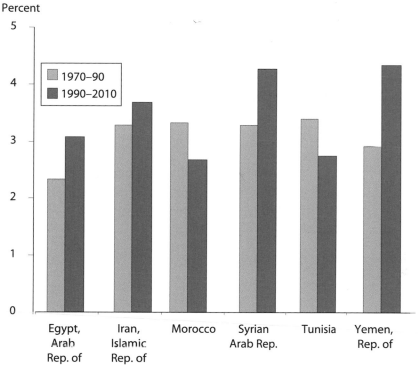

Sources: ILO 1996; United Nations Population Prospects 2002.

grow faster than the national average, whereas rural populations experience low or even negative growth. In fact, rural-to-urban migration accounts for an estimated one-third to one-half of population growth in cities (Adams 2003a).

As a result of this migration, MENA is one of the most urbanized regions in the world. The percentage of people living in rural areas is lower in all MENA countries, with the exception of the Republic of Yemen, than in low- and middle-income developing countries as a whole (table 3.2). The Islamic Republic of Iran, Lebanon, and Tunisia, in particular, show signs of negative rural population growth largely because of migration. Egypt exhibits rural population growth rates that reflect a low rate of migration, whereas rural population growth rates in Jordan, Syria, and the Republic of Yemen, though lower than urban growth rates, do not suggest the high rates of rural-to-urban migration of other countries in the region.

Migration from rural to urban areas has had a substantial effect on rural labor markets in MENA. Most notably, it has reduced labor supply pres-

TABLE 3.2

Rural and Urban Population in Selected MENA Countries

Country	Rural population (percent of total population)	Employment in agriculture (percent of total employment)	Urban population growth (percent), 2000	Rural population growth (percent), 2000
Algeria	42.9	12.0 (1995)	2.7	0.1
Egypt, Arab Rep. of	57.3	30.0 (2000)	2.3	2.1
Iran, Islamic Rep. of	36.0	23.0 (1996)	2.3	−0.7
Jordan	21.3	6.0 (1993)	3.8	2.7
Lebanon	10.3	7.3 (1990)	1.8	−2.9
Morocco	44.5	44.0 (1999)	3.1	0.1
Syrian Arab Rep.	48.6	28.2 (1991)	3.3	1.9
Tunisia	34.5	21.6 (2000)	2.2	−1.0
Yemen, Rep. of	75.3	54.0 (1999)	3.6	2.4
Low- and middle-income countries	58.9	46.3 (1995)	2.6	0.5
MENA	42.7	26.8 (1990)	2.5	1.0

Sources: ESCWA 2001; World Bank 2003h.

sures in rural areas and lowered the number of workers who need to be absorbed by the agricultural sector. As of 2000, only 27 percent of the labor force in MENA was engaged in agriculture. In fact, only the Republic of Yemen has more than half of its population employed in agriculture. In Jordan and Lebanon, less than 10 percent of the population works in agriculture. Furthermore, all evidence suggests that the share of workers engaged in the agricultural sector will continue to decline (chapter 4).

Effect of Young Working Adults Is Growing

The share of young adults (ages 15–29) in the working-age population and their participation in the labor force yield important insights into the dynamics of labor supply, since this segment of the working-age population constitutes the bulk of new entrants into labor markets. The share of young cohorts in the working-age population has remained high throughout the past half-century at no less than 47 percent (figure 3.11). It reached its peak in the 1980s at 51.5 percent but will remain above 40 percent until at least 2020.

Young adults, however, have not composed as large a weight in the labor force as they have in the population. Their share has been consistently below their share in the working-age population, averaging 45 percent between 1950 and 2000 and peaking in 1980 at 47 percent. This trend results largely from the fact that youths in MENA, like their counterparts elsewhere, are remaining in school longer and delaying their entry into the work force.

FIGURE 3.11

Actual and Projected Share of Young Adults (Ages 15–29) in MENA's Population and Labor Force, 1950–2010

Percent

Sources: ILO 1996; United Nations Population Prospects 2002.

Still, the pressure of young adults on labor force growth has been persistently high in MENA, with their growth in the labor force averaging almost 3 percent a year between 1950 and 1990 (figure 3.12). The period 1990–2010 will witness the greatest labor force pressures from young adults, as the share of young workers in the total labor force exceeds their share in the total population for the first time. Rising participation rates are driving this trend, and there is an important gender dimension to this increase.

Gender Profile of the Labor Force Is Changing

While young males have been staying longer outside the work force, young females are choosing to participate in greater numbers (Assaad 2002b). Participation rates for young men in the age group 15–29 fell from 77 percent in 1970 to 67 percent in 2000, whereas participation rates for the same cohort of women rose from almost 23 percent to 32 percent (figure 3.13). Thus, while growth rates of young male entrants have declined, those of young female entrants have accelerated. As a result, labor force pressures from young adults will remain as high over the 1990–2010 period as they were during 1970–90.

The rising participation of women in the labor force since the 1980s constitutes one of the most important developments affecting the size

FIGURE 3.12

Actual and Projected Growth of Young Adults (Ages 15–29) in MENA, 1950–2010

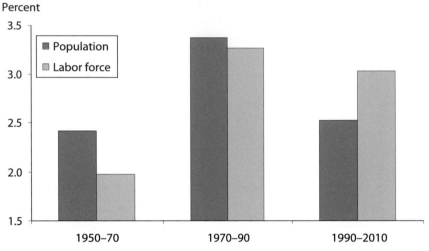

Sources: ILO 1996, United Nations Population Prospects 2002.

FIGURE 3.13

Female Labor Supply in MENA, 1950s–2010s

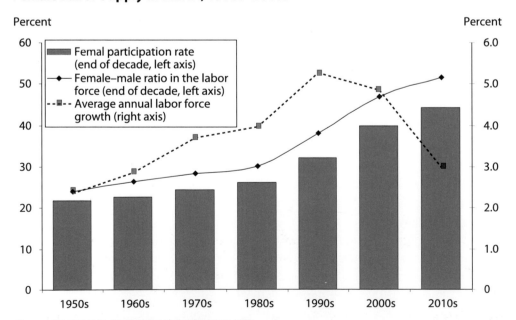

Sources: ILO 1996, United Nations Population Prospects 2002.

and gender composition of the region's labor supply in recent years (World Bank 2003c). The trend, while particularly evident among young females, cuts across all age cohorts. Female labor force participation rose from about 22 percent in 1960 to almost 25 percent in 1980, 27 percent in the 1990s, and 32 percent in 2000. Furthermore, female participation is forecast to reach 43 percent in 2020. The rate of growth of female labor supply accelerated to 5 percent in the 1990s and is at 4.9 percent in the present decade. As a result, the low female share in the total labor force of 18 percent in the 1950s rose to 27 percent in 2000 and will expand to 32 percent by 2010.

Female labor force participation is traditionally high in agrarian societies, and accordingly, Egypt, Morocco, and the Republic of Yemen have historically high participation rates (figure 3.14). However, not all employment has the same effect on women's choices. Those who participate in agricultural or informal work do not face the opportunity costs associated with children that women working in the formal sector do. In these cases, it is the change in female participation over the long run that matters because it reflects their exit from agriculture.

FIGURE 3.14

Female Labor Participation Rates in MENA, 1970 and 2000

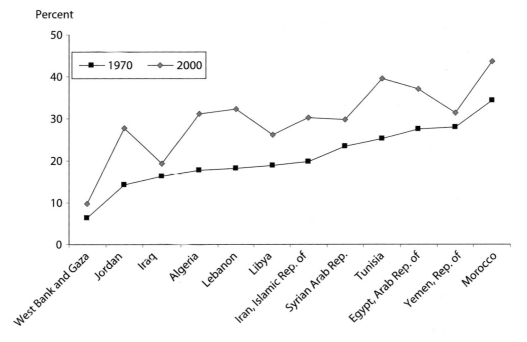

Sources: ILO 1996, United Nations Population Prospects 2002.

Labor Force Is Increasingly More Educated

Not only are young adults entering the labor force in greater numbers, they also are increasingly more educated, a consequence of the considerable resources devoted by governments in MENA to human capital accumulation. In the 1960s, educational attainment in the region was the lowest in the world, with less than a year of education per adult age 15 or older (table 3.3). By 1980, MENA had begun closing the gap with other developing regions, and in the past 20 years, the effect of the policy commitment to education has been impressive. The educational attainment of the adult population in MENA increased more than 150 percent, faster than in any other region or income group in the world. With an average 5.3 years of schooling among those age 15 and older, MENA is ahead of South Asia and Sub-Saharan Africa and is a little more than a year behind East Asia and Latin America.

Recent surveys in Egypt and Morocco provide greater detail on the expansion of educational attainment (figure 3.15). In Egypt, for example, people currently between the ages of 65 and 69 received slightly more than 3 years of education, whereas people ages 45 to 49 received 5–6 years of education. Those now between 30 and 35 have attained nearly 8 years of education.

TABLE 3.3

Average Years of Schooling in Developing Regions and Countries (Adults Age 15 and Older), 1960–99

Region	1960	1980	1999
East Asia	4.3	4.9	6.6
Eastern Europe	4.9	6.5	7.3
Industrial countries	7.2	9.1	10.0
Latin America and the Caribbean	3.8	4.9	6.4
MENA	0.9	2.6	5.3
South Asia	1.5	3.0	4.6
Southeast Asia	2.2	4.1	5.5
Sub-Saharan Africa	1.7	2.3	3.5
Country	1960	1980	1999
Algeria	1.0	2.7	5.4
Bahrain	1.0	3.6	6.1
Egypt, Arab Rep. of	—	2.3	5.5
Iran, Islamic Rep. of	0.8	2.8	5.3
Iraq	0.3	2.7	4.0
Jordan	2.3	4.3	6.9
Kuwait	2.6	4.3	7.1
Syrian Arab Rep.	1.4	3.6	5.8
Tunisia	0.6	2.9	5.0

— Not available.
Note: East Asia includes China. Eastern Europe does not include the Russian Federation. South Asia includes India. Regional data are weighted by population.
Source: Barro and Lee 2000.

FIGURE 3.15

Schooling by Year of Birth in Egypt and Morocco, 1926–76

Average years of schooling

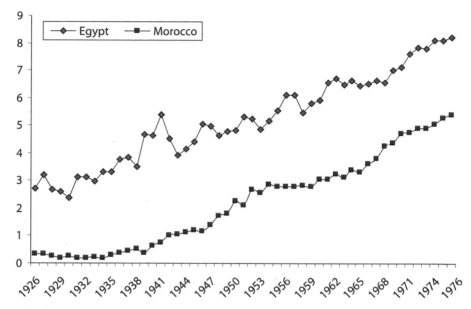

Sources: Arab Republic of Egypt, CAPMAS 1998; Morocco 1999.

Gender Gaps Are Narrowing by International Standards

MENA's success in educating its female population is as impressive as the aggregate record. Starting from the lowest average years of schooling in the world, women in the region have either narrowed the gap or surpassed their counterparts in other regions. An examination of specific levels of attainment confirms the depth of this achievement. In 1960, MENA ranked below Sub-Saharan Africa, East Asia, and Latin America in terms of the ratio of women with higher or secondary education to women with only primary or no education (figure 3.16). Between 1980 and 2000, this ratio grew faster in MENA than anywhere else.

More importantly, the gender gap in education in MENA has been shrinking rapidly. The ratio of male-to-female years of schooling fell from 2.5 in 1960, to 1.9 in 1980, and to 1.4 in 2000. Rising female enrollment rates at all levels of education since the 1970s are responsible for this trend and, at the current pace, will push educational outcomes toward greater gender parity. In Syria, for example, primary enrollment rates in the 1970s were 84 percent for boys and 54 percent for girls. By 2000, they were 99 percent for boys and 94 percent for girls. It is not surprising, then, that MENA's gender gaps in education are smaller now than those in East Asia and South Asia.

FIGURE 3.16

Female Education in Developing Regions, 1960–2000

Ratio of secondary- and tertiary-educated women
to primary-educated and uneducated women

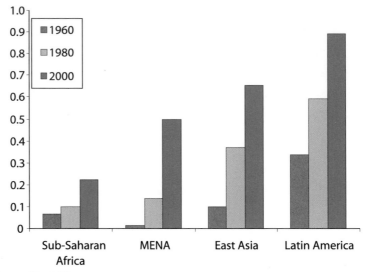

Source: Barro and Lee 2000.

Education Matters More for Female Labor Participation

There is little doubt that the rising educational attainment of women in the region has contributed to their growing participation in the economy (Assaad and El-Hamidi 2002). Education affects labor force participation directly by raising the opportunity costs of remaining outside the work force and by providing greater access to better job opportunities. It affects labor force participation indirectly by reducing fertility. As the trends in Egypt and Morocco show, female labor force participation rises with the level of education, doubling or tripling as women move from illiteracy to postsecondary levels (figures 3.17 and 3.18).

Greater educational attainment has coincided with the growing size of female cohorts in their prime working years because of the dynamics of demography in the region. The two forces have interacted positively to raise female labor participation, in line with the experience of Latin America in the 1980s and East Asia in the 1970s: changing age structure and education together explain close to 55 percent of the rise in female labor participation rates in MENA in the past 20 years.

Male labor force participation rates are generally higher than female participation rates at every level of education, in part because of men's traditional role as primary breadwinners. But what is striking from recent evidence in Egypt and Morocco is the V-pattern of male participa-

FIGURE 3.17

Female Labor Force Participation in Egypt, by Education Level, 1998

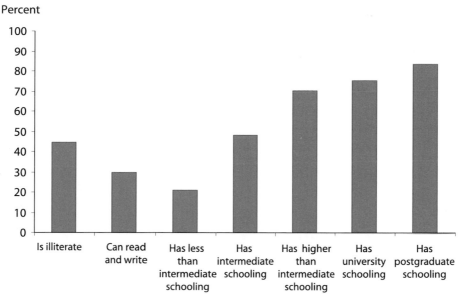

Source: Arab Republic of Egypt, CAPMAS 1998.

FIGURE 3.18

Female Labor Force Participation in Morocco, by Education Level, 1999

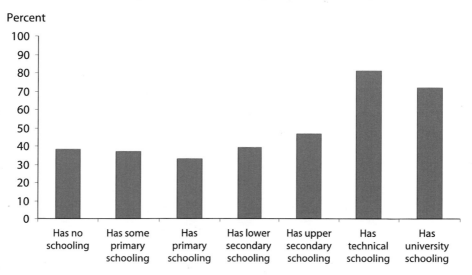

Source: Morocco 1999.

tion and education profiles (figures 3.19 and 3.20). Participation rates are higher at the extremes of educational attainment but low at intermediate levels. The stability of this pattern in the 1980s and 1990s suggests that the participation rates for men with intermediate levels of education are

FIGURE 3.19

Male Labor Force Participation in Egypt, by Education Level, 1998

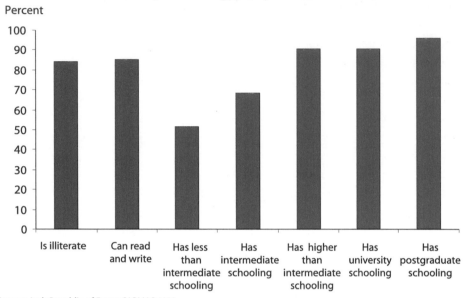

Source: Arab Republic of Egypt, CAPMAS 1998.

FIGURE 3.20

Male Labor Force Participation in Morocco, by Education Level, 1999

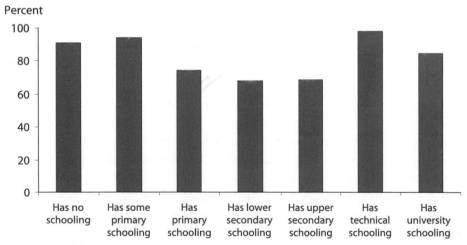

Source: Morocco 1999.

a reflection of high unemployment rates among this category of workers and the low demand for their skills in labor markets (chapters 4 and 6).

Labor Market Outcomes in the 1990s

The dynamics of demography in MENA have created some of the most intense pressures on labor markets observed anywhere in the world in the post–World War II period. The growing supply of workers constitutes one of the fundamental forces driving employment outcomes in the region (Duryea and Székely 1998). But since employment outcomes are determined by the interaction of supply and demand, no complete account of labor markets can be made without an assessment of labor demand as determined by economic conditions and policies internal and external to the region. From this perspective, the strong economic performance of MENA before the mid-1980s and its weaker performance in the subsequent period have been fully reflected in labor market outcomes. In contrast to the 1960s and 1970s, labor supply growth against a backdrop of anemic economic performance and an outdated development model in the 1980s and 1990s has resulted in the emergence of high and persistent unemployment (Shaban, Assaad, and Al-Qudsi 2001).

High Unemployment Emerges

By definition, if labor supply exceeds the level of employment, the unemployment rate rises. Over the past decade, growth in the labor force has exceeded growth in employment in Algeria, Egypt, the Islamic Republic of Iran, and Morocco, which together account for two-thirds of the region's labor force (figure 3.21). In Jordan and Tunisia, where rates of unemployment were already moderately high, employment growth has just kept pace with labor force growth.

Accordingly, unemployment in MENA is, at present, among the highest in the world, second only to that in Sub-Saharan Africa. A conservative estimate places unemployment at about 15 percent of the work force. Also, young cohorts are disproportionately affected by unemployment. Youth unemployment rates are more than twice the rates of total unemployment in many countries in the region. The majority of unemployed workers are relatively well-educated, first-time job seekers (chapter 4).

The problem of unemployment affects almost every country in the region (figure 3.22). Recently, even the oil-exporting countries that traditionally imported expatriate labor to supplement the national work force have begun to experience increasing rates of unemployment. Unofficial estimates put rates of unemployment at much higher levels, and the regionwide

FIGURE 3.21

Labor Force Growth versus Employment Growth in the 1990s

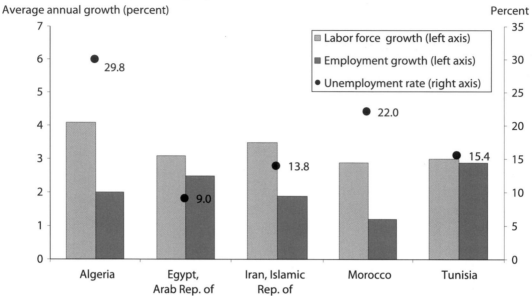

Source: Compiled by World Bank staff from ILO and country sources.

FIGURE 3.22

Unemployment Rates in MENA

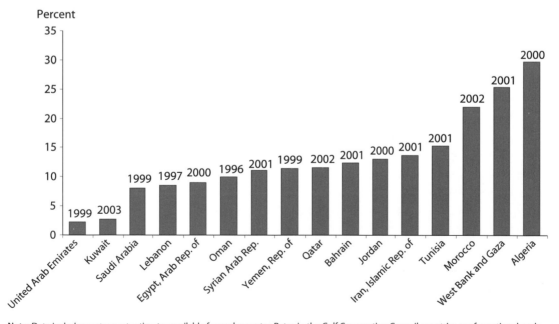

Note: Data include most recent estimates available for each country. Rates in the Gulf Cooperation Council countries are for nationals only.
Source: Compiled by World Bank staff from ILO and country sources.

estimate would also rise if Iraq were included. Moreover, official estimates do not include underemployment and disguised employment, which, if taken into account, would raise the estimates even further (Fergany 2001).

Real Wages Have Stagnated or Declined

MENA's poor labor market outcomes in the 1990s affected employment and real wages. Although real wages increased marginally in some countries, they either stagnated or declined in most, extending a trend that began in the 1980s (chapter 4). Worker productivity, which forms the basis for the long-term behavior of real wages, improved in only a handful of countries in MENA (figure 3.23). In Egypt, the Islamic Republic of Iran, and Tunisia, productivity per worker increased by an average of 1.8 percent a year. For MENA as a whole, worker productivity increased by an average of about 0.7 percent a year in the past decade. This growth is less than in any other region except Europe and Central Asia, which has been undergoing significant economic restructuring. Worker productivity soared in East Asia, with output per worker growing at more than 7.0 percent a year (figure 3.24).

Many Factors Lead to Adverse Labor Market Outcomes

Labor supply pressures in MENA, while important, cannot alone account for the adverse labor market outcomes in the 1990s. After all, had

FIGURE 3.23

Average Annual Growth in Output per Worker in MENA Countries, 1990s

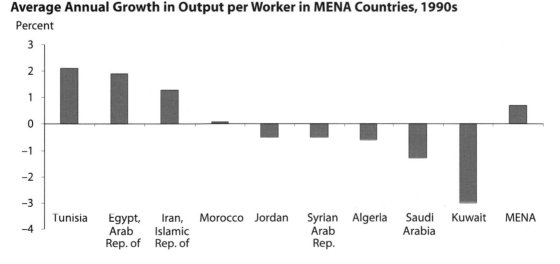

Note: The average for MENA is weighted.
Source: World Bank staff estimates.

FIGURE 3.24

Average Annual Growth in Gross Domestic Product per Employed Person, by Region, 1990s

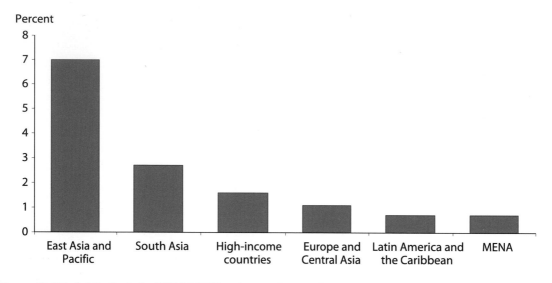

Sources: World Bank staff estimates for MENA, ILO 2002 for other countries.

employment growth in the 1990s simply matched labor force growth, the rates of unemployment would have stabilized instead of rising. Although the supply of first-time job seekers, who are traditionally vulnerable to high unemployment, has grown since the 1980s, this growth has not necessarily led to high unemployment rates for young adults. In some MENA countries where youth unemployment is high, participation rates among young males fell in the 1990s, implying that not all potential workers entered the labor market (figure 3.25). International experience suggests that overall economic conditions matter more than demographic forces alone in shaping labor market outcomes (O'Higgins 2003). Where unemployment rates are high, they tend to affect young as well as older workers (figure 3.26).

Employment and Output Trends Are Linked

Labor demand appears to have slowed the pace of job creation in the 1990s, leading to high unemployment. The most important indicator of trends in labor demand is output growth. Strong output growth both reflects and leads to employment growth and lower unemployment because

FIGURE 3.25

Youth Unemployment and Youth Population as a Share of Total, 1990s

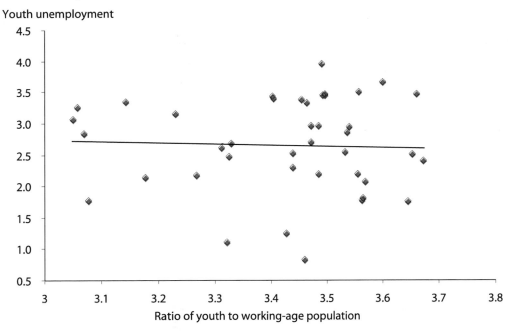

Note: The data are the average value for the 1990s in logs.
Source: ILO 2002.

FIGURE 3.26

Adult Unemployment and Youth Unemployment Rates, 1990s

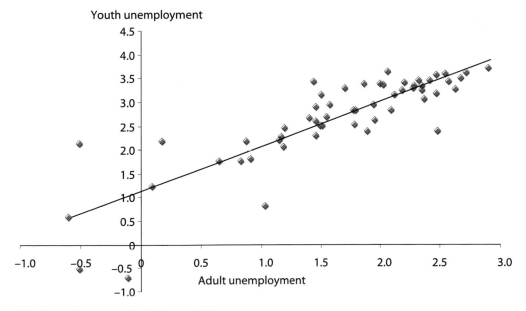

Note: The data are the average value for the 1990s in logs.
Source: ILO 2002.

the work force is an essential factor of production that contributes directly to the expansion of output. Thus, faster output growth has generally gone hand in hand with lower unemployment, whereas growth stagnation has invariably implied higher levels of unemployment. In most MENA countries, the economies that have grown the fastest since the mid-1980s today exhibit the lowest unemployment rates (figure 3.27).

The interplay among output, employment, and unemployment can be summarized in a simple accounting framework that conceptualizes the two basic characteristics of good labor market outcomes: high employment and wage growth. The sum of the two objectives is captured by the behavior of output per laborer over time:

$$Growth\left(\frac{Output}{Labor\,force}\right) = Growth\left(\frac{Employment}{Labor\,force}\right) + Growth\left(\frac{Output}{Employment}\right)$$

Accordingly, creating employment opportunities for those who want to work is equivalent to increasing the ratio of employed persons to the total labor force. Boosting wage growth, however, depends on raising worker productivity, or output per employed person. Faster employment and productivity growth go hand in hand with the expansion of output growth per laborer. Conversely, slower output growth reflects rising unemployment, productivity slowdowns, or both.

FIGURE 3.27

Changes in Unemployment and Output, 1980–99
(percent)

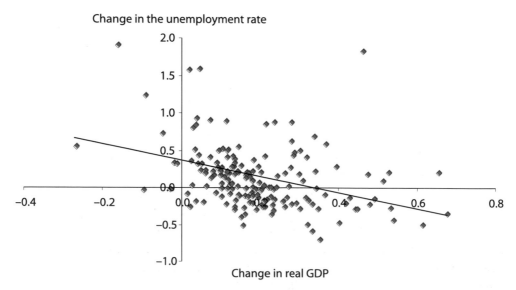

Change in the unemployment rate

Change in real GDP

Sources: Rama and Artecona 2000; World Bank 2002e.

Trends in the growth of output per laborer are fairly consistent with trends in productivity growth and reductions in unemployment in MENA countries. Countries that experienced faster growth in output per laborer in the 1990s witnessed an increase in worker productivity, a decline in unemployment, or both. Tunisia's growth in output per laborer of 1.9 percent was achieved through higher worker productivity, which averaged 2.1 percent, and a modest reduction in the unemployment rate from 16 percent to 15 percent. Egypt's more modest growth in output per laborer, 1.4 percent, reflected productivity gains but lower employment growth and, hence, increased unemployment. For countries such as Algeria, Jordan, and Morocco, negative growth in output per laborer over the 1990s was the result of either worsening unemployment or lower worker productivity.

Those findings suggest that trends in output growth per laborer reflect labor market outcomes in MENA. The story in the 1990s was one of weak output performance in the face of rapid labor force growth, with the result that output per laborer barely improved—if at all (Nabli and Keller 2002). Although there is a modest difference in labor force growth rates between MENA in the 1990s and the fast-growing Asian economies in the 1970s, the real difference between the regions is that labor force growth was accompanied by enormous increases in real output in East Asia but not in MENA. Real gross domestic product (GDP) growth in East Asia averaged 7.4 percent a year during 1970–80—more than double its labor force growth rate for the same period. In MENA, however, the combination of low worker productivity and high unemployment in the 1990s implied that output growth averaged only about 3.7 percent a year—only marginally higher than the growth rate of its labor force.

MENA's Growth Performance Needs Closer Examination

Although anemic growth in output per laborer has resulted in and reflected the poor labor outcomes in MENA in the past decade, it does not explain the reasons behind the growth slowdown. Output growth (and output growth per laborer) is driven by the accumulation of physical and human capital embodied in the work force, as well as by how these factors of production are used in production. A fuller understanding of the dynamics of growth requires a closer examination of the underpinnings of output. Furthermore, MENA's recent record, which has elicited the concern of policymakers and outside observers, should be assessed in the context of the MENA region's long-run development trajectory and the policies and events shaping it since 1960 (table 3.4).

TABLE 3.4

Growth in Output, Capital, and Total Factor Productivity, by Region
(percent per laborer)

Region	Decade	Gross domestic product	Physical capital	Human capital	Total factor productivity
East Asia and the Pacific	1960s	2.6	2.9	0.7	1.0
	1970s	3.7	6.2	0.9	0.7
	1980s	5.9	6.1	1.0	2.9
	1990s	7.0	8.4	0.7	3.2
High-income countries and Organisation for Economic Co-operation and Development	1960s	3.3	3.8	0.7	1.4
	1970s	1.5	2.2	1.5	−0.2
	1980s	1.6	1.9	0.2	0.7
	1990s	1.6	2.0	0.6	0.4
Latin America and the Caribbean	1960s	2.7	2.9	0.5	1.2
	1970s	2.9	4.0	0.6	1.0
	1980s	−1.7	0.2	0.9	−2.3
	1990s	2.7	2.9	0.5	1.2
MENA	1960s	6.0	5.4	0.7	3.4
	1970s	3.8	10.0	1.3	−1.0
	1980s	0.3	2.4	1.4	−1.5
	1990s	0.7	0.1	1.3	−0.2
South Asia	1960s	2.1	4.0	0.6	0.2
	1970s	0.6	1.9	1.0	−0.7
	1980s	3.6	3.1	0.9	1.9
	1990s	2.7	3.3	0.9	0.9
Sub-Saharan Africa	1960s	2.8	3.6	0.3	1.2
	1970s	1.4	3.2	0.3	−0.1
	1980s	−0.9	0.6	0.7	−1.6
	1990s	0.4	0.7	0.6	−0.2

Note: Regional averages weighted by average labor force over period.
Source: Nabli and Keller 2002.

MENA Had Exceptional Performance before the 1980s

In the 1960s, MENA began two decades of massive public investments in infrastructure, health, and education that translated into high growth. Heavy investments were also made in state-owned enterprises in protected industries. These efforts helped the region to make better use of underused capacities and provided a boost to industrialization. As a result, MENA's economic growth performance in the 1960s was the highest in the world, averaging 7.1 percent a year, equivalent to an annual 4.7 percent growth per laborer (World Bank 1995a). Strong output growth continued in the 1970s, though at a lower annual average of 5.8 percent. However, the conditions spurring growth in the 1970s included some undesirable departures from the previous decade in terms of accumulation and productivity. Growth in the 1970s was driven only by high rates of accumulation, made possible by the availability of resources during the oil boom, while productivity growth slowed. During that decade, MENA realized the highest rates of growth in the world in both physical capital and human capital per laborer, but growth on a per laborer basis was 2 percentage points lower on an average annual basis than it was in the 1960s.

Thus, although workers were equipped with more physical and human capital, the efficiency in using these inputs was declining. Algeria's rate of physical capital accumulation almost quadrupled between the 1960s and 1970s, but total factor productivity (TFP) growth went from 1.9 percent a year to –0.7 percent (table 3.4). Jordan tripled its rate of physical capital accumulation, but TFP growth declined by 40 percent (from 2.8 percent a year to 1.7 percent). Morocco doubled its rate of accumulation, but TFP growth fell from 1.8 percent a year to –0.3 percent per year. In the Gulf, Saudi Arabia's doubling of its physical capital accumulation was accompanied by a decline in average annual TFP growth from 4.7 percent in the 1960s to zero in the 1970s.

Oil Bust Signaled the Beginning of Economic Crisis

As international oil prices plummeted in the 1980s, the foundations of positive labor market outcomes in MENA collapsed. Output growth per laborer slowed, even becoming negative in some cases. With eroding macroeconomic balances and growing debt burdens, and despite external assistance that permitted spending, investments declined dramatically. Growth in physical capital per laborer fell by 75 percent from the previous decade.

Every country in the region experienced a dramatic deceleration in the rate of accumulation between the 1970s and 1980s, and almost every economy experienced a decline in TFP growth. Only the Islamic Republic of Iran, Kuwait, and Morocco saw improvements in TFP growth between the 1970s and 1980s, though in Syria TFP growth remained essentially the same (table 3.5). Negative productivity growth was most prevalent in the oil-producing economies of the region—within most of the GCC and in Algeria. With massive declines in the rate of accumulation and with corresponding declines in TFP growth for most countries, output growth per laborer collapsed, a change of almost –3.5 percent a year over the 1970s (Page 1998).

Stabilization and Reform Programs Followed

The growth slowdown and large macroeconomic imbalances prompted a handful of countries, including Morocco, Jordan, and Tunisia, to em-

TABLE 3.5

Growth in Output, Capital, and Total Factor Productivity in MENA, 1970s and 1980s
(percent per laborer)

Region or country	Decade	GDP growth	Physical capital growth	Human capital growth	Total factor productivity growth
MENA	1970s	3.8	10.0	1.3	−1.0
	1980s	0.3	2.4	1.4	−1.5
Algeria	1970s	2.7	6.8	1.1	−0.7
	1980s	−1.0	1.4	1.6	−2.5
Egypt, Arab Rep. of	1970s	7.3	10.2	1.6	2.2
	1980s	2.9	5.7	1.9	−0.5
Iran, Islamic Rep. of	1970s	0.3	16.4	1.2	−7.0
	1980s	−0.3	0.8	1.2	−1.3
Jordan	1970s	9.3	17.3	1.0	1.7
	1980s	−2.8	4.2	1.7	−5.5
Kuwait	1970s	−7.4	−4.8	1.4	−6.3
	1980s	−5.2	−4.0	1.7	−4.6
Morocco	1970s	1.9	4.4	0.8	−0.3
	1980s	1.2	1.5	0.8	0.1
Saudi Arabia	1970s	4.4	8.9	1.4	0.0
	1980s	−6.0	0.0	1.7	−7.0
Syrian Arab Rep.	1970s	6.5	7.8	1.5	−2.5
	1980s	−1.0	1.5	1.5	−2.4
Tunisia	1970s	3.6	3.4	1.5	1.4
	1980s	0.8	1.9	1.0	−0.6

Source: Nabli and Keller 2002.

bark on programs of stabilization and policy reform in the mid-1980s. By the early 1990s, after the Gulf War, nearly all non-oil-exporting countries followed suit, as did several of the Gulf economies. The hope was that such measures would improve the efficiency of resource allocation, would attract investment, and would ultimately create an environment in which the private sector could emerge as an engine of faster and sustainable economic growth and employment creation.

Did these efforts pay off? By and large, countries in the region experienced improvements in productivity and, hence, faster growth in output per laborer in the 1990s than in the 1980s (table 3.6). Saudi Arabia, Jordan, and Kuwait experienced the largest improvements in productivity growth from the 1980s to 1990s. Although productivity remained stagnant in the 1990s, these countries succeeded in stabilizing the productivity declines of the previous decade. Syria benefited over the decade from increased oil production, better agricultural performance, and an aid windfall that allowed it to undertake key infrastructure investments. Three of the four earliest reformers in the region (Egypt, Jordan, and Tunisia) also experienced improvements in their average TFP growth between the 1980s and 1990s, while Morocco, another early reformer, saw productivity growth deterioration.

Crisis in Accumulation Deepened

Despite stabilization efforts, the declines in capital accumulation that marked the 1980s continued into the 1990s, with nearly every country in the region realizing lower rates of physical capital accumulation than it did in the previous decade. As a result, despite the productivity gains and the positive contribution of human capital accumulation, growth performance in MENA remained significantly below past levels in the region and significantly below the overall global pattern. Had MENA maintained the rates of capital accumulation per laborer of the 1980s into the 1990s, and had TFP growth and human capital accumulation remained fixed, output per laborer would have grown by as much as 3.4 percent a year instead of 0.7 percent. Assuming that such growth performance would have affected wages and employment proportionately, unemployment across the region would have been much lower than the observed levels.

Investment by the Public Sector Is Not the Answer

Could MENA have marshaled the necessary resources to achieve faster growth and better labor market outcomes? The investment rates required to achieve these outcomes are inconsistent with the policy setting

TABLE 3.6

Change in Growth in Output, Capital, and Total Factor Productivity in MENA between the 1980s and 1990s
(percent per laborer)

Country	GDP growth in the 1990s	Change from 1980s to 1990s			
		GDP	Physical capital	Human capital	Total factor productivity
Algeria	−2.0	−1.0	−3.8	−0.3	0.7
Egypt, Arab Rep. of	1.4	−1.5	−5.7	−0.5	1.1
Iran, Islamic Rep. of	1.9	2.2	0.4	0.4	1.8
Jordan	−0.5	2.3	−4.9	−0.6	4.6
Kuwait	−2.6	2.6	0.8	−0.5	2.6
Morocco	−0.2	−1.5	−0.7	0.1	−1.3
Saudi Arabia	−0.3	5.7	−0.5	−0.5	6.2
Syrian Arab Rep.	0.8	1.8	−0.7	−0.7	2.5
Tunisia	1.9	1.1	−0.8	0.2	1.3

Source: World Bank staff estimates.

of the region in the past decade. Absent significant structural reforms to the investment climate that would have facilitated greater private and foreign investment, the public sector would have had to contribute most of the investment. Such a contribution would have entailed a serious deterioration in fiscal balances or external accounts, undermining the hard-won macroeconomic stability in the 1990s. Inflation would have accelerated, and exchange rates would have become even more overvalued, all of which could have led to the sort of financial crisis that East Asia experienced in the late 1990s, especially given the slow reforms of the financial sector in MENA countries.

Response of Private Investment Was Limited

The faster rates of accumulation needed to improve the growth and employment performance of the 1990s would have had to come from the private sector, both domestic and foreign. Furthermore, the focus should have been on the new sectors of the economy, where employment and productivity growth were taking place. The failure of a strong response from the private sector stemmed primarily from the slow and protracted pace of policy reforms launched in the late 1980s and early 1990s. Although the early macroeconomic and structural reforms improved economic outlooks, most countries failed to follow through on reforms. The private sector in MENA countries remains stifled by the systems of governance, the size and scope of government intervention in the economy, and the limited progress in integrating the region into the world economy through trade and investment (chapter 6).

The slow pace of economic reforms and the weak investment response largely explain MENA's poor growth performance in the 1990s (Dasgupta, Keller, and Srinivasan 2002). The record accords with the predictions of standard cross-country determinants of economic growth. Macroeconomic stability delivered a positive growth dividend, while the limited investment response held overall performance to modest levels (figure 3.28).

A stronger investment response would likely have been elicited from the private sector had the reform agenda been fully implemented. Even if reforms did not lead to the high accumulation rates of the 1980s, the greater dynamism and efficiency of the private sector should have resulted in better TFP growth. If MENA's TFP growth in the 1990s had matched the global average of 1.6 percent a year, even with just half the accumulation rates of the 1980s, the region would have experienced impressive annual growth of nearly 4 percent per laborer. The implications for wages and employment growth would have been strikingly positive (Fawzy 2002).

FIGURE 3.28

Public and Private Investment in MENA as a Share of Gross Domestic Product, 1980–2000

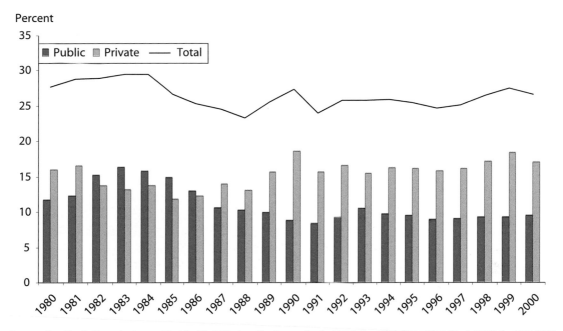

Sources: For Algeria, Egypt, Jordan, and Tunisia: World Bank staff estimates; for the Islamic Republic of Iran: World Bank 2003h for 1991–2000 and World Bank 2003f for 1980–90; and for Morocco: World Bank 2003h.

External Instability Correlates Negatively with Private Investment

It would be a mistake, however, to completely blame conditions endogenous to the region or to the policy formulation process for the limited investment response by the private sector and perhaps even for the policy setting in MENA. In a few countries, notably Jordan and Morocco, policy reforms should have elicited a response at home and abroad. The dilemma of reforms taken with little payoff in investment and growth has bedeviled several MENA countries just as it did Latin America throughout the 1990s. In MENA, the answer lies partly in regional instability and volatility. The Intifadas in the West Bank and Gaza, the Iran–Iraq War, the Gulf War of 1991, and the U.S. war in Iraq in 2003 cast a shadow of persistent instability on the region's economic prospects (Elbadawi 2002). Instability, as well as multiple sanctions regimes imposed on several large economies in the region, disrupted trade and investment, hence slowing integration into global capital markets. Furthermore, oil-exporting countries faced considerable oil price volatility in the 1990s, and the Moroccan economy was subject to severe droughts (box 3.4).

BOX 3.4

Volatility and Economic Performance in MENA

Like most developing regions, MENA suffers from high economic volatility relative to industrial countries. Volatility has been high during the past three decades, whether measured by aggregate output, private consumption (which better reflects volatility in living standards), or investment. High volatility, whether related to economic policy or external shocks, has negatively affected the economic performance of many countries in the region, including reformers such as Jordan and Morocco.

There are several reasons behind the high volatility in the region. First, MENA economies remain relatively undiversified and dependent on a few export markets or commodities that often experience strong fluctuations in relative prices. Oil prices, in particular, have led to sharp fluctuations in fiscal and external accounts, either because of direct dependence on oil revenues or because of strong linkages between oil producers and other countries in the region through trade, labor, and financial flows, including workers' remittances.

Second, countries in the region are subject to frequent droughts that sharply reduce rural incomes and agricultural production. Morocco was severely affected during the 1990s as its GDP growth fluctuated widely with the drought patterns (see figure).

Third, MENA countries are affected by the unstable security situation, whether directly or through various economic linkages within the region. In Egypt, Jordan, and other countries, the security situation has affected the tourism industry, trade and labor markets, and prospects for foreign direct investment. Although there is little that countries like Jordan or Morocco can do to significantly alter the frequency of external shocks or the variability of the weather, policy can be implemented that allows these economies to better manage such effects on the domestic economy.

Agricultural Production and Gross Domestic Product Growth in Morocco, 1990–2000

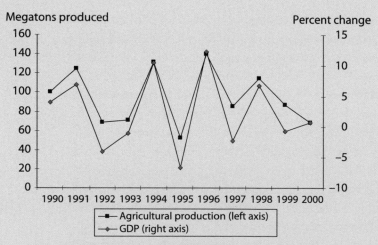

Note: Agricultural production includes cereals, vegetables, and fruits.

Source: Johansson, Silva-Jauregui, and Yousef 2003.

Insecurity Affects Labor Markets Directly

At times, regional instability transmitted shocks that directly affected labor market outcomes, as with Israel's border closures (box 3.5). The repatriation of millions of expatriate workers from the Gulf in 1990 created huge pressures on the labor forces of the labor-exporting countries, thus causing sharp, temporary increases in unemployment in addition to the loss of remittance income (Stanton Russell 1992). Among the repatriated workers were an estimated 150,000 Palestinians, 300,000 Jordanians, 500,000 Egyptians, and 800,000 Yemenis, who fled the conflict.

In all, some 2 million migrants returned to their countries of origin from Iraq, Kuwait, and Saudi Arabia in the 5 months preceding the Gulf War in 1991. Many of the returnees to Egypt, most of whom had worked in Iraq, were absorbed into the Saudi Arabian economy within several months; thus, the shock of Egypt's returning workers was largely temporary. In the other countries, these pressures were partly alleviated as returning workers invested their repatriated savings in housing and businesses. However, the positive effects of such investments were primarily long term and did little to ease the short-term pressures associated with the immediate rise in unemployment and the loss of income.

BOX 3.5

Border Closings and Unemployment in the West Bank and Gaza

Given the close integration of the Palestinian and Israeli economies since Israel's 1967 occupation of the West Bank and Gaza, Israel's border policies have had a significant effect on the Palestinian economy, especially its labor market. Palestinian employment and overall income levels depend largely on Israeli labor demand and workers' ability to commute to Israel. When workers are prevented from entering Israel because of border closures, unemployment levels rise in Palestine. And because the earnings of Palestinian workers in Israel have accounted historically for nearly a third of Palestinian labor earnings, such closures result in significant reductions in household income within the West Bank and Gaza.

Since 1991, the Israeli government has required permits for Palestinians to work in Israel. This policy has restricted the mobility of Palestinian workers, which together with uneven enforcement over time, has increased volatility in the Palestinian economy. Although the political and economic thaw following the 1993 Oslo Accords temporarily relieved some labor pressures, increased political violence, security clampdowns, and border closings since 1995 have led to heightened volatility and higher levels of unemployment within the Palestinian economy.

(Box continues on the following page.)

BOX 3.5 (continued)

The travel restrictions imposed in the wake of the most recent Intifada, in particular, have further limited the ability of Palestinian workers to enter Israel. Hence, since 2000, per capita incomes in the West Bank and Gaza have declined more than 30 percent, and unemployment rates have risen dramatically, soaring from an estimated 9.9 percent in the first three quarters of 2000 to 28.0 percent in the final quarter of 2000. Rates of unemployment are higher in Gaza, at 36.3 percent in 2002, largely because of the more severe border restrictions imposed on that area. The relatively more porous border between the West Bank and Israel has allowed some workers to illegally cross the border to work, so that unemployment rates in the West Bank in 2002 were 25.5 percent (see figure).

These labor market outcomes highlight the importance of a solution to the long-standing conflict between the Palestinians and the Israelis. As policymakers negotiate the final status of a peace settlement, their decisions will have major implications for the future stability of the Palestinian economy and labor market. Any settlement that does not provide for a flow of workers across the border between Palestine and Israel will likely result in burgeoning unemployment levels, declining economic returns, and rising poverty in the West Bank and Gaza.

Unemployment in the West Bank and Gaza, 1980–2002

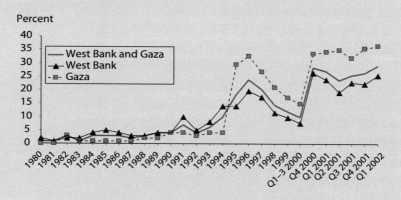

Source: Ruppert Bulmer 2003.

Toward a Fuller Understanding of Labor Market Outcomes

The foregoing analysis of labor market outcomes in MENA has emphasized the interplay between labor supply and demand in explaining the emergence of high unemployment in the 1990s. The region's poor growth performance in the past decade reflected its inability to reap the demographic dividend embodied in the rapid growth of a young and educated labor force. Slow progress with structural reforms aimed at encouraging an investment response from the private sector combined with episodes of high volatility and regional instability to deepen the crisis of accumulation that began in the late 1980s. Rising unemployment and low productivity were the result.

This aggregate perspective on growth and employment is an important building block toward a fuller understanding of labor market outcomes in MENA. A more complete picture, however, requires exploring the microeconomic foundations of these trends. The next chapter will attempt to explore these foundations and to set the stage subsequently for the analysis of policy options for faster job creation and growth in the future.

CHAPTER 4

Structure of Employment and Earnings in the 1990s

Labor supply pressures in the Middle East and North Africa (MENA) are at their apex, with one of every three people of working age a youth (ages 15–24) and a potential new entrant to the labor market. This young generation has benefited from large-scale investments in education and health. However, evidence shows that, despite significant investment in human capital, MENA has reaped less than its potential in terms of economic growth and job creation. As a result, the region experienced high unemployment and low growth in productivity in the 1990s. Chapter 3 explored the macroeconomic trends underpinning these outcomes. This chapter investigates the microeconomic and institutional reasons for the poor labor market outcomes. It explores rigidities in education, wage-setting, and regulatory regimes that arise largely from the dominance of the public sector in labor markets. In addition to the dynamics of employment and wages, it looks at equity in the labor market, including wage determination and wage inequality, gender differentials in wages and access to employment, and links between labor markets and poverty.

Structure of Unemployment

Reduced labor demand from the public sector, slow growth of the private sector, and high job expectations of educated workers after years of guaranteed public sector employment have resulted in alarmingly high unemployment rates in MENA (Shaban, Assaad, and Al-Qudsi 2001, ILO 2003a, UNDP 2002). Unemployment is generally concentrated among youths with intermediate levels of education and is more limited among workers with low levels of education, who are generally not eligible for government employment. This pattern suggests that a significant part of unemployment results from high job expectations by workers with some formal education and a low valuation of these credentials by the private sector because education systems have concentrated on making public sector jobs accessible rather than on building skills.

Youth and Female Unemployment Are High

Unemployment in MENA falls disproportionately on the young (ILO 2003a). Youth unemployment ranges from 37 percent of total unemployment in Morocco to 73 percent in the Syrian Arab Republic, with a simple average of 53 percent for all countries for which data are available (figure 4.1). Except in Jordan and Lebanon, first-time job seekers make up more than 50 percent of the unemployed in all countries for which data are available, further confirming that unemployment in MENA is essentially a labor market insertion phenomenon for youth (figure 4.2).

There is a gender dimension as well to the profile of unemployment. Unemployment rates tend to be higher for women, in part because of the growth in the female working-age population and rising labor force participation rates brought about by higher educational attainment. Unemployment rates for the region as a whole are nearly 50 percent higher for women than for men (figure 4.3).

FIGURE 4.1

Youth Unemployment as a Share of Total Employment in MENA Countries

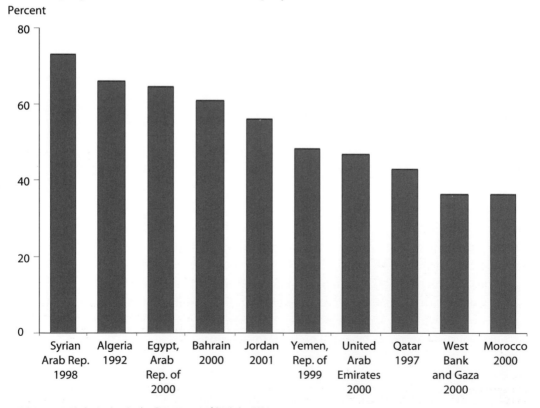

Sources: ILO 2002, 2003b; for Jordan: Jordan Department of Statistics 2001.

FIGURE 4.2

First-Time Job Seekers among the Unemployed in MENA Countries

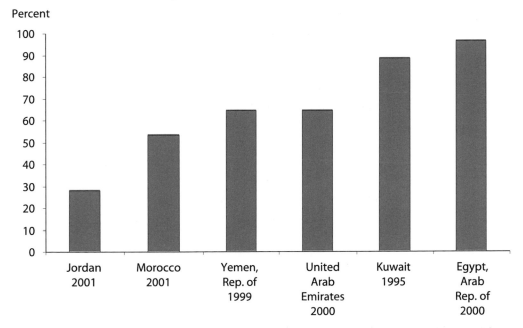

Percent

Sources: ILO 2003b; for Kuwait: Kuwait 2001; for Jordan: Jordan Department of Statistics 2001.

FIGURE 4.3

Unemployment Rates in MENA Countries, by Gender

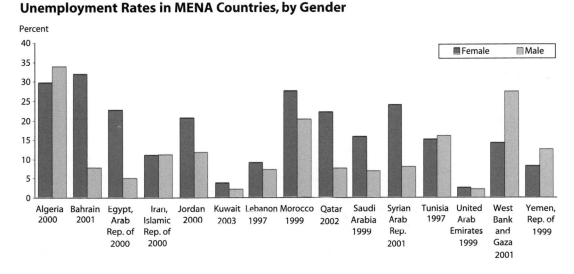

Percent

Sources: For Algeria, Jordan, Syria, Egypt, and the West Bank and Gaza: ILO 2003b; for Tunisia: INS 2001; for Bahrain, Kuwait, Qatar, Saudi Arabia, and the United Arab Emirates: Girgis, Hadad-Zervos, and Coulibaly 2003; for the Islamic Republic of Iran: Statistical Center of Iran 2000; for Morocco: Morocco 1999; for the Republic of Yemen: Central Statistical Organization 1999.

Working-age children of heads of households are much more likely to be unemployed than are heads of households or other members of the household. For men, this effect is stronger in urban areas, whereas for women it is stronger in rural areas. For women, household size is positively correlated with a higher probability of unemployment in both urban and rural settings. In addition, a higher dependency ratio within the household is associated with a greater likelihood of unemployment for men but a lower likelihood for women. These patterns support the claim that unemployment among younger workers of both sexes is to some extent voluntary, facilitated by support from their families while they search for acceptable employment.

Unemployment and Education Are Strongly Linked

Unemployment is also strongly linked to education, with unemployment rates highest for groups in the middle and upper end of the education distribution. The educational attainment of the adult population has increased more than 150 percent in the past three decades, making educated youths the fastest-growing segment of the population. In nearly all countries for which data are available, most of the unemployed have primary or secondary education certificates. In Algeria, Jordan, and Tunisia, more than half of the unemployed have a primary education certificate, and in the Arab Republic of Egypt more than two-thirds have a secondary certificate.

University graduates constitute a small fraction of the unemployed, except in Jordan, where they make up about a third. In Algeria and Morocco, university graduates compose a small share of the unemployed, although they have the highest unemployment rates. Those without formal school certificates are a small share of the unemployed, except in Djibouti and Morocco. Those with no formal education in Morocco had an unemployment rate of 9.4 percent in 1999, significantly below unemployment rates at higher education levels, although they made up more than 40 percent of the unemployed (box 4.1, table 4.1, figure 4.4).

The conclusion that emerges from these stylized facts is that unemployment in MENA is a phenomenon that primarily affects young new entrants and women at the middle and upper ends of the educational distribution. Thus, the unemployed are essentially those who would have had a chance at a formal job in the public sector in the past and continue to have expectations of acquiring such a job (Assaad 1997, Radwan 2002). To survive, those with no education must either accept whatever employment is available to them, no matter how casual, or create their own job. Although they might be underemployed, they are less likely to be openly unemployed.

BOX 4.1

Profiles of the Unemployed in Morocco and the Arab Republic of Egypt

Survey data for Morocco and Egypt provide a detailed profile of the unemployed and the reasons for their status. In Morocco, about a third of the unemployed in 1999 said that they were unemployed because of "firm closure," up from 22 percent in 1991. This fact suggests that economic restructuring may be emerging as an important contributor to unemployment. That new entrants make up a larger majority of the unemployed in Egypt suggests that economic restructuring is not as important a reason for unemployment in that country. In Egypt, 66 percent of unemployed men and 54 percent of unemployed women claimed that they were unemployed because no jobs were available, which suggests that their unemployment may be involuntary.

In Morocco, unemployment is highest among primary school and lower secondary school graduates. In Egypt, the highest probability of unemployment is among upper secondary school graduates, followed by graduates of 2-year postsecondary institutions. However, in interpreting this differential, it is important to note that educational attainment is significantly lower in Morocco than in Egypt. In 1999, 68 percent of working-age Moroccans had less than a primary education, compared with 35 percent of Egyptians in 1998. In both countries, unemployment significantly affects people in the upper third of the educational distribution, perhaps because unemployment affects primarily young people, who tend to be more educated than older cohorts. However, even if the sample is limited to those ages 20 to 24, unemployment is significant only for people in the top half of the education distribution.

The average age of the unemployed in Morocco has increased slightly, from 26.5 in 1991 to 27.4 in 1999, and the average number of years of schooling went from 6.8 to 8.2. In Egypt, the average age of the unemployed is 25, the same as in 1988, and the average number of years of schooling increased from 9.4 to 11, reflecting the national increase in educational attainment. There is little evidence from either country that unemployment is spreading to older or less-educated groups. This finding is important because the older and the less educated an unemployed worker is, the more vulnerable the worker's household is to poverty.

The average duration of unemployment has increased sharply in both countries, rising in Egypt from 29 weeks in 1988 to 158 weeks in 1998 and from 79 weeks in 1991 to 178 weeks in 1999 in Morocco. Although recall and reporting problems may cloud these figures, the increase in duration is unmistakable. The data also suggest that unemployment is longer among first-time job seekers than among those with previous work experience.

Data on labor market transitions in Egypt confirm that the unemployed are mostly seeking wage employment, especially in the public sector. More than 90 percent of the unemployed who transitioned into employment from 1991 to 1998 in Egypt went into wage work, 80 percent of them in the public sector. In the 1980s, this proportion was even higher, at 96 percent, indicating that securing employment in the public sector is becoming more difficult.

Sources: Assaad 2002b; World Bank staff estimates.

TABLE 4.1

Unemployment Rates in MENA Countries, by Gender and Education Level
(percent)

Country	Year	None			Primary			Secondary			Tertiary			All		
		T	M	F	T	M	F	T	M	F	T	M	F	T	M	F
Algeria	1995	9.6	—	—	30.9	—	—	30.9	—	—	68.4	—	—	27.9	26.0	38.4
Egypt	1998	4.1	3.6	6.6	5.7	4.7	18.2	22.4	12.9	42.1	9.7	6.5	17.0	11.4	6.9	26.9
Morocco	1999	9.4	9.7	8.9	26.3	24.9	31.1	32.4	30.4	37.3	37.6	31.8	48.2	15.6	15.7	15.4
Oman	1996	5.6	5.6	5.6	13.4	12.2	29.6	24.8	13.5	79.4	2.8	2.3	5.0	10.8	8.7	28.6
Tunisia	1997	10.2	—	—	20.8	—	—	15.4	—	—	6.4	—	—	15.7	15.4	16.7

— Not available.
Note: T = total; M = male; F = female.
Sources: For Algeria and Oman: ILO 2002; for Egypt: Arab Republic of Egypt, CAPMAS 1998; for Morocco: Morocco 1999; for Tunisia: INS 1997.

FIGURE 4.4

Distribution of the Unemployed, by Level of Education
(percent)

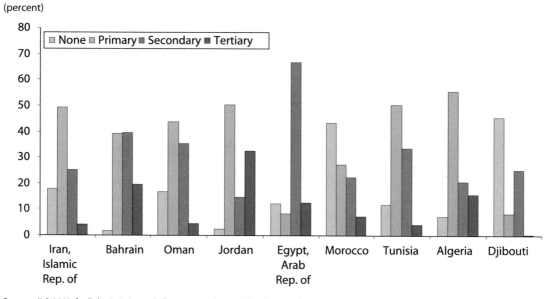

Sources: ILO 2002; for Bahrain: ILO 2003b; for Egypt: Arab Republic of Egypt, CAPMAS 1998; for Morocco: Morocco 1999.

Public Sector Employment in the 1990s

The prospect of work in the public sector affects the expectations of young workers and shapes unemployment in the region. However, governments in MENA have continued to maintain their dominant position in the structure of production and employment. MENA countries entered the

1990s with a high share of public employment in total employment. The share of civilian government employment is high by international standards, exceeding averages for both industrial countries and other developing regions (figure 4.5). In countries for which data are available, the share of the public sector in total employment in the late 1990s ranged from 8 percent in government and 2 percent in public enterprises in Morocco to 32 percent in government and 7 percent in public enterprises in Egypt (Schiavo-Campo, de Tommaso, and Mukherjee 2003).

Significant queuing continues for public sector jobs, especially among educated workers. Sluggish growth in the private sector, the perpetuation of implicit and explicit employment guarantees in government hiring, and mismatched wage expectations resulting from generous public sector compensation and benefits policies have all contributed to the continued preference for public sector jobs. This phenomenon is strongest among the oil exporters, where a high youth unemployment rate coexists with a large inflow of foreign workers. In the long run, the most detrimental impact of such government hiring practices is that they trap human capital in unproductive public sector jobs, thus limiting its contribution to growth.

FIGURE 4.5

Size of Government around the World in the 1990s

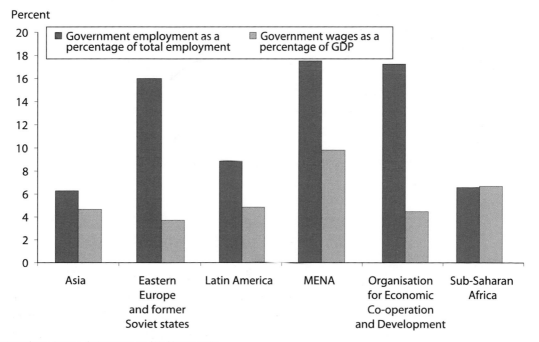

Source: Schiavo-Campo, de Tommaso, and Mukherjee 2003.

Dynamics of Public Sector Employment

Public sector employment as a share of total employment is highest among Gulf Cooperation Council (GCC) countries, such as Bahrain, Kuwait, Oman, and Saudi Arabia, followed by Algeria and the Islamic Republic of Iran and the more diversified economies of Egypt and Jordan. Tunisia and Morocco have the lowest public employment ratios. The share of public sector employment declined in the late 1990s except in the oil-exporting countries (box 4.2) and in Egypt (figure 4.6). In Egypt, civil service expansion resulted in an increased public sector share despite contraction of the public enterprise sector. Only in Algeria and Egypt did public employment growth outstrip growth of total employ-

---

BOX 4.2

Special Conditions of the Oil-Exporting Countries

The expansion of public sector employment in MENA has resulted in an employment structure skewed toward women and educated groups, segmenting the labor market along gender and education lines. In the oil-exporting countries, however, the main axis of segmentation resulting from public sector hiring is along the national–expatriate dimension. With a rapidly growing number of young nationals entering the labor force at a time when governments are no longer able to act as employers of first and last resort, nearly all oil-exporting countries in the region are attempting to institute policies to increase the employment of nationals in the private sector. These policies range from mandatory quotas and employment targets to wage subsidies and taxes on foreign workers.

Although the contribution of government employment growth to total employment growth has been low in the oil-exporting countries compared with the contribution in Algeria, Egypt, and Tunisia, the low shares primarily reflect the decline in expatriate hiring and conceal the continued importance of government employment for nationals. The public sector accounted for nearly all net job creation for nationals in Kuwait and 40 to 45 percent in Bahrain and Oman (see box figure 1).

Yet private sector job growth has been vigorous in all the oil-exporting countries for which data are available (see box figures 1 and 2 below). The private sector created 90 percent of new jobs in all four countries for which data are available. Most of these jobs were in relatively low-skill, low-wage sectors of the economy, however, and in most cases nationals appeared to prefer the slow-growing public sector. This pattern can help to explain the high rates of unemployment among educated nationals in these countries.

The extent of the labor market challenge differs by country. Kuwait and the United Arab Emirates have small working-age populations that rely almost exclusively on government jobs. Unemployment has been kept in check by using fiscal resources to provide employment for nationals. In Bahrain and Saudi Arabia, nationals account for a

BOX 4.2 (continued)

larger share of the labor force and are more active in the private sector, but these economies are not able to absorb the growing numbers of new entrants. This problem has led to higher rates of unemployment, especially for women. In Oman, bolder policies, including retrenchment in the public sector, have allowed the economy to generate high employment growth rates, by creating job opportunities for nationals in the private sector and by reducing the level of unemployment (Girgis 2002).

BOX FIGURE 1

Employment Growth of Nationals in the Public and Private Sectors

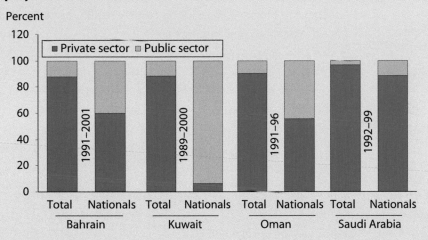

BOX FIGURE 2

Annual Employment Growth in the Public and Private Sectors

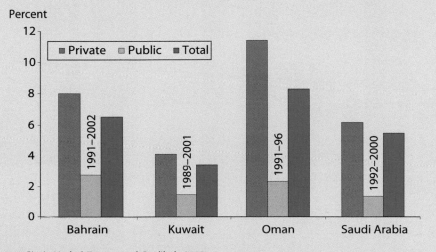

Source: Girgis, Hadad-Zervos, and Coulibaly 2003.

ment. In both countries, Egypt over the period 1988–98 and Algeria over the period 1996–99, the public sector accounted for well over a third of job creation (figure 4.7).

Efforts to Downsize: Some Countries Falter, a Few Succeed

With the increasing realization that large public sectors have become unsustainable, countries attempted in the 1990s to reduce the size of the public sector. But most still employ a large civil service, and the state continues to participate directly in—and even to dominate—industrial activities through public enterprises. In the mid-1990s, for example, Egypt had 200 public enterprises operating 936 establishments in the manufacturing sector, with public enterprises accounting for two-thirds of formal manufacturing employment.

A few countries, however, have succeeded in reducing public sector employment. The most far-reaching rationalization of public employment occurred in the government sector of Jordan and in the government and public enterprise sectors of Morocco. In Jordan, government

FIGURE 4.6

Public Sector Employment as a Share of Total Employment in MENA Countries

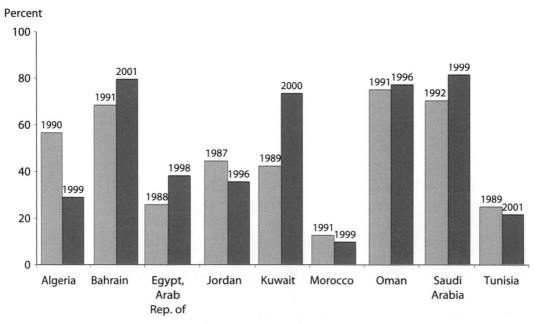

Note: Percentages for Bahrain, Kuwait, Oman, and Saudi Arabia include only nationals.
Sources: For Morocco: Morocco 1991, 1999; for Tunisia: Said 2001, World Bank 2003e; for Bahrain, Kuwait, Oman, and Saudi Arabia: Girgis, Hadad-Zervos, and Coulibaly 2003; for Jordan: ILO 1996, Jordan Department of Statistics 1997; for Algeria: ILO 1996, ONS 1990; for Egypt: Arab Republic of Egypt, CAPMAS 1988, 1998.

FIGURE 4.7

Contribution of the Public Sector to Total Employment Growth in MENA Countries

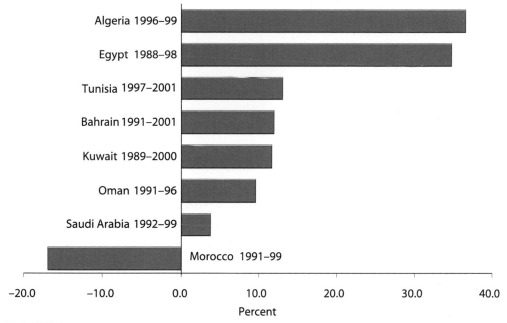

Sources: For Algeria: ILO 2003b; for Egypt: Arab Republic of Egypt, CAPMAS 1988, 1998; for Morocco: Morocco 1991, 1999; for Tunisia: World Bank 2003e; for Bahrain, Kuwait, Oman, and Saudi Arabia: Girgis, Hadad-Zervos, and Coulibaly 2003.

grew at only 0.5 percent a year in 1995–2000, and the share of overall public sector employment in total employment declined from 45 percent in 1987 to 36 percent in 1996. In Morocco, public sector employment declined in relative and absolute terms. Public employment declined by 1.8 percent a year in 1991–99, and its share in total employment fell from 12.6 percent to 9.9 percent. Both government and state-owned enterprise (SOE) components declined, with SOEs declining more rapidly. The high unemployment rate of 38 percent among Moroccan university graduates in 1999 can be directly attributed to the suspension of government hiring.

Gender and Occupation in the Public Sector

The privileged position of the public sector in MENA labor markets has had important gender and education effects. The rise in female labor force participation in many countries is due primarily to the expansion of educational opportunities and to the government employment of educated workers, as well as to explicit government policies to facilitate the participation of women in the labor force (Assaad and El-Hamidi 2001).

In Jordan, the rise in female labor force participation from 4.8 percent in 1984 to 15 percent in 1996 resulted mostly from the expansion of public sector employment for educated women, who benefited from generous maternity leave and childcare policies (Miles 2002). Although such policies in MENA ostensibly apply to both public and private employers, private employers evade them by not hiring women on a formal basis and by encouraging women to quit jobs upon marriage.

The role of the public sector as a major employer of women was only marginally reduced in the 1990s (figure 4.8). Algeria has the highest concentration of female employment in the public sector, with more than 85 percent of the female labor force in public employment in 1990. In the late 1980s, both Jordan and Egypt also had comparatively high shares: 54 percent and 66 percent respectively, although by 1998 that share had dropped to 57 percent in Egypt. Syria's ratio of female employment in the public sector relative to total employment remained stable at about 42 percent, whereas in Morocco, the share was much smaller at 7 percent through the 1990s.

FIGURE 4.8

Female Employment in the Public Sector as a Share of Total Female Employment in MENA Countries

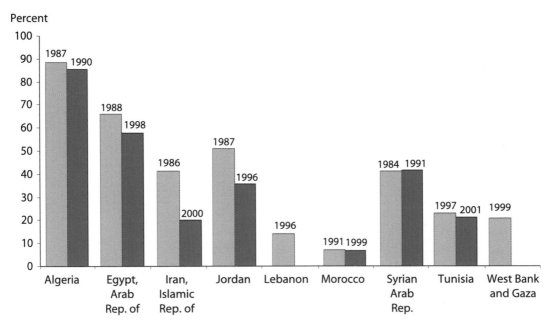

Sources: For Algeria: ILO 2003b, ONS 1990; for Egypt: Arab Republic of Egypt, CAPMAS 1988, 1998; for the Islamic Republic of Iran: Shaban, Assaad, and Al-Qudsi 2001, Statistical Center of Iran 2000; for Jordan: Jordan Department of Statistics 1997; for Lebanon: Lebanon Ministry of Social Affairs, 1996; for Morocco: Morocco 1991, 1999; for Syria: ILO 2003b; for Tunisia: INS 1997, 2001; for the West Bank and Gaza: Palestinian Central Bureau of Statistics 1999.

Research on Egypt suggests a number of reasons for the public sector's large share of female employment in MENA. First, the public enterprise sector, which has proportionately fewer women, is declining as a share of overall public sector employment. Second, because of less desirable options in the private sector, women are less likely to drop out of the public sector employment queue than are men. Finally, as public sector jobs have become more difficult to secure, women have tended to hold on to these jobs longer than to jobs in the private sector, remaining more often, for example, after marriage. Women also face fewer barriers to entry and experience less occupational segregation and wage discrimination in the public sector, thanks to more standardized wage-setting and hiring procedures. And many nonwage benefits valued by women are more common in the public sector (greater job security, shorter working hours, and earlier pensions).

Role of the Public Sector Reinforced by Education

Education has been a principal driver of the expansion of public employment in MENA. In Egypt, for example, the expansion of education has driven the growth in public employment seen since 1990, as it has made more people eligible for the public sector employment guarantee. Teachers were the fastest-growing occupational group in government employment in Egypt, accounting for more than a third of government employment growth. There was also a rapid growth in clerical workers, which appears to be the result of continued pressure to hire graduates.

In contrast to findings in Egypt, data on relative wages in Jordan indicate that the public sector is more attractive to workers with lower skills and educational levels. In 1997, wages were 17 percent higher in the public sector than in the private formal sector for workers with a secondary degree and less-educated workers but were 9 percent lower for workers with an intermediate diploma or higher (Ruppert Bulmer 2000). Until the mid-1990s, before Civil Service Bureau clearance was required, central government hiring accelerated for low-skilled jobs and absorbed proportionately fewer university graduates. However, government employment was more favorable for educated women, whose public sector employment grew by 9 percent during 1992–97, compared with 4 percent growth for less-educated women.

Structure of Labor Markets

Rising rates of unemployment are a clear indicator that employment growth in MENA has not kept up with labor force growth. Unemploy-

ment statistics may even understate the employment creation problem
because they do not include the discouraged unemployed (people who
would be working had employment been available but who have quit
searching). What are the sources of employment growth in MENA, and
what sectors are contributing to labor absorption?

Agriculture Declines While Manufacturing Is at a Standstill

The distribution of employment and value added (output) reveals a decline in the share of agriculture during the oil boom, followed by a slowdown or reversal of that trend after the collapse of oil prices in 1986
(table 4.2). For the diversified economies, the share of agriculture in
value added declined during the 1970s, recovered somewhat in the 1980s
as the share of oil fell, and then declined again in the 1990s as oil prices
recovered. Similarly, the share of agriculture in employment declined
rapidly up to the mid-1980s, stabilized in the late 1980s, and then re-
sumed its decline in the 1990s.

TABLE 4.2

Structure of Employment and Production in MENA Countries
(percent)

Country	Year	Agriculture	Manu-facturing	Other industry	Services and similar sectors	Year	Agriculture	Manu-facturing	Other industry	Services and similar sectors
		Employment				Value-added production				
Mixed oil producers										
Algeria	1977	31	12	20	36	1977	8	10	45	36
	1991	24	12	16	48	1980	9	11	47	34
	1995	12	30[a]	n.a.	58	1991	10	12	41	37
						2000	9	8	52	31
Iran, Islamic Rep. of	1976	42	19	16	23	1986	24	9	13	54
	1986	30	14	12	44	1990	24	12	16	48
	1996	23	31[a]	n.a.	45	1996	20	15	22	44
						2000	19	16	6	59
Iraq	1977	24	10	14	52					
	1987	14	7	12	67					
	1990	16	18[a]	n.a.	66					
Diversified economies										
Egypt, Arab Rep. of	1976	47	14	5	33	1976	28	16	10	46
	1986	39	13	9	39	1986	21	13	14	52
	1995	34	14	8	44	1995	17	17	15	51
	2000	30	12	9	49	2000	17	19	15	49

TABLE 4.2 (continued)

Country	\<Employment\> Year	Agriculture	Manu-facturing	Other industry	Services and similar sectors	\<Value-added production\> Year	Agriculture	Manu-facturing	Other industry	Services and similar sectors
Jordan	1979	11	8	18	63	1979	7	14	14	65
	1987	6	7	11	76	1987	7	11	13	69
	1993	6	12	13	69	1993	6	13	14	67
						2000	2	16	9	73
Morocco	1971	58	11	6	25	1971	20	16	11	53
	1982	44	17	9	31	1982	15	17	15	53
	1991	49	13	5	33	1991	20	17	14	49
	1999	44	14	7	33	2000	14	18	15	54
Syrian Arab Rep.	1970	50	13	9	29	1970	20	25[a]	n.a.	55
	1981	25	16	19	39	1981	19	26[a]	n.a.	55
	1991	28	14	11	46	1991	22	18	13	48
						2000	24	27	3	46
Tunisia	1975	39	18	13	30	1975	18	9	17	56
	1984	28	19	23	30	1984	14	15	19	52
	1994	22	34[a]	n.a.	43	1994	12	19	11	59
	2001	22	21	13	44	2000	12	18	11	59
West Bank and Gaza	1980	23	18[b]	23	36	1987	19	14[b]	22	46
	1992	20	12[b]	34	34	1993	13	8[b]	22	57
	1996	14	16	12	57	1996	16	15	10	59
	2000	14	14	20	52	2000	8	15	11	66
Gulf Cooperation Council										
Bahrain	1971	7	7	27	58	1980	1	16	43	40
	1991	1	13	16	68	1991	1	16	24	59
	1994	1	54[a]	n.a.	43	1995	1	19	21	59
Kuwait	1975	3	8	15	74	1975	0	6	73	22
	1988	1	7	17	74	1988	0	14	32	54
						1995	0	11	43	46
United Arab Emirates	1975	5	6	36	52	1975	1	1	78	20
	1985	8	7	21	64	1985	1	9	55	35
	1995	8	11	23	58	1993	2	8	49	40
	2000	8	11	22	59					

n.a. Not applicable.

Note: Other industry includes mining, construction, and electricity, water, and gas, except as noted in notes a and b. For Iraq, value-added production data were not available.

a. Manufacturing includes all other industry.

b. Manufacturing includes utilities and mining, but not construction (which is included in other industry).

Sources: Employment data for Bahrain, Egypt (1976, 1986), Iraq, Jordan, Kuwait, Syria, and the United Arab Emirates (1975, 1985) are from ESCWA 1994. Employment data for Algeria, Egypt (1995, 2000), the Islamic Republic of Iran, Morocco, the United Arab Emirates (1995, 2000), and the West Bank and Gaza (1996, 2000) are from ILO 2003a. Employment data for the West Bank and Gaza (1980, 1992) are from Palestinian Central Bureau of Statistics 1999. Value-added data are from World Bank 2002e, except for the West Bank and Gaza (1987, 1993), which are from Shaban, Assaad, and Al-Qudsi 2001.

Despite massive efforts to promote industrialization in many countries, manufacturing's share in employment and output was either stagnant or declining in the 1970s and 1980s, a victim of the Dutch Disease phenomenon. A general increase in expenditures and appreciation of the real exchange rate brought about by the oil windfall resulted in a boom in nontradables, adversely affecting the production of tradable goods (Corden 1984, Richards and Waterbury 1998). Several of the diversified economies were also affected by the Dutch Disease phenomenon, as significant oil-related resources flowed into their economies as remittances and aid flows. In Jordan, for instance, the share of agriculture in employment fell from 42 percent in 1961 to 6 percent in 1987, and agriculture's share in value added collapsed by similar proportions. Manufacturing also declined, only to recover in the 1990s after the oil boom ended. Egypt and Syria experienced similar trends but to a lesser extent.

The diversified economies that were more insulated from the 1970s oil boom, Morocco and Tunisia, fared differently. They also saw a decline in the share of agriculture in employment and value added, but the share of manufacturing increased in both countries in the 1980s as they implemented structural adjustment programs. Their economic structures were more stable in the 1990s, with manufacturing and services maintaining a relatively constant share of employment. By the end of the 1990s, Tunisia had the highest share of employment in manufacturing among MENA countries for which data are available.

Services Are the Most Dynamic Sector

With agriculture shedding workers and no longer absorbing surplus labor and manufacturing stagnant except in Morocco and Tunisia, services are playing the lead role in labor absorption in most countries. The private sector is gradually taking the lead from the public sector in employment creation in much of the region, but most new jobs are (a) jobs in the informal sector, (b) informal jobs in the formal sector in the non–oil economies, or (c) jobs filled by expatriate workers in oil-exporting countries. Private employers appear unwilling to hire workers under the highly protective labor regimes in most countries (chapter 5). And many governments have chosen lax enforcement of labor laws over the politically treacherous process of reform.

Mixed Patterns Exist in Job Creation

The availability of microeconomic data for Egypt, Morocco, and Tunisia allows a more detailed analysis of employment creation over the past decade. Overall employment growth was more rapid in Egypt and

Tunisia than in Morocco (table 4.3). The difference between data for Morocco and for Egypt is almost entirely accounted for by changes in public sector employment, which declined in Morocco while growing in Egypt. The difference between data for Tunisia and for Morocco is largely attributable to differences in agricultural performance. Morocco suffered from severe drought, whereas agriculture was the fastest-growing segment of the economy in Tunisia. In Morocco, paid employment in agriculture grew, while in Tunisia, both segments of the agricultural sector grew, with the unpaid segment growing slightly faster. Egypt's agricultural sector appears to be more dynamic than that of Morocco, but the difference is attributable entirely to the hard-to-measure female employment in subsistence agriculture. Male employment in agriculture in Egypt declined, as did paid employment, which corresponds roughly to the commercial agriculture sector.

Private sector paid employment outside agriculture was the most dynamic segment of the Moroccan economy, growing at an annual rate of 6.2 percent (five times the average) and accounting for more than 100 percent of net employment creation in the 1990s. The sector was also dynamic in Egypt, growing at 1.7 times the average and accounting for about a third of net employment creation in 1988–98. In Tunisia, nonag-

TABLE 4.3

Employment Growth in Egypt, Morocco, and Tunisia

(percent)

Sector	Egypt (1988–98)		Morocco (1991–99)		Tunisia (1997–2001)	
	Share of growth	Annual rate of growth	Share of growth	Annual rate of growth	Share of growth	Annual rate of growth
Government	41.8	4.8	–9.0	–1.2	7.1	1.0
State-owned enterprise	–7.0	–2.6	–7.9	–4.5	–2.5	–1.5
Subtotal public	34.7	3.0	–16.9	–1.8	4.6	0.5
Private agriculture wage work	–0.4	–0.2	8.2	1.7	24.4	4.2
Private agriculture nonwage work	27.4	1.9	–5.0	–0.1	12.4	5.3
Subtotal agriculture	26.9	1.6	3.2	0.1	37.1	4.5
Private nonagriculture wage work	31.6	4.3	110.1	6.2	20.4	3.4
Private nonagriculture nonwage work	6.7	1.3	–5.5	–0.3	45.7	3.2
Subtotal private nonagriculture	38.3	3.0	104.7	3.1	66.2	3.3
Other	n.a.	n.a.	9.0	10.0	–7.9	–38.3
Total	100.0	2.5	100.0	1.2	100.0	2.7

n.a. Not applicable.
Note: Totals may not be exact because of rounding.
Sources: For Egypt: Arab Republic of Egypt, CAPMAS 1988, 1998; for Morocco: Morocco 1991, 1999; for Tunisia: INS 1997, 2001.

ricultural paid employment grew more slowly but still accounted for more than 20 percent of employment growth. Most employment growth occurred in the broad services, manufacturing, mining, and utilities in all three countries. In Tunisia, but not in Morocco or Egypt, the nonwage component of nonagricultural employment, an important component of the informal sector, grew at about the same pace as paid employment and accounted for nearly 46 percent of employment growth. This finding suggests that the informal sector is significantly more dynamic in Tunisia than in Egypt or Morocco.

Informalization of Work in the 1990s

In the state-led era, most countries in MENA adopted protective labor regulations providing workers with lifetime job security, generous retirement packages, and other job-related benefits (chapter 5). These regulations were generally enforced in the public sector but much less so in the private sector. As countries began to reform in the past decade, they made few attempts to explicitly deregulate labor markets to encourage employment creation. Instead, there appears to have been a tacit agreement between the authorities and private business that labor laws would not be strictly enforced for new labor market entrants. Thus, the growing informalization of labor markets spread beyond self-employment and wage employment in small informal sector enterprises to include further unregulated employment in the formal private sector. In the oil-exporting countries, lax enforcement extended to low-paid expatriate workers, whose employment and compensation levels are largely unregulated.

Challenge of Measuring the Informal Sector

While the conventional wisdom is that the informal sector has become a leading source of employment in MENA in the 1990s, data limitations make it difficult to study the size and dynamics of this sector (Charmes 1999). Informal employment is typically estimated as a residual: employment in establishments of more than 10 workers (obtained from establishment surveys) is subtracted from total nonagricultural employment (obtained from household surveys). This method misses workers in large firms who are hired informally without the benefit of employment contracts or social insurance. Estimates of informal employment in MENA range from a low of 42 percent of nonagricultural employment in Syria to a high of 55 percent in Egypt (figure 4.9). Although moderate compared with other developing regions, these estimates are high given the large share of public sector employment.

FIGURE 4.9

Informal Sector Employment as a Share of Nonagricultural Employment, 1994–2000

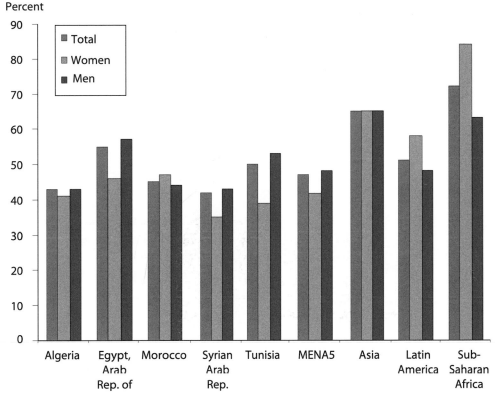

Source: ILO 2002.

Self-employment accounts for about half of informal employment in Egypt and Tunisia, two-thirds in Algeria and Syria, and up to four-fifths in Morocco, with wage employment in enterprises of fewer than 10 workers accounting for the rest. Although the informal sector is generally an important source of employment for women in developing countries, in MENA the proportion of men in informal employment exceeds that of women. And although female self-employment as a share of total female nonagricultural employment has increased in most developing countries, it has fallen in MENA, probably because women are increasingly concentrated in public sector employment.

Dynamic Informal Sector or Informalization?

At one end of the spectrum, the informal economy involves productive, small-scale activities with the potential for growth and technical upgrading. Such small and microenterprises may employ several workers for wages. They tend to use capital more efficiently and rely on labor-intensive technologies (Abdel-Fadil 2002, Handoussa and Potter 1992). At the other end of the spectrum, the informal economy includes survival activities that employ people without any particular skills. In the middle are family enterprises that rely primarily on household labor, self-employed workers with close subcontracting or piece-rate relationships with others, and artisans who have acquired some craft skills. Informal employment further includes casual wage workers who work intermittently or seasonally, often outside fixed establishments, and regular wage workers who work for large firms without employment contracts or social insurance coverage.

Expansion of Informal Employment for Everyone

Although it is difficult to determine how much each of these categories of work is growing or shrinking, household surveys provide information on the proportion of employment that is not covered by legal employment contracts or social insurance. Such surveys are the broadest measure of informality in the labor market because they cover self-employment and family labor, as well as unregulated employment in the private sector and sometimes the public sector.

Evidence from Egypt indicates that nonagricultural informal employment increased in the 1990s, whether informality is measured by lack of an employment contract or by lack of social security coverage. The proportion of nonagricultural workers (over 18 years old) engaged in informal jobs increased by about 5 percentage points in the 1990s. In 1998, more than half the working labor force (54 percent) and about 44 percent of nonagricultural workers were not covered by legal employment contracts. Nearly 47 percent of all workers and 36 percent of nonagricultural workers did not have social insurance coverage (Wahba 2002).

The evidence from Egypt for increased informalization remains even after controlling for individual characteristics, including the tendency for some workers to transition out of the informal sector with age and experience. For a worker with average characteristics, the probability of being an informal worker was 5 percentage points higher in 1998 than in 1990. Although the probability of informality increased for both male and female workers, the increase was greater for women, albeit from a lower initial level (figure 4.10). Informal employment affected people at all education levels, with the largest increase in informality among workers with an intermediate education—those with the lowest eligibility for the public employment guarantee for graduates (figure 4.11).

Another indication of the gradual informalization of the Egyptian labor market is the shift in the type of jobs that first-time job seekers

FIGURE 4.10

Probability of Informal Employment in Egypt, by Gender, 1990 and 1998

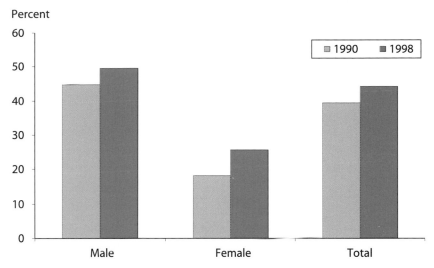

Source: Wahba 2002.

FIGURE 4.11

Probability of Informal Employment in Egypt, by Education Level, 1990 and 1998

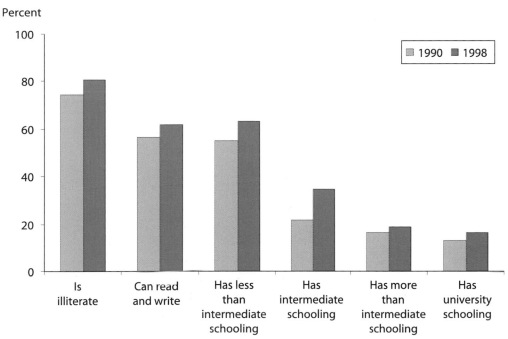

Source: Wahba 2002.

have been able to secure. In the 1970s, the proportion of new job market entrants going directly into public sector employment hovered between 60 and 70 percent, but by 1998 that share had fallen to 25 percent (figure 4.12). The share of new entrants whose first jobs were informal increased from less than 20 percent in the 1970s to 60 percent in the late 1990s, nearly matching the decline in the public sector share. The share of formal private sector employment also increased in the 1980s and early 1990s but remained well below 20 percent.

The increased informalization of employment among new entrants would not necessarily indicate overall informalization of the labor market if new entrants were able to transition quickly to formal jobs. This, however, is not the case. Some 95 percent of nonagricultural workers without employment contracts or social insurance in 1990 were still without contracts or social insurance in 1998 (Wahba and Mokhtar 2002). Such high levels of persistence in informal employment show that informality is not just a transient state for new entrants on their way to a formal job.

In conjunction with the analysis on unemployment trends at the beginning of this chapter, the foregoing analysis demonstrates that, at least in Egypt, the slowdown in government hiring in the late 1980s and 1990s resulted in higher levels of unemployment among new entrants

FIGURE 4.12

Share of New Entrants into Formal and Informal Employment in Egypt, 1969–98

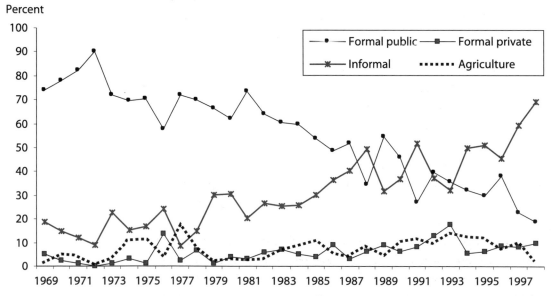

Note: Figure includes persons ages 18 or older.
Source: Wahba and Mokhtar 2002.

and an increased reliance on informal employment arrangements. If formal private sector firms were hiring, they were doing so by skirting regulations on employment contracts and social insurance.

Gender Equity in Access to Labor Markets

Female labor force participation rates are rising (chapter 3) and, coupled with growth in the working-age population, will lead to unprecedented growth in the female labor force of 5 percent a year in the next decade. In this context, and given the increasing feminization of government employment, a question remains about the extent to which paid employment outside the government is accessible to women in MENA (Standing 1999). The region's bureaucracies are already large by international standards and are likely to grow only slightly, if not contract, in the upcoming period. If the projected rapid increase in the female labor force is to be accommodated, paid employment outside of government will have to be the major source of growth. And yet as job opportunities in the more egalitarian public sector are dwindling, women continue to face significant barriers to entry in the private sector, contributing to higher female unemployment rates and larger gender gaps in wages (CAWTAR 2001, Moghadam 2002).

Household survey data for Egypt and Morocco enable a closer examination of "feminization" and "defeminization" trends in nongovernment paid employment. Egypt is probably more representative of the general trend in MENA, whereas Morocco appears to be an exception (Assaad 2002a). The data help to identify the job types (such as blue-collar workers in textile manufacturing and professional and managerial workers in finance and business services) in each country with higher-than-average shares of female employment at the beginning of the period. The analysis looks first at the change in the overall share of female employment between 1991 and 1999 in Morocco and between 1988 and 1998 in Egypt from each job type (total effect). It then examines the components of that change: that from a change in women's share in that job type (feminization effect), that from growth of the job type compared with overall growth of nongovernmental paid employment (growth effect), and that from the interaction of the feminization and growth effects (interaction effect).

Except for agriculture, all the job types highlighted in tables 4.4 and 4.5 had higher-than-average female employment at the beginning of the period. Several disproportionately female job types are the same in the two countries, including teachers and health workers, domestic servants and other personal service workers, blue-collar workers in food processing and textiles and garment manufacturing, white-collar workers out-side retail trade, and professional and managerial workers. The most feminized job types in both countries are teachers and health workers and domestic and other personal service workers. Blue-collar manufac-turing outside textiles and food processing and white-collar work in re-tail trade are disproportionately female in Egypt but not in Morocco.

In Egypt, all job types became defeminized from 1988 to 1998, whereas in Morocco all but two job types increased their female shares, including the "other" category that covers all job types with a lower than average female share. In Egypt, agricultural work, which constitutes nearly a fifth of the total, accounted for 40 percent of the defeminization of nongovernmental paid employment. Within agriculture, three-quar-ters of the effect was from defeminization of the sector, and most of the rest was from the sector's slow growth. After agriculture, the largest con-tributors to defeminization were white-collar work outside retail trade (19 percent) and professional and managerial work outside finance, in-surance, and real estate (14 percent). In white-collar work in retail trade, the growth effect was positive and substantial, but the defeminization ef-fect canceled it out.

TABLE 4.4

Decomposition of the Change in the Female Share of Nongovernmental Paid Employment in Egypt, 1988–98

(percent)

Type of job	1988		1998		Contribution to change in female share in total employment			
	Female share	Share in overall employment	Female share	Share in overall employment	Total effect	Feminization effect	Growth effect	Interaction effect
Agricultural worker	16.1	21.6	9.7	15.9	−1.9	−1.4	−0.9	0.4
Blue-collar in food processing	16.8	2.7	13.7	3.2	0.0	−0.1	0.1	0.0
Blue-collar in textiles and garment manufacturing	21.0	5.0	19.9	4.2	−0.2	−0.1	−0.2	0.0
Blue-collar in other manufacturing	17.1	4.0	8.8	4.6	−0.3	−0.3	0.1	0.0
White-collar in retail trade	32.1	4.9	23.2	6.9	0.0	−0.4	0.7	−0.2
White-collar not in retail trade	36.7	5.6	23.8	4.7	−0.9	−0.7	−0.3	0.1
Teachers and health workers	90.8	1.8	78.6	1.6	−0.4	−0.3	−0.2	0.0
Domestic and other service workers	59.0	1.8	34.4	1.9	−0.4	−0.4	0.1	0.0
Professional and managerial workers	16.5	13.2	13.9	11.4	−0.6	−0.3	−0.3	0.0
Other	2.3	39.5	1.6	45.6	−0.2	−0.3	0.1	0.0
Total	15.0	100.0	10.2	100.0	−4.9	−4.9	0.0	0.0

Note: Only sectors other than agriculture with a disproportionately higher share of females are identified.
Source: World Bank staff estimates from Arab Republic of Egypt, CAPMAS 1988, 1998.

TABLE 4.5

Decomposition of the Change in the Female Share of Nongovernmental Paid Employment in Morocco, 1991–99

(percent)

Type of job	1991		1999		Contribution to change in female share in total employment			
	Female share	Share in overall employment	Female share	Share in overall employment	Total effect	Feminization effect	Growth effect	Interaction effect
Agricultural worker	15.3	18.6	16.2	14.6	−0.5	0.2	−0.6	0.0
Blue-collar in food processing	30.8	3.1	17.8	2.3	−0.6	−0.4	−0.3	0.1
Blue-collar in textiles and garment manufacturing	39.9	7.5	62.3	9.9	3.2	1.7	0.9	0.5
White-collar not in retail trade	29.4	7.6	35.9	6.2	0.0	0.5	−0.4	−0.1
Teachers and health workers	63.9	1.9	52.7	0.9	−0.7	−0.2	−0.6	0.1
Domestic and other service workers	55.9	8.9	60.6	10.3	1.3	0.4	0.8	0.1
Professional and managerial workers	32.9	1.8	34.9	0.9	−0.3	0.0	−0.3	0.0
Other	4.3	50.5	7.5	54.9	1.9	1.6	0.2	0.1
Total	18.0	100.0	22.3	100.0	4.3	4.3	0.0	0.0

Note: Only sectors other than agriculture with a disproportionately higher share of females are identified.
Source: World Bank staff estimates from Morocco 1991, 1999.

In Morocco, the exceptions to the increased feminization effect were blue-collar workers in food processing and teachers and health workers, which together constituted only 5 percent of nongovernmental paid employment. Blue-collar work in textile and garment manufacturing accounted for 74 percent of feminization. Just over half the effect was from feminization of the sector, 30 percent from its faster-than-average growth, and the rest from the interaction of feminization and growth. The second-highest contributor to overall feminization was the "other" category. Although this large category has a much lower than average female share, its female share has increased substantially over the period. Domestic and services work, always predominantly female, was next, with about two-thirds of the effect on overall feminization from the sector's growth and one-third from the feminization effect. Some job types, including agriculture workers, blue-collar workers in food processing, teachers and health workers, and professional and managerial workers, went counter to the overall feminization trend because they were slow growing.

While in Egypt defeminization occurred across all job types, in Morocco the feminization of jobs can be attributed largely to developments in the textile and garment sector. Although the sector accounted for only 7.5 percent of nongovernmental paid employment in 1991, it accounted for 74 percent of job feminization during 1991–99 because it grew faster than average and became more feminized. There is also evidence that job types traditionally closed to women, which constitute more than half of all nongovernmental employment in Morocco, are becoming more accessible to women.

The findings suggest that increased access of women to the labor market can initially be achieved by promoting sectors that have traditionally been open to female participation, such as textile and garment manufacturing. This finding conforms to international trends in the feminization of employment that accompanies an increase in export-processing zones and assembly-type production (Joekes 1995, Ozler 2000). Over time, jobs that have been closed to women can gradually be opened in order to increase women's share in overall employment. Thus, it is not surprising that the countries that have experienced significant growth in manufactured exports, such as Tunisia and Morocco, have done considerably better in increasing women's share in employment than countries that have relied on remittances, service exports, and oil for their foreign exchange earnings.

Real Wages and Wage Formation

Real wages in most countries in the region tracked the oil boom–bust–stabilization cycle of the past three decades, either through the direct effect of oil on the economy or through cross-border movement of labor in response to these fluctuations. Real wages in manufacturing rose sharply from 1970 to 1975 in oil-exporting and diversified economies as a result of the first oil shock and resultant waves of migration. During this period, real manufacturing wages rose at a torrid rate of 20 percent a year in Kuwait and at the only slightly lower rate of 17 percent a year in the diversified economies.

Flexibility Suggested among Trends in Real Wages

Real wages rose again following the second oil shock of 1979, which led to an acceleration of growth in the region's economies. From 1980 to 1985, real wages rose 5 percent a year in the diversified economies and 3 percent a year in the oil exporters (figure 4.13). Most of the increases occurred in the early 1980s and were followed by greater stability in 1982–85. However, there were several exceptions. Real wages collapsed in the Islamic Republic of Iran after the 1979 revolution, falling more than 7 percent a year in 1980–85. They also fell in Morocco by 3.8 percent a year, as phosphate prices dropped and stabilization policies were introduced.

The collapse in oil prices in 1986 ushered in a period of generalized wage decline across the region. Real wages fell by 5.5 percent a year in

FIGURE 4.13

Real Hourly Manufacturing Wages in MENA, 1980–98

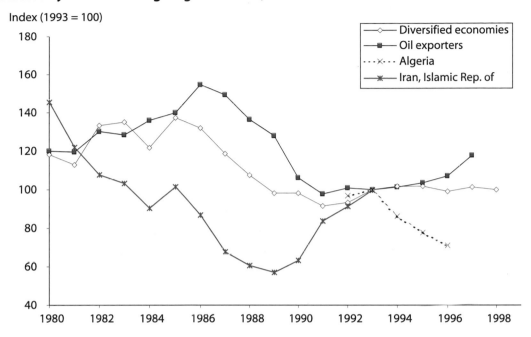

Note: The diversified economies are represented by Egypt (1980, 1985–97), Jordan (1980–98), Morocco (1980–97), Syria (1980, 1987–95), and Tunisia (1980–81). The oil exporters are represented by Bahrain (1999), Kuwait (1980–96), Oman (1993–97), and Qatar (1986–94). Since the data for the Islamic Republic of Iran and Algeria are available only for different periods, they are presented separately rather than aggregated in a mixed oil producers group.
Source: UNIDO 2002.

the diversified economies, by 6.7 percent a year in the oil exporters, and by as much as 14.4 percent a year in the Islamic Republic of Iran. By 1990, real wages in the diversified economies and the oil exporters had fallen to 70 percent of their peak levels in 1985–86 and remained below their 1975 levels. In the Islamic Republic of Iran in 1989, real wages had dropped to 40 percent of their 1980 level. Exceptions to this overall declining trend were Morocco and Tunisia, where real wages were fairly stable in the second half of the 1980s.

Real wages were more stable in the 1990s than in the two previous decades. Among oil exporters, average real wages remained virtually unchanged from 1990 to 1995, with rising wages in Oman, falling wages in Bahrain and Kuwait, and relatively stable wages in Qatar. In the diversified economies, real wages were virtually flat as well. Nearly all countries in this group had stable wages with the exception of Syria, which had significant increases in the early 1990s. Real wages recovered in the Islamic Republic of Iran from 1990 to 1993 (the last date for which data are available) but remained significantly lower in 1993 than they were just after the revolution. Algeria, for which data are available only from 1992 to 1996, experienced significant wage erosion, with real wages declining by more than 30 percent in 4 years.

Higher Returns to Education in the Public Sector

Wages tend to be more egalitarian in the public sector than in the private sector, leading to a narrower range of wages (Said 2002). Public sector wage-setting rules also place considerable emphasis on formal education and seniority. As the state's role as employer of first or last resort shrinks, wages would be expected to increasingly reflect productivity differences among workers.

How these considerations would affect returns to education over time is less clear. If educational differences reflect productivity differences and if public sector wages are contracting, returns to education would be higher in the private sector and rising as the private sector expands. But if educational credentials do not translate into productivity differences, yet still are well rewarded in the public sector, a reduction in the role of the public sector will lead to lower returns to education in the private sector and falling returns over time. Given that the region's education systems have catered for years to the needs of growing bureaucracies, the second situation is much more likely in MENA. However, a reduction in educational premiums does not necessarily mean that wage inequality is reduced. Wage inequality along other dimensions, such as gender, skill, region, and occupation, may, in fact, increase as public sector wage-setting rules become less salient.

Estimates of returns to education for selected MENA countries are generally higher in the public sector than in the private sector at nearly all education levels except the university level (table 4.6). Only in the Republic of Yemen, a country with low educational attainment and low returns in general, are the returns comparable or slightly higher in the private sector. This finding suggests that the private sector places less value on basic and secondary education. Returns are higher for general secondary education, which is more selective than vocational secondary schooling, but since those who pass the general secondary exam usually go on to postsecondary studies, there are few workers in this category.

Decline of Public–Private Wage Differences

Rates of return to education in the private sector have been fairly stable in Egypt, but they have declined in Morocco, matching estimates of more rapid increases in unemployment of educated workers in Morocco, where the public sector has contracted, than in Egypt, where it continues to expand. Rates of return, however, appear to be declining in the public sec-

TABLE 4.6

Rates of Return to Schooling in MENA Countries, by Gender and Sector

(percent per year)

Education level/ description	Egypt, Arab Rep. of 1988	Egypt, Arab Rep. of 1998	Morocco 1991	Morocco 1999	Jordan 1997	Yemen, Rep. of 1997
Primary						
Male public	8.2	6.4	12.4	6.1	3.5	2.7
Male private	2.3	3.6	3.0	3.4	2.0	2.7
Female public	1.9	5.3	28.2	10.5	−3.9	5.1
Female private	0.9	7.2	8.5	9.4	14.7	8.0
Lower secondary						
Male public	7.0	4.9	10.7	8.2	2.9	2.7
Male private	2.5	4.4	6.4	6.3	5.5	2.7
Female public	7.7	8.2	22.3	13.4	5.2	3.7
Female private	3.2	−11.2	13.9	10.0	9.8	7.4
Upper secondary, general						
Male public	8.6	8.8	10.6	8.8	2.8	2.2
Male private	6.3	7.3	10.4	7.7	6.0	2.2
Female public	8.6	9.7	18.1	12.1	4.6	3.9
Female private	3.8	−1.5	16.4	11.0	10.4	12.1
Upper secondary, vocational						
Male public	9.6	7.2	8.4	6.8	3.8	3.3
Male private	5.3	5.0	6.9	5.8	3.2	3.3
Female public	7.9	9.6	16.5	11.9	4.3	4.3
Female private	4.4	4.9	11.1	11.3	8.6	10.7
University			*			
Male public	10.1	8.8	10.8	8.9	4.6	3.8
Male private	8.5	7.3	12.5	9.5	10.2	5.2
Female public	8.9	10.7	15.0	12.8	6.8	4.4
Female private	9.1	10.9	15.2	9.3	12.9	6.8

Note: Derived from regressions that control for potential experience and potential experience squared, urban–rural location, and part-time and casual work status in the private sector. The Republic of Yemen regressions control for age and age squared instead of potential experience and potential experience squared. All regressions control for sample selection using the Heckman procedure, except for the Morocco regressions.
Source: World Bank staff estimates.

tor in both countries. This finding suggests that, as inflation has eroded public sector wages, policymakers have tried to partially protect the wages of the lowest-paid workers, leading to a contraction of the wage range.

Rates of return to schooling in the private sector appear to be higher for women than for men. Moroccan and Jordanian women, in particular, seem to reap significant benefits from schooling in the private sector. This finding does not mean, however, that educated women fare better than educated men, but simply that the gender gap in wages declines with education (discussed in the subsequent section).

By rewarding educational credentials in public employment with higher wages, governments have encouraged investment in types of human capital that are not necessarily valued in the private sector. The problem is most acute in primary and secondary education, which has expanded significantly to accommodate growing numbers of enrollees, often at the expense of quality. The recent decline in the number of school-age children in many countries provides an opportunity to refocus efforts on quality improvements and greater responsiveness to the need for productive skills (chapter 6).

Measurement of the Gender Wage Gap

One dimension along which wages in MENA are likely to become more unequal over time is gender. Since public sector wage setting is generally based on educational credentials and seniority, it tends to be fairly egalitarian along gender lines. Gender wage differentials in the private sector, however, persist in MENA, just as they do throughout the world, even after adjusting for education and experience (Assaad and Arntz 2002). Some wage differences may result from productivity differences, as in physical labor, but most relate to gender norms about the division of labor in both the domestic and market spheres.

Because women bear the bulk of household responsibilities, they are generally unable to commit as much time to market work. Their need to work shorter hours or to withdraw periodically from the labor force during their childbearing years may consign women to lower-paid, part-time, or temporary employment and may reduce their advancement opportunities. Gender norms about the division of labor in the work sphere can also result in lower wages for women. If gender norms force women into a small number of occupations, these occupations can become overcrowded, thus lowering wages. And if gender norms limit women's mobility, thereby confining their job search to a limited local labor market, their employment options may be limited to lower-paying jobs (Karshenas and Moghadam 2002, Miles 2002). For all these reasons, gender gaps in wages are likely to be larger in the private sector than they are in the public sector. As economies in the region shift toward greater reliance on the private sector for job creation, the gender gap in wages is likely to grow, unless these shifts are accompanied by changes in gender norms.

Without adjustments for differences in experience, education, and other observable attributes, the (crude) gender wage gap ranges from 79 percent in the West Bank and Gaza in 1999 to 4 percent in Egypt in 1998, meaning that average male wages are 79 percent higher than female wages in the West Bank and Gaza and 4 percent higher in Egypt (table 4.7). These crude gaps can be highly misleading, since the composition of the female labor force is usually quite different from that of the male labor force. Female workers are often more educated and less experienced than their male counterparts. Similarly, while men tend to work until the age of retirement or later, many women withdraw from

TABLE 4.7

Decomposition of Gender Wage Differentials in Selected MENA Countries
(percent)

Category	Egypt, Arab Rep. of 1988	Egypt, Arab Rep. of 1998	Morocco 1991	Tunisia 2001	West Bank and Gaza 1999	Yemen, Rep. of 1997
Gender wage gap (male – female)/female	0.20	0.04	0.25	0.21	0.79	0.16
Gender wage gap adjusted for gender differences	0.28	0.15	0.27	0.15	0.86	0.36
Proportion of gap explained by differences in characteristics	–0.35	–2.37	–0.05	0.27	–0.07	–1.10
Proportion not explained	1.35	3.28	1.09	0.73	1.07	2.10

Source: World Bank staff estimates.

wage labor when they marry or during their childbearing years, which tends to lower their average work experience.

Adjusting for these differences yields gaps that range from 0.86 in the West Bank and Gaza in 1999 to 0.15 in Egypt in 1998, meaning that if women's characteristics, such as education and experience, were compensated equally to those of men, women's average wages would be 86 percent higher in the West Bank and Gaza in 1999 and 15 percent higher in Egypt in 1998. That wage gaps generally increase when these adjustments are made means that female wage workers are more highly selected than male wage workers, according to observables such as education and experience. In essence, this finding suggests that less-educated women have limited access to the paid labor market. Only in Tunisia does the adjustment lead to a lower gap, which means that the educational profiles for male and female wage workers in Tunisia are fairly similar.

The adjusted wage gap appears to have fallen in Egypt from 28 percent to 15 percent from 1988 to 1998. That finding does not necessarily mean that labor markets are becoming more equitable along gender lines. If private sector labor markets become more defeminized and government employment becomes more feminized, and if government pay structures are more gender neutral than private pay structures, as is the case in Egypt, the adjusted gender gap would fall even if the private sector were becoming less gender equitable.

When the gender wage gap data for Egypt are disaggregated by public and private sector, a different picture emerges (figure 4.14). There is essentially no differential in the government sector, which has a nearly gender-neutral wage-setting system. In the private sector, however, the adjusted differential increases from 29 percent to 41 percent. The public enterprise sector occupies an intermediate position, but as firms gain more

FIGURE 4.14

Crude and Corrected Gender Wage Differentials in Egypt, by Sector of Ownership, 1988 and 1998

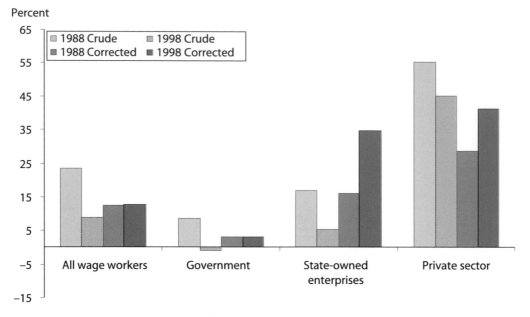

Note: Male–female wage differential is measured in percent.
Sources: Arab Republic of Egypt, CAPMAS 1988, 1998.

flexibility in wage setting, the sector looks more like the private sector. The overall male–female differential has remained stable, however, because as nongovernmental wage employment in Egypt was defeminized, government employment became more feminized, by shifting some of the female work force toward the more equitable government sector. With government employment unlikely to expand significantly in the future, the increasing gender inequity in the private sector is cause for concern.

Income Inequality That Remains Moderate

MENA and South Asia are the only developing regions with improvements in income inequality over the past three decades (table 4.8). MENA, which had one of the highest rates of income inequality in 1970, now has one of the most equal income distributions in the world, with an estimated Gini coefficient of 0.357 (Adams and Page 2001). The Gini coefficient for individual countries in the region ranges from 0.35 to 0.47, compared with 0.44 to 0.61 in a sample of Latin American countries. The mean income of the bottom fifth of the population in MENA rose rapidly in 1975–79 and 1985–89 and, after a decline in the early

TABLE 4.8

Gini Coefficient and Share of the Poor in Income, by Region

Region	Gini coefficient	Income share of bottom quintile (percent)
East Asia	0.397	6.4
Europe and Central Asia	0.343	7.4
Latin America and the Caribbean	0.484	4.3
MENA	0.357	7.5
South Asia	0.336	8.4
Sub-Saharan Africa	0.448	5.3

Source: Adams and Page 2001.

1990s, recovered again at the end of the decade. The pattern closely parallels the region's economic performance and the trend in real wages.

Growth and Redistribution Protect Welfare Gains

Postcolonial political ideologies, which dictated the redistribution of assets, helped to promote more egalitarian income distribution. Furthermore, the rapid growth in worker remittances and aid flows associated with redistribution of oil rents helped to finance public investments and commodity-based subsidies. During the period of rapid growth, the poor benefited both from income growth and from an increasing share of income. These income and distribution gains for the poor appear to have withstood the region's economic downturn after 1985 (Adams and Page 2001, Ali and Elbadawi 2002), although trends have diverged in some countries.

In Egypt, there was a decline in the percentage of expenditures going to the lowest quintile of the population and an increase in poverty during 1985–99. The opposite happened in Morocco and Tunisia. Income going to the lowest fifth rose by 0.65 percent a year in Morocco and 1.71 percent in Tunisia. These patterns are confirmed by changes in real wages. In Tunisia, wages grew fastest in agriculture, where many of the poor work, helping them to work their way out of poverty. In Egypt, real wages fell in all sectors in 1981–95, including those in which the poor work.

Wage Inequality Remains Greater than in Other Regions

Although MENA exhibits one of the most equal income distributions in the world, it has had, since the 1990s, one of the highest wage inequality levels of all developing regions, according to data compiled by the United Nations Industrial Development Organization (UNIDO 2002) for the manufacturing sector (figure 4.15). If oil-exporting countries are

FIGURE 4.15

United Nations Industrial Development Organization (UNIDO) Theil Measure of Wage Inequality, by Region, 1965–97

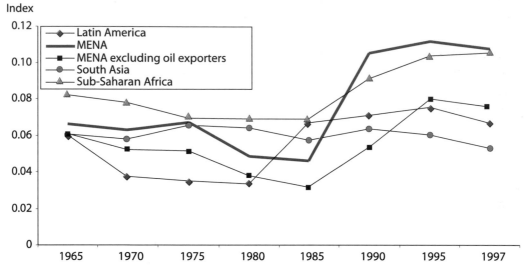

Source: UNIDO 2002.

excluded from the MENA sample, income inequality improves, putting MENA ahead of Sub-Saharan Africa but behind Latin America and South Asia. In 1995, wage inequality was lowest in Jordan (0.05) and highest in Kuwait (0.34).

Observations of the wage inequality data for three separate groups of MENA countries reveal a consistent trend. Wage inequality declined steadily between 1965 and 1985, and then rose again until 1995 only to decline thereafter. These results conform with the general trend reported around the world. However, although the three groups of countries exhibit similar trends, the measure is much higher in oil-exporting economies, compared with diversified economies.

Poverty Rates Are among the Lowest in the World

By developing country standards, poverty rates are low in MENA. On the basis of a poverty line of US$1.08 per person per day in 1993 purchasing power parity exchange rates, only 2 percent of the MENA population fell below the poverty line in the 1990s (table 4.9). Although that figure represents an increase of about 18 percent over the poverty rate in the 1980s, it is still low compared with poverty rates in other developing regions. Poverty reduction before the 1980s can be credited to the rapid growth during the oil boom. The continued low poverty rates are remarkable, however, considering the slow gross domestic product (GDP) growth since 1985. Two reasons have been advanced for the low incidence of poverty: government employment and remittances from international migration. Cross-country regressions for MENA show that a 10 percentage point increase in remittances as a share of GDP reduces poverty by 5.7 percent, and a 10 percentage point increase in the share of government in total employment reduces poverty by 6.2 percent (Adams 2003b).

Although high levels of government employment have clear efficiency implications for MENA, they have served an important social function in redistributing wealth. Among oil exporters and the diversified economies, government employment has been the primary mechanism for distributing oil rents. Even in several of the diversified economies, such as Egypt, Jordan, and Syria, a large portion of oil-related revenues has flowed to the government in the form of aid or export proceeds, thereby allowing these governments to expand their work forces. Government employment also has served as a social safety net because it shields a significant portion of the work force from economic fluctuations. With government employment concentrated among the more educated portion of the population, however, this safety net does not extend to some of the most vulnerable members of society. The distribution of wages in Egypt and Morocco suggests that between 40

TABLE 4.9

Poverty in Developing Regions, 1990–99

Region	Less than US$1/day (millions)		Less than US$1/day (percent of population)	
	1990	1999	1990	1999
MENA	5	6	2.1	2.2
East Asia and the Pacific	486	279	30.5	15.6
Europe and Central Asia	6	24	1.4	5.1
Latin America and the Caribbean	48	57	11.0	11.1
South Asia	506	488	45.0	36.6
Sub-Saharan Africa	241	315	47.4	49.0
Region	Less than US$2/day (millions)		Less than US$2/day (percent of population)	
	1990	1999	1990	1999
MENA	50	68	21.0	23.3
East Asia and the Pacific	1114	897	69.7	50.1
Europe and Central Asia	31	97	6.8	20.3
Latin America and the Caribbean	121	132	27.6	26.0
South Asia	1010	1128	89.8	84.8
Sub-Saharan Africa	386	480	76.0	74.7

Source: World Bank 2003h.

and 60 percent of public sector employees belong to the highest income quintile, whereas less than 5 percent are found in the poorest segment of the population (figure 4.16).

Poverty Is Not Associated with Unemployment

Data from household surveys in five MENA countries show that the relationship between poverty and employment status varies across countries and by urban and rural location. Working in the public sector appears to be effective protection against falling into poverty. Public sector workers are much less likely than the average person to be in the bottom quintile of the income distribution. Regular private sector wage work also appears to offer protection from poverty. In all countries except Jordan, regular private sector workers are less likely to be in the bottom fifth. Rural residents are more likely to be in the bottom fifth of the income distribution than urban residents—three times more likely in Egypt and the Islamic Republic of Iran and 2.3 times more likely in the Republic of Yemen. The difference is smaller in Morocco and Jordan. Protection from poverty is somewhat lower in rural areas than in urban areas.

FIGURE 4.16

Wage Distribution and Public Sector Employment in Egypt and Morocco, by Quintile

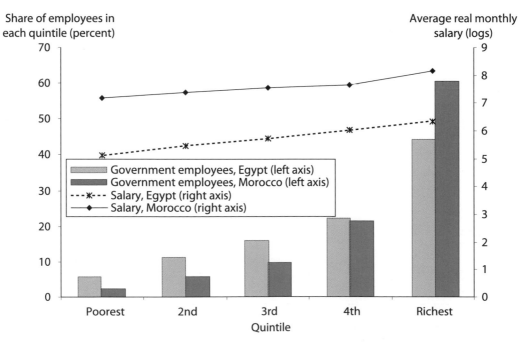

Sources: Arab Republic of Egypt, CAPMAS 1998; Morocco 1999.

The relationship between poverty and unemployment is more complex (table 4.10). In Egypt, Jordan, and Morocco, for example, unemployed individuals are not much more likely to be in the bottom quintile of the income distribution than other working-age adults. In the Islamic Republic of Iran and the Republic of Yemen, however, unemployed individuals are more likely to be in the bottom fifth. (Some of this effect may be caused by the use of a short reference period of one day to identify the unemployed, which would capture casual wage workers when they are out of work.) The rural unemployed in these countries appear to be especially vulnerable to poverty.

In most countries, casual wage workers are disproportionately represented in the bottom fifth, with Morocco as an exception. In urban Egypt, a casual wage worker is more than twice as likely to be in the bottom fifth than an average person and 1.7 times as likely as an unemployed person. Nonwage work is strongly associated with poverty in Morocco (in rural and urban areas) and in Jordan (rural areas), but it is weakly associated with poverty elsewhere. Finally, nonparticipation in the labor force moderately increases the chance of being in the bottom fifth in nearly all countries discussed.

Poverty is, therefore, not strongly associated with an absolute lack of work (the unemployed and those who are out of the labor force) but

TABLE 4.10

Percentage of Working Adults (Ages 15–64) in Each Work Status Who Are in the Lowest Per Capita Income Quintile

| Country | Year | Urban | | | | | | |
		Private casual	Private regular	Private nonwage	Public	Unemployed	Inactive	All
Egypt, Arab Rep. of [a]	1997	23.1	5.8	13.0	5.9	13.8	11.1	11.0
Iran, Islamic Rep. of [b]	2000	9.3	—	6.1	0.6	14.6	8.8	7.9
Jordan	1997	18.2	14.0	16.9	5.9	18.1	15.0	14.2
Morocco	1999	4.6	4.7	37.1	1.5	20.3	22.7	19.0
Yemen, Rep. of	1999	15.6	6.0	10.7	2.7	16.1	10.0	9.2

| Country | Year | Rural | | | | | | |
		Private casual	Private regular	Private nonwage	Public	Unemployed	Inactive	All
Egypt, Arab Rep. of [a]	1997	44.5	26.7	30.4	23.6	28.9	33.5	32.7
Iran, Islamic Rep. of [b]	2000	22.4	—	21.9	3.9	32.5	24.3	22.9
Jordan	1997	13.7	26.9	26.0	6.8	16.5	15.6	15.0
Morocco	1999	3.0	8.3	25.7	1.3	17.0	22.2	21.2
Yemen, Rep. of	1999	28.5	15.9	17.7	6.5	35.2	24.8	21.4

— Not available.
a. Data for Egypt are based on per capita expenditure rather than per capita income quintile.
b. Data for private casual and private regular are combined for the Islamic Republic of Iran.
Source: World Bank staff estimates based on country poverty assessments.

rather with unstable or inadequate employment. In general, the extremely poor cannot afford to be unemployed for long. The classification used here fails to distinguish those who are not working because of disability, old age, or youth and, therefore, does not capture those potential sources of vulnerability to poverty. Besides casual wage work, which is strongly associated with poverty, self-employment and work for family-run enterprises appear to be highly vulnerable to poverty in some contexts, such as in Morocco and rural Jordan.

What We Have Learned

MENA's high youth unemployment rates are intimately linked to the accumulated effect of years of virtually guaranteed employment in the government for educated youth. Although hiring has been curtailed in recent years, educated new entrants continue to queue for government jobs because of nonwage benefits that are rare in the private sector. Although wages appear to be flexible, the dominant role of government as employer introduces rigidities in the wage structure that distort labor market incentives. Higher returns to education in the public sector encourage the accumulation of such credentials even if they are undervalued by the private sector.

With the slowdown in government hiring, unemployed workers are increasingly relying on informal employment arrangements in the private sector, where labor regulations are evaded. Within the private sector, the labor market is highly segmented along gender lines. Countries that have pursued policies conducive to labor-intensive manufactured exports, such as Tunisia and Morocco, have succeeded in raising the female share in nongovernmental paid employment. The other countries of the region have experienced defeminization of paid employment outside government.

MENA has fared well relative to other regions in income inequality and poverty levels, thanks in large measure to the redistribution of oil rents through labor remittances or increased government employment. Although fairly effective in reducing poverty, government employment is an inefficient safety net because most of the benefits go to educated workers, who are underrepresented among the poor. Moreover, the costs of excessive government employment in reduced economic and total factor productivity growth can limit poverty reduction over the long run.

CHAPTER 5

Labor Market Reforms: Opportunities and Constraints

The high unemployment rates of the 1990s and stagnant worker productivity mirrored weak output growth. These outcomes were caused by the crisis in accumulation and weak total factor productivity (TFP) growth (chapter 3). Underlying these trends were the slow pace of structural reforms and a volatile external environment, reinforced by public sector hiring and wage-setting policies and other institutionalized sources of labor market segmentation (chapter 4). The limited response from the private sector and the persistence of structural rigidities in the labor market have implications not only for aggregate labor market outcomes, but also for developments at the microeconomic level.

Policy proposals that aim to alleviate current pressures and to generate better outcomes must address these structural rigidities, including the state's role as both employer and labor market regulator. International experience suggests that labor market institutions and policies matter in shaping employment and wage outcomes. Where labor markets are flexible, demographic transitions that entail rapid expansion in the labor force are associated with stronger growth performance (figure 5.1). Where labor markets are more rigid, countries tend to experience deeper recessions before adjustment and slower recoveries (Forteza and Rama 2001). Reforming the institutional and regulatory setting is integral to better functioning labor markets.

Reforming the Labor Market in a Dynamic Setting

This chapter looks at the scope for policy intervention in the labor markets of the Middle East and North Africa (MENA) to address the structural rigidities driving unemployment and slowing job creation. Much of the analysis focuses on the need to rationalize public sector hiring and wage-setting practices. Doing so will reduce the effect of guarantees for public sector employment on human capital formation and wage expec-

FIGURE 5.1

Gross Domestic Product Per Capita Growth and the Demographic Gift, by Labor Market Rigidity

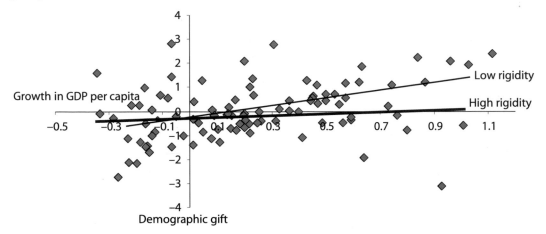

Note: The figure shows the relationship between gross domestic product per capita growth and the demographic gift conditional on a set of geographic, economic, and policy variables. Data are averages of the period 1965–90. The relationship is shown for countries with high and low levels of labor market rigidity.
Sources: Estimated using data from Sachs and Warner 1997; labor market rigidity data from Forteza and Rama 2001.

tations among first-time job seekers, who face the highest unemployment rates. But there are fiscal and efficiency reasons as well for tackling the neglected agenda of public sector reform. The analysis also extends to institutionalized rigidities in the private sector that impede flexibility in hiring and dismissal, raise indirect labor costs, and protect unionized workers.

Because labor market reforms are politically difficult and, when attempted, tend to be slow and piecemeal, quantitative estimates of their effects can advance the agenda of reform (Gill, Montenegro, and Dömeland 2002). Thus, this chapter examines the challenge of reforming labor markets in MENA by using empirical simulations generated by a general equilibrium modeling framework that is designed to replicate the effect of policies in the labor-abundant (labor-exporting) countries of MENA (Agénor and others 2003a; see chapter 5 appendix). The simulations offer insight not only into the direct effect of policy reforms on labor market outcomes (wages, unemployment, informal sector), but also into the implications for macroeconomic aggregates, including output, investment, and the fiscal balance. The chapter also looks at the special case of the labor-importing countries, where labor market segmentation along national–expatriate lines creates additional complexities for policy reform.

Rationalizing the Role of the Public Sector

There are many reasons to rationalize the role of the public sector in MENA's labor markets. The most well known—and the subject of past reform efforts—is the financial burden placed on the government and the rest of the economy by high public sector employment. MENA governments continue to employ a higher share of the population than any other developing region. This trend remains a concern, with government wage bills averaging 11.3 percent of gross domestic product (GDP) in the late 1990s and reaching fiscally unsustainable levels in several oil-exporting countries. Despite reform efforts over the past decade, only a few countries reduced the size of the public sector wage bill, and in many countries the wage bill has even increased (figures 5.2, 5.3, and 5.4). Wage expenditures are a significant drain on fiscal revenues, reducing the resources available for other sectors of the economy and potentially crowding out spending and investment by the private sector.

Wage Bills Are High but Productivity Is Low in the Public Sector

Efficiency losses attributable to falling productivity in the public sector are another concern. Across MENA, most branches of the public sector remain overstaffed, even in countries that have tried to shed public sector labor. In the early 1990s, the share of underused workers in the pub-

FIGURE 5.2

Average Government Wage Bill as a Share of Gross Domestic Product in MENA Countries

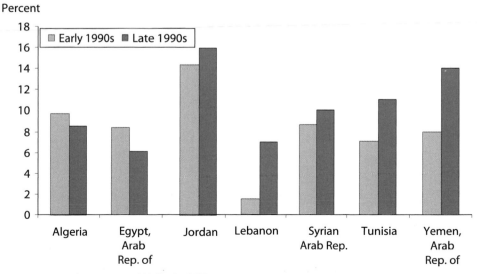

Source: Schiavo-Campo, de Tommaso, and Mukherjee 2003.

FIGURE 5.3

Central Government Wage Bill as a Share of Gross Domestic Product, by Region

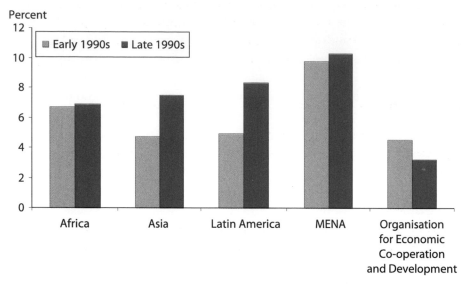

Source: Schiavo-Campo, de Tommaso, and Mukherjee 2003.

FIGURE 5.4

Public Sector Wage Bill in Gulf Cooperation Council Countries, Late 1990s

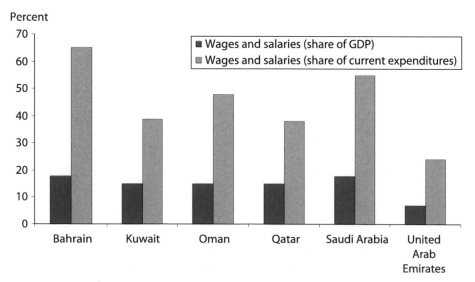

Sources: IMF 1997; World Bank estimates.

lic sector ranged from 17 percent in Algeria to 21 percent in the Arab Republic of Egypt to even higher shares among the oil-exporting countries. These estimates suggest that the scale of overstaffing is greater than ever. Recent estimates put labor redundancies in public enterprises alone at about 35 percent in Egypt and nearly 40 percent in Jordan (Ruppert Bulmer 2002). In Algeria, redundancy remains a concern despite layoffs of more than half a million workers during the 1990s.

Public Sector Reforms Are Critical for Reducing Unemployment

Significant financial savings and efficiency gains would result from rationalizing public sector employment. These considerations alone would justify scaling back the state's presence in labor markets. But even more important, the dominance of the public sector is linked to the structure of unemployment and the supply of skills in the economy (chapter 4). The need for public sector reform stems less from the financial and overstaffing implications and more from the rigidities that state dominance introduces into labor markets. Implicit and explicit employment guarantees in government hiring and mismatched wage expectations resulting from generous public sector compensation policies perpetuate market segmentation and ensure continued queuing for public sector jobs, especially among educated first-time job seekers.

Wages and Benefits Drive Preferences for Public Employment

In some countries, workers prefer government jobs because wages are higher than those in the private sector (figure 5.5). In other countries, workers are attracted to such nonwage factors as job security, worker protections, and social allowances unlinked to productivity (Said 2001). These considerations, as well as special provisions on work hours and maternity leave, make public sector employment especially attractive to women. Although large nonwage benefits are a mechanism for distributing wealth, they are distortionary, contributing to structural rigidities that reinforce the segmented structure of employment. In the labor-importing countries, public–private segmentation that results from wage and nonwage advantages for nationals in the public sector is further reinforced by distinctions in employment between nationals and expatriates. Private sector wages are considerably lower in countries that rely on foreign laborers who are not covered by social protection legislation and benefits. Low reservation wages reflect conditions in the sending country, such that only foreign workers are competitive in the private sector.

FIGURE 5.5

Public versus Private Wages, by Region, Late 1990s

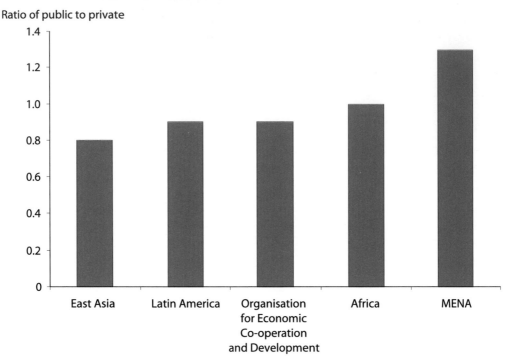

Source: Schiavo-Campo, de Tommaso, and Mukherjee 2003.

Menu of Policy Options Is Large and Flexible

Policymakers have several instruments for reducing public employment, containing the public wage bill, and—most important—directing new labor market entrants toward private sector employment (Rama 1999). To be most effective and sustainable in the long run, the realignment of incentives toward work in the private sector should rely on both push and pull factors. The menu of policies ranges from natural attrition and hiring freezes, to accelerated attrition through substantial wage adjustments or benefit cuts, to explicit retrenchment through layoffs. Because these options imply tradeoffs between the costs and benefits to workers and the public sector on different time horizons, they may be introduced separately, sequentially, or simultaneously. The optimal combination of policies would vary by initial conditions, specific objectives, and political economy considerations.

Natural attrition rates can be high as employees leave public employment for private sector jobs or withdraw from the labor force because of disability, retirement, or other reasons. The age structure of public employment can provide some notion of natural outflow rates. In Egypt and

Morocco, for example, nearly 15 percent of public sector employees are more than 50 years old, and in Bahrain, Kuwait, and Oman, the equivalent figure is 10 percent. The average age of public sector employees is also rising as inflows of younger workers have decelerated. Thus, there is significant potential for employment reductions as workers retire over the next 10 years. Combined with a hiring freeze, attrition alone could translate into substantially reduced employment levels in the public sector.

Reducing remuneration can accelerate the process of attrition and can shift a greater supply of labor to the private sector. Lower compensation in the public sector raises the appeal of private sector employment for job seekers as the reservation wage falls and for current employees as the wage differential with the private sector shifts. Because cutting the wages of existing employees is likely to be politically untenable, especially when applied to tenured civil servants, alternative measures may be needed for reducing government employment and the wage bill. These measures include lowering remuneration for new entrants, adjusting the pay scale to strengthen the link between compensation and productivity, and focusing on nonwage benefits that distort labor decisions, such as generous pension systems and family allowances that add to the lure of employment in the public sector.

Algeria, for example, has no ceiling on the number of dependents eligible for family allowances, and in Kuwait the ceiling is seven dependents. The effect of these policies is distortionary, because workers can increase their remuneration by increasing family size rather than by increasing productivity. The nonwage benefit premium in the public sector represents a significant share of total public sector compensation (up to 50 percent) and represents the only variable that can be manipulated to reduce total compensation other than nominal wage cuts and pay-scale reforms.

Although lowering public sector remuneration can induce labor reallocation toward the private sector through the price mechanism, public sector downsizing can also be facilitated through layoffs or voluntary separations. Most countries in MENA have enabling legislation or precedents for such an approach. Because laid-off workers and dependents incur income losses through no fault of their own, but for broader economic reasons, retrenchment is typically accompanied by some income support to smooth consumption over the period of joblessness. Severance packages also reward workers for years of past service. In addition to these equity and social protection considerations, there are macroeconomic stabilizing effects from severance packages, because large-scale layoffs lead to declines in income that depress aggregate demand.

In reducing public employment, policymakers may need to define a number of elements, including the targeted number of layoffs, the level of necessary compensation, the means of financing layoff costs, and the redistribution or equity objectives. Retrenchment schemes vary, but governments typically adopt a national system that covers the entire labor force in the formal sector and defines uniform terms and conditions for layoffs and unemployment compensation. Private or union-sanctioned retrenchment schemes may exist alongside national schemes, and employers may establish their own voluntary schemes with more generous benefits, providing greater flexibility at higher cost.

Most countries in MENA have some type of severance requirement (table 5.1). Compensation can take the form of severance pay delivered in a lump sum or in periodic payments, as is common in Organisation for Economic Co-operation and Development (OECD) countries. Lump-sum severance involves high upfront costs to employers, which may discourage layoffs. In Algeria, for example, until 1994, the law required employers to compensate laid-off workers with 1 month's salary per year of tenure (up to 15 months) in a lump-sum payment. The Islamic Republic of Iran and Tunisia have legislation covering unemployment assistance, but only Algeria and Egypt have unemployment insurance in which formal sector workers participate through a mandatory payroll tax. In Egypt, there has been only modest use of this legislation, because layoffs are allowed only when an enterprise is liquidated. Thus, within MENA, Algeria alone has a functioning unemployment insurance system under which significant retrenchment has occurred (box 5.1).

Rationalizing the Public Sector Has Effects

The effects of reforms that target public sector employment and the wage bill can be illustrated using the framework outlined in the appendix to this chapter. The model offers a detailed treatment of the labor market, explicitly accounting for public sector employment and the "leadership effects" of public sector wages. Consider, for example, a 5 percent permanent reduction in the number of unskilled workers in the public sector (table 5.2). In the short run, the empirical simulations suggest that the unemployment rate of unskilled workers will increase even though, as unskilled wages fall, the private sector increases its hiring of workers and informal sector employment expands. In the long run (over 10 years), however, reducing public sector employment increases private sector investment and unskilled employment in the formal private sector. These positive outcomes are due to the crowding-in effect of lower public sector borrowing on private investment and the effect of higher private sector investment on demand for formal sector goods and, by extension, on demand for both skilled and unskilled workers. As a result, the initial increase in unemployment of unskilled workers is partially re-

TABLE 5.1

Severance Legislation in MENA Countries

Country	Level	Maximum	Notes
Algeria	1 month per year of tenure	3 months of salary	Before 1994, maximum was 15 months of salary; current unemployment insurance system pays monthly benefits for 1–3 years, ranging from 0.75 to 3 times the minimum wage.
Egypt, Arab Rep. of	No layoffs allowed except for firm liquidation	n.a.	Unemployment insurance pays benefits for 28 weeks at 60 percent of salary; benefits are financed by a 2 percent employer payroll tax.
Iran, Islamic Rep. of	1 month per year of tenure for justified dismissal, voluntary resignation, disability, or retirement	n.a.	Social insurance benefits are available for some period, financed by 3 percent social security payroll tax.
Jordan	1 month per year of tenure; civil servants entitled to 1 month per year of tenure for years 1–10, 1.5 months per year for > 10 years	n.a.	Benefits are available for voluntary resignation; they are paid by Social Security Corporation.
Lebanon	1 month per year of tenure	10 months of salary	n.a.
Morocco	1 week per year up to 5 years, 1.5 weeks per year for 6–10 years, 2 weeks per year for 11–15 years, 2.5 weeks per year for > 15 years	n.a.	n.a.
Tunisia	Minimum: 12 days per year of tenure (under the Labor Code); sectoral collective agreements stipulate 15 days to 1 month per year of tenure	3 months of salary (Labor Code); 6 months of salary (sectoral collective agreements)	Most common severance is 1 month per year of tenure; unemployment benefits are available for 3 months at twice the minimum wage; benefits are subject to strict eligibility criteria.
West Bank and Gaza	None	n.a.	n.a.
Yemen, Rep. of	1 month per year of tenure unless covered by Social Insurance Act	n.a.	Layoffs are allowed for economic reasons; legislation is pending for civil servants.

n.a. Not applicable.
Note: Information current as of 2002.
Source: Ruppert Bulmer 2002.

versed over time, whereas output expands in the formal, informal, and rural sectors together with private consumption and investment.

A permanent 5 percent reduction in the wages of skilled workers in the public sector has similar but stronger effects: it crowds in private investment and leads to an expansion in output in the long run. The effects are especially strong in the case of skilled workers because of the leadership effect of wages in the public sector on private wages. Lower public sector wages spill over into lower wages and higher employment of skilled workers in the formal private sector. Both skilled and unskilled workers benefit in the long run through lower unemployment rates. Skilled workers benefit from increased insertion into the formal private sector, and unskilled workers benefit from higher employment in the in-

BOX 5.1

Unemployment Insurance in Algeria

Algeria introduced unemployment insurance in July 1994 as part of a broader retrenchment program. The system was implemented relatively quickly and efficiently by tying it to the existing social security infrastructure. Benefits consist of an upfront, firm-financed severance payment equivalent to 1 month's salary per year of tenure up to 3 years, followed by a monthly benefit paid by the unemployment insurance fund at a level proportional to salary. Payments are made as a share of the reference wage, calculated as the average of the monthly and minimum wages, and they decline over the period of eligibility from 100 to 50 percent. Benefit levels also are subject to a minimum (three-fourths the minimum wage) and a maximum (three times the minimum wage) standard.

The system is financed by payroll tax contributions, which are shared by employers (2.5 percent) and employees (1.5 percent), and by an initiation fee paid by firms on behalf of each dismissed employee, proportional to that worker's salary and job tenure. Workers who are laid off for economic reasons, who have been affiliated with the social security system for at least 3 years, and who receive no alternative earnings are eligible to collect benefits, subject to their employer's payment of the initiation fee. The system covers workers and firms in the formal sector only.

Obstacles to implementation of the unemployment insurance system included strong union opposition, regulations limiting an employer's ability to retrench workers, and a high payroll tax burden. To win support for the new system, the Algerian government agreed not to raise the employer's portion of the payroll tax and extended the duration of benefits, which now ranges from 1 to 3 years and averages 22 months. The government also took on the financing of the program's family allowances, which, as initially proposed, were to be paid by a 3 percent employer contribution. The employee portion of the payroll tax rose by 2.5 percentage points (including 0.5 percent to finance early retirement, which was implemented concurrently with unemployment insurance), thus resulting in a higher total payroll tax burden of 34 percent.

The system has stimulated labor reallocation, and employers have gained some flexibility in their labor decisions; however, the unemployment insurance program has numerous flaws. Employers' total costs associated with retrenchment have not changed much. Instead of one upfront severance package, costs for the employer are spread out over a 1- to 2-year period. Also, the long duration of the benefits package may discourage job searching. There is some evidence that an influx of applications and complex administrative procedures have overwhelmed the system. Finally, the unemployment insurance system appears to suffer from inadequate monitoring. Revenues amply cover costs, indicating that the system is financially viable, but a weak investment strategy and poor regulatory oversight have somewhat undermined an initially high level of reserves. Lowering the payroll tax or the initiation fee could improve the financial efficiency of the program.

Source: Ruppert 1999a.

TABLE 5.2

Effect of Changes in Government Employment and Wages—Policy Experiment: 5 Percentage Point Reduction

Outcome	Skilled labor wages		Unskilled labor employment	
	Short run	Long run	Short run	Long run
Output				
Urban formal sector[a]	+	+	+	+
Urban informal sector[a]	+	+	+	+
Rural sector[a]	+	+	+	+
Private investment	+	+	+	+
Employment				
Unskilled labor in formal private sector	+	–	+	+
Skilled workers in formal private sector	+	+	+	+
Informal sector	+	+	+	+
Wages				
Unskilled labor in formal private sector	+	+	–	+
Skilled workers in formal private sector	–	–	+	+
Informal sector	+	+	–	+
Unemployment rate				
Unskilled labor in formal sector[b]	–	–	+	+
Skilled labor in formal sector[b]	–	–	+	+

Note: The short run reflects the effect in the first year, and the long run reflects the effect over 10 years. Percentage deviations from baseline unless otherwise stated.
a. Real terms.
b. Absolute deviations from baseline.
Source: Agénor and others 2003b.

formal sector. Although skilled workers face lower wages in the private sector, unskilled workers earn higher wages in both the informal and formal sectors. These dynamics also have important effects on migration. The substitution of skilled for unskilled workers in the formal private sector reduces the incentive to migrate to urban areas, while rising wages in the informal sector lower international migration pressures. Output expands in both urban and rural sectors.

Looking at Labor Market Institutions in the Private Sector

In MENA, government intervention in labor markets has extended to the private sector. Labor market regulations were adopted in MENA, as in much of the developing world, some half-century ago to provide social protection and justice to workers (figure 5.6). Whether covering hiring contracts, severance pay, grounds for dismissal, the right to unionize, or the scope for collective bargaining, labor market regulations aim to protect workers from arbitrary, unfair, or discriminatory actions by their employers while addressing potential market failures stemming from insufficient information and inadequate insurance against risk. Together, regulations encompassing employment and industrial relations laws constitute a broad and complex framework for managing labor markets (El-Mikawy and Posusney 2002). These laws at the national level received broad sanction from international labor conventions and regional agreements on labor regulations.

Although there are common tendencies in MENA toward providing workers with lifetime job security and generous retirement, health, and other job-related benefits, individual countries differ considerably in the extent of intervention, reflecting specific historical trajectories (figure 5.7). Thus, trade unions are permitted in Egypt and the North African countries but are either banned or absent in most labor-importing countries. Similarly, restrictions on hiring and firing are more stringent in Algeria, Egypt, and Tunisia than in Jordan, Morocco, and the expatriate-

FIGURE 5.6

Labor Market Regulation in Developing Regions

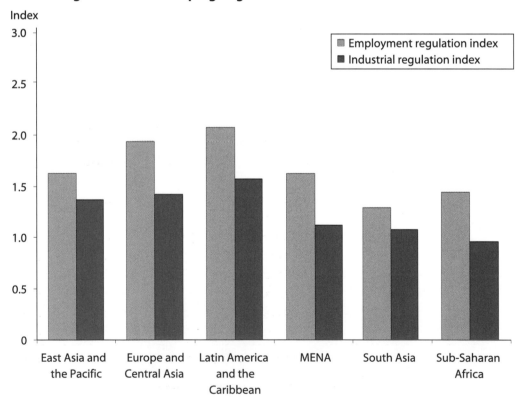

Note: On a scale of 1 to 3. The average is weighted.
Source: World Bank 2003b.

dominated private sectors of labor-importing countries. Minimum wage laws have been legislated in Egypt, the Islamic Republic of Iran, and the North African countries but not elsewhere. Specific differences exist not only in legislation but also in enforcement and coverage. The highly protective rules adopted in the state-run era are more or less universally enforced in the large public sectors, but they are imperfectly enforced in the private sector and, in the labor-importing countries, in jobs filled by low-paid expatriate workers.

Social Protection That Balances with Flexibility

There have been sharp differences of opinion concerning the costs and benefits of labor regulations (Freeman 1993). One perspective supports regulations for providing important social protection for workers, while an opposing perspective emphasizes that such regulations raise the cost

FIGURE 5.7

Labor Market Regulation in MENA Countries

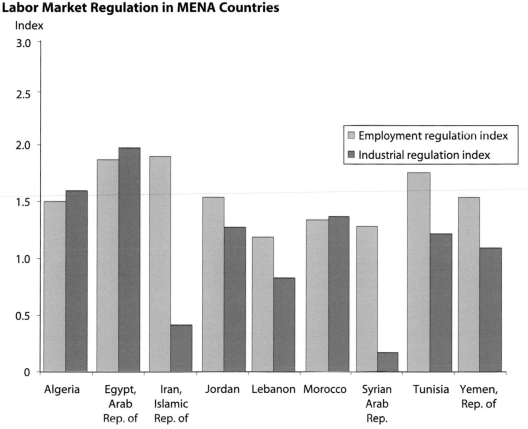

Note: On a scale of 1 to 3.
Source: World Bank 2003b.

of labor and favor more privileged insiders (figures 5.8 and 5.9). These contrasting views suggest that what matter from a policy perspective are the economic and social effects of different approaches to labor market regulations. But clear empirical evidence for assessing the effects of regulation has been lacking. Furthermore, there has been the perception that in most developing countries, including MENA, employment laws are often ineffective because of evasion, weak enforcement, and failure to reach the informal sector (World Bank 1995c).

Recent international evidence suggests that the regulatory framework can strongly influence labor market outcomes, by affecting job creation and the structure of employment as well as the degree of social protection of workers. Although regulation generally increases the tenure and wages of incumbent workers, it also limits job creation and reduces flexibility in the work force. With excessive regulation, workers endure long unemployment spells, which lead to skill degradation and lack of work experience. Unemployment of women and youths also rises, which may limit the opportunities of disadvantaged groups to emerge from poverty. With few job opportunities in the formal economy, workers are pushed

FIGURE 5.8

Labor Regulation and the Informal Economy

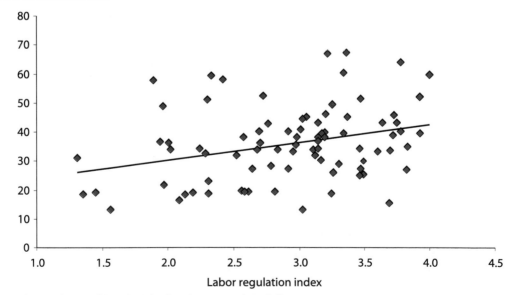

Note: Labor regulation is the sum of the industrial and employment regulation indices.
Source: World Bank 2003b.

FIGURE 5.9

Unemployment and Employment Regulation

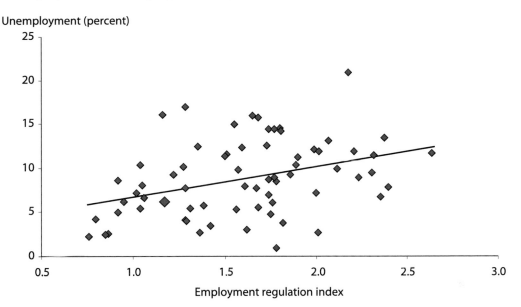

Source: ILO 2002; World Bank 2003b.

into the informal sector where social protection is lacking altogether (Maloney 1999). MENA has not been immune to these undesirable effects, as the evidence presented in chapter 4 demonstrates. Even minimum wage laws, which are thought to be ineffective because of weak coverage and lack of enforcement, have been shown to have significant effects on unemployment, as Morocco's experience illustrates (El-Hamidi 2002, see box 5.2).

By reducing flexibility in the work force, stringent regulations can also reduce productivity and growth of firms. Rigid rules and procedures discourage enterprise restructuring by imposing excessive costs and large administrative burdens. Stringent rules on dismissal may push managers to reorganize the production process to continue to employ unneeded workers, thus also reducing incentives to adopt the latest technologies. Hiring and firing restrictions may also result in smaller firms and unexploited economies of scale. These combined effects—longer unemployment spells and the related skill obsolescence of workers, less job creation, less investment in research and development, and smaller company size—reduce overall productivity growth.

BOX 5.2

Effects of the Minimum Wage in Morocco

Minimum wage legislation in Morocco, first adopted in 1936, sets different wage floors for rural and urban labor markets. Officially, the minimum wage is to be adjusted whenever the consumer price index increases by 5 percent. In practice, however, political discretion and pressure by labor unions tend to determine increases. Evidence suggests that the urban minimum wage is observed by the public sector and is well enforced in the formal private sector.

During 1970–2000, the urban minimum wage rose an average of 6 percent a year, which translates into a 1.1 percent annual increase in real wages in urban areas. In the 1990s, growth of the real minimum wage in urban areas rose to 1.3 percent a year, exceeding the growth in labor productivity in the formal sector. By 2000, the minimum wage was close to half the average wage in the formal private sector and 178 percent of GDP per capita.

Several observers have argued that the increases in the urban minimum wage (a) reduced demand for unskilled labor; (b) contributed to a rise in unit labor costs, thus reducing Morocco's external competitiveness; and (c) encouraged the informalization of production. These factors may have pushed more unskilled workers outside the formal sector, where compensation is lower than the official minimum wage.

In simulations of a dynamic general equilibrium model for Morocco, a permanent 5 percent reduction in the urban minimum wage leads to a 3.7 percent increase in the demand for unskilled labor in the private sector in the first year. As a result, the unemployment rate for unskilled workers drops by about 2.4 percentage points each year. Employment of unskilled workers in the informal sector, as well as rural–urban migration, declines. By reducing the costs of unskilled labor, the reduction in the minimum wage also leads the private sector to substitute labor for capital. The effects on private consumption and output are also positive.

Source: Agénor and El Aynaoui 2003.

Strong Dynamic Effects of Labor Market Regulations

International evidence shows that rigid employment rules are potentially more harmful when the dynamics of labor market outcomes—including job creation, job destruction, and unemployment duration—are considered, especially in countries undergoing restructuring and reform and rapid labor force growth as in MENA (Betcherman, Luinstra, and Ogawa 2001). In this regard, the much higher unemployment rates over three decades in Latin America, where labor markets are highly regu-

lated, than in East Asia, where regulations are more flexible, are reveal-
ing (figure 5.10). Labor regulations became a focus of attention in countries enduring long unemployment spells, leading to efforts to reform
employment laws. More flexible employment arrangements are likely to
facilitate adjustment to macroeconomic shocks and support restructuring programs because rigid labor regulations impede the necessary relocation of workers across sectors (table 5.3).

FIGURE 5.10

Labor Force Growth and Unemployment in Asia and Latin America and the Caribbean

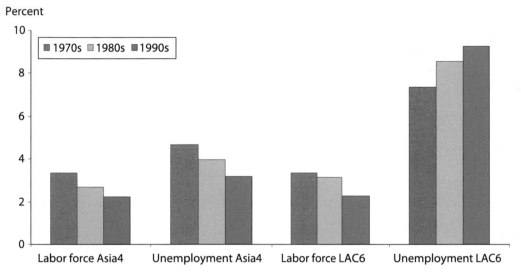

Note: Asia4 = Hong Kong, Republic of Korea, Malaysia, and Singapore; LAC6 = Argentina, Brazil, Chile, Colombia, Mexico, and Uruguay.
Sources: Asia 4, ADB 2001; LAC6, ILO 2002 for labor force and ECLAC 2001 for unemployment.

TABLE 5.3

Summary of Effects of Employment Protection Regulations

Indicator	Effects of strict limitations regarding	
	Fixed-term and temporary agency work	Termination of permanent employees for economic reasons
Employment level	Somewhat lower	Somewhat lower
Labor force participation	n.a.	Somewhat lower
Unemployment level	Insignificant	Insignificant
Unemployment duration	Longer	Longer
Informal employment	Higher	Higher
Job creation	Lower	Lower
Job destruction	Lower	Lower
Job tenure	n.a.	Longer
Groups benefiting	—	Prime-age males, skilled workers
Groups losing	Women, youths	Women, youths, unskilled workers

n.a. Not applicable.
— Not available.
Source: Betcherman, Luinstra, and Ogawa 2001.

Hiring and Dismissal Procedures That Influence Employment

More flexible hiring and dismissal procedures are the most relevant policy issues in the reform of labor market regulations in MENA, where low job creation and long-term unemployment are major problems (chapter 4). Firms are reluctant to hire workers when it is unduly costly to terminate them as economic conditions change. As a result, to get the hiring flexibility they need, firms are likely to rely increasingly on fixed-term, temporary contracts or even unregistered contracts that are beyond the reach of regulations (figures 5.11 and 5.12).

Although MENA has generally had a regulatory preference for permanent employment contracts in the formal sector, several countries have recently taken steps to make hiring arrangements more flexible. Egypt's new labor code of April 2003 allows defined-duration contracts to be renewed an unlimited number of times without becoming a permanent contract, whereas Egypt's 1981 labor law required such contracts to be converted to permanent contracts if employment extended beyond the initial period (box 5.3). Morocco and Tunisia recently have implemented legislation that expands the possibilities for part-time work and fixed-term contracts, which are the main source of flexibility on the hiring side in these countries (box 5.4).

FIGURE 5.11

Share of Temporary Employment in Morocco, by Enterprise Size

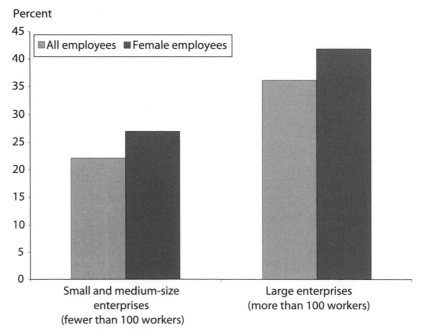

Percent

Source: Morocco 1999.

FIGURE 5.12

Share of Temporary Employment in Morocco, by Sector

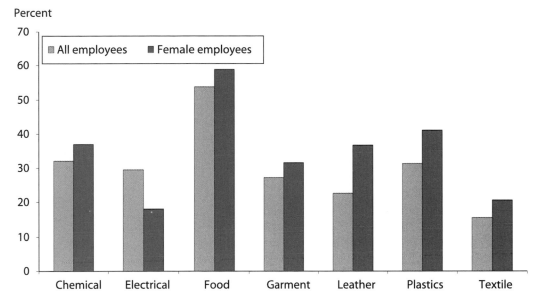

Source: Morocco 1999.

Uneven Progress with Labor Reforms

Although countries are starting to provide more flexible employment arrangements on the hiring side, they are paying less attention to restrictions on dismissal and layoffs. This asymmetry in hiring and firing regulations introduces further rigidities in labor markets. Most countries either ban dismissal for economic reasons (shrinking markets, increasing competitiveness) or make it administratively cumbersome. In Morocco and Tunisia, dismissed workers can pursue legal measures that can result in heavy costs for firms and that subject firms to the unpredictable and inconsistent legal process. And in some countries, wage agreements boost severance costs, overriding provisions of the labor code. As a result, private enterprises are not restructuring, and small firms often find solutions outside the legal framework. Some firms get around restrictions on dismissals by making employees sign undated letters of resignation, which are held in reserve in case layoffs are required.

High Indirect Labor Costs

High nonwage labor costs in some MENA countries reinforce the incentive to hire workers on a temporary basis or to avoid registration requirements, which trigger mandatory contributions (table 5.4). In Morocco

BOX 5.3

Labor Reform in the Arab Republic of Egypt

Law 12, passed in April 2003, addresses major shortcomings in Egypt's United Labor Code (Law 137) of 1981, including its inflexible hiring and firing provisions, and addresses the concerns of labor. Important provisions of the new law include

- *Contract termination.* Law 12 allows for temporary contracts that can be renewed repeatedly and allows companies to fire workers during times of economic hardship or for dereliction of duty. Previous legislation allowed defined-duration contracts, but upon renewal, these contracts had to be made permanent. It was virtually impossible for employers to fire permanent employees, regardless of their performance or economic conditions.

- *Right to strike.* The new code permits "peaceful demonstrations," but only if mediation has failed. Workers in "vital" and "strategic" establishments, as determined by the prime minister, are still prohibited from striking. Previous legislation did not guarantee workers the right to strike.

- *Wages and compensation.* Law 12 establishes a minimum wage for the first time. The newly created National Council on Wages is to reevaluate the minimum wage at least every 3 years. Automatic annual increases of 7 percent are required for all workers, unless the council reaches another decision.

- *Safety measures.* Law 12 establishes safety standards for industry and articulates standards to ensure that workers are physically and mentally fit to perform their jobs and that they have proper training to carry out their duties.

- *Vocational training.* The new code requires that vocational training programs be managed by limited liability or joint venture companies and that they be licensed. It also creates a government oversight group to ensure high standards of training.

Source: World Bank staff.

and Tunisia, nonwage costs paid by employers and employees make up on average 25 percent of the wage bill. In Algeria, contributions to the social security system alone constitute more than 36 percent of total labor costs. In Morocco, employers' share of social security payments is about 19 percent of the wage bill, whereas in Tunisia, it is about 16 percent. Other surcharges range from medical coverage, injury insurance, and safety provisions to vocational training. The many small charges add up to a substantial indirect cost on labor. The investment incentives that reduce the user cost of capital may have encouraged firms to adopt more capital-

---

BOX 5.4

Labor Regulation Reforms in Morocco and Tunisia

Morocco's Labor Code of 2003 introduced the following provisions:

- *Term contracts.* Nonagricultural sector firms that are newly established or are producing a new product may set up term contracts for 1 year, which may be renewed one time. If renewed again, the contract becomes open ended. Agricultural sector firms may conclude term contracts for a 6-month period, which may be renewed up to three times before becoming an open-ended contract.

- *Open-ended contracts.* The new labor code permits a 3-month probation period for high-level employees, a 1.5-month period for middle-level employees, and 15 days for lower-level employees. The probation period is renewable one time.

Tunisia's Labor Code of 1996 introduced the following provisions:

- *Fixed-term contracts.* The Labor Code of 1996 establishes two categories of fixed-term contracts or contrats à durée déterminée (CDDs). The first category is work of a definite term, which is stipulated as work stemming from (a) a temporary increase in activity, (b) the replacement of an absent employee, (c) seasonal activities, or (d) work that is by definition fixed in duration. In these cases, employers have no restrictions on CDDs. The second category is work of indeterminate length. In this case, fixed-term contracts are permitted for a maximum of 4 years and are subject to the agreement of both parties. CDD workers have the same rights as indeterminate-contract employees.

- *Part-time work.* This new category of work is defined as work for fewer than 70 percent of normal hours. It is intended to promote freedom of choice for all employees and equal treatment for part-time employees. According to the most recent Tunisian Employment Survey, 14 percent of all employment in 2001 was part time.

Source: World Bank 2003e and World Bank staff.

---

intensive processes in order to improve flexibility in the face of high indirect labor costs and other rigidities in the labor market (table 5.4).

In theory, being subject to social security contributions and payroll taxes puts employers at no disadvantage to their competitors if the workers themselves end up paying for those benefits in the form of lower salaries, because workers should then be indifferent to getting a job with or without social security coverage. Evidence from Egypt and Tunisia suggests, however, that employers in the formal sector are not able to pass these nonwage costs onto employees (Assaad 1996, World Bank

TABLE 5.4

Financial Indicators of Pension Funds in MENA Countries

Fund	Percent of GDP		Contribution share of gross wage bill (percent)			
	Pension spending	Revenues from contributions	Employee	Employer	Government	Total
Algeria (1999)	2.9	1.8	—	—	—	—
National Retirement Fund [a]	1.7	1.7	6.5	9.5	0	16.0
National Social Insurance Fund [b]	1.2	0.1	7.5	7.5	0	15.0
Bahrain (1996)	1.2	2.4	5.0	7.0	0	12.0
Egypt, Arab Rep. of (1998)	2.9	3.6	13.0	17.0	1.0	31.0
Iran, Islamic Rep. of (2001)	1.8	2.0	—	—	—	—
Civil Servant Retirement Organization [c]	0.8	0.7	8.5	12.8	0	21.3
Social Security Organization [c]	1.0	1.3	7.0	23.0	3.0	33.0
Jordan (2001)	4.8	2.4	—	—	—	—
Social Security Corporation [d]	1.3	2.4	5.5	9.0	0	14.5
Public System (Military)	2.8	—	8.8	0	0	8.8
Public System (Civil Service)	0.7	—	8.8	0	0	8.8
Kuwait (1996)	5.9	8.5	5.0	10.0	10.0	25.0
Morocco (1998)	2.1	2.3	—	—	—	—
National Fund for Social Security [d]	0.1	0.6	3.0	6.1	0	9.1
Moroccan Pension Fund [c]	1.0	1.3	7.0	7.0	0	14.0
Retirement Benefits Collective Plan [c]	0.1	0.2	6.0	12.0	0	18.0
Interprofessional Pension Fund [e]	0.3	0.2	3.0–6.0	3.0–6.0	0	6.0–12.0
Syrian Arab Rep. (1999)	0.6	1.3	7.0	14.0	0	21.0
Tunisia (1998)	4.8	—	—	—	—	—
National Fund for Social Security [d]	—	—	6.3	17.5	0	23.8
National Fund for Retirement and Social Protection [c]	—	—	7.5	9.7	0	17.2
Yemen, Rep. of (1994)	0	0.1	6.0	9.0	0	15.0

— Not available.
a. Applies to public and private employees.
b. Applies to self-employed.
c. Applies to public employees.
d. Applies to private employees.
e. Voluntary fund.
Source: World Bank 2002c.

2003e). Thus, together with restrictions on dismissal, social protection costs force employers to reduce their labor costs by hiring fewer workers or by employing more workers on a temporary or illegal basis. Generous maternity leave provisions in the formal sector, which are required by many labor codes, further reduce female employment.

It is straightforward to show that lower indirect labor costs lead to increased employment of unskilled workers in the formal private sector (figure 5.13). Under this policy scenario, a permanent 5 percentage point reduction in payroll taxes for unskilled workers would provide a strong incentive for the private formal sector to substitute unskilled for skilled workers. Wages for unskilled workers would rise as unskilled workers are drawn from the rural sector and from the informal sector into the formal private sector. To the extent that employment in the formal private sector implies greater social protection for workers, lower payroll taxes confer this benefit on unskilled workers in addition to lowering their overall unemployment rate. These effects go hand in hand with a strong positive effect on real output in the formal sector and at the aggregate level. The benefits under this payroll tax reduction scenario are stronger when the government takes offsetting budgetary measures to keep the budget deficit unchanged. For example, by keeping the budgetary effect neutral through an increase in sales taxes, the government minimizes the crowding out of private investment and the negative effects on employment and output.

FIGURE 5.13

Simulation Results for a Reduction in Payroll Taxes

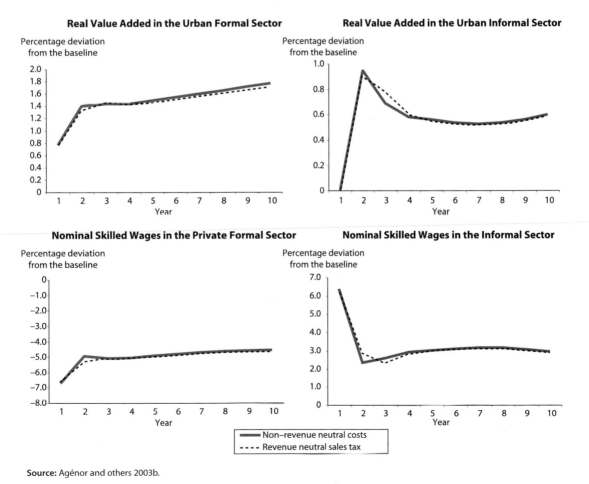

Source: Agénor and others 2003b.

Quantifying the Effects of Labor Reforms

However pressing labor market reform might be, it is often among the most challenging reforms to implement—witness the experience of Latin America and MENA in the past decade. Conflicting views about the employment benefits and unemployment costs of downsizing the public sector and deregulating markets are partly to blame, because they send mixed signals to policymakers, who are often reluctant to undertake reforms. Greater labor market flexibility brings with it greater employment volatility, with more firing than hiring during recessions and the opposite during booms. In environments where economic volatility is already high and unemployment is a problem, as in MENA, concerns about employment volatility may amplify workers' fears about the effects of reforms.

Political Economy of Labor Market Reforms

Existing labor regulations protect older workers in the formal sector, both public and private (Dömeland and Gill 2002). Better represented in the policy arena through unions and political parties, these workers are able to exert considerable pressure to maintain job security (figures 5.14 and 5.15). Unionized workers in MENA have often hijacked the public debate and impeded labor market reforms despite their declining share in the labor force and the political control governments subject them to. Resistance to reform not only has slowed progress in privatizing public enterprises, where labor retrenchment is a concern, but also has delayed bringing the legal code into alignment with current practices in labor markets, such as the use of temporary contracts. The recent labor legislation in Egypt and Morocco was the culmination of decades of effort. As a result of all these factors, labor market reforms have been absent from the policy agenda in MENA for much of the past decade.

Model simulations shed some light on the political economy driving organized labor's resistance to reforms (figure 5.16). If the bargaining power of unions is reduced, wages drop for skilled workers, who dominate the ranks of organized labor. But the lower wages lead to increased employment and reduced unemployment of skilled workers in the formal private sector, both unionized and nonunionized. As incomes rise, so does aggregate demand, which together with the lower wage bill boosts the profitability of firms in the private sector. The level of private investment rises, and with it formal sector and total output. The effects also extend to unskilled workers, who experience lower unemployment and higher wages.

FIGURE 5.14

Share of Unionized Workers in Algeria, by Enterprise Ownership

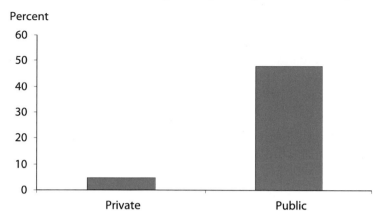

Source: Assaf and Benhassine 2003.

FIGURE 5.15

Share of Unionized Workers in Algeria, by Enterprise Size

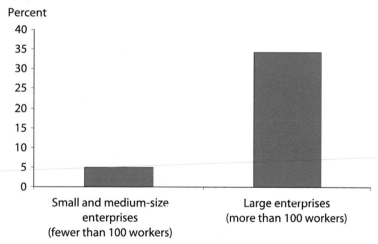

Source: Assaf and Benhassine 2003.

Aggregate Effects of Reforms: Positive but Modest

Most of the simulations reported in this chapter indicate that labor market reforms should lower overall unemployment, increase formal sector employment, and expand output. With all the political economy considerations governing labor market reform, however, policymakers also need to know more precisely what payoffs can be expected from the

FIGURE 5.16

Simulating the Effects of a Reduction in the Bargaining Power of Labor Unions

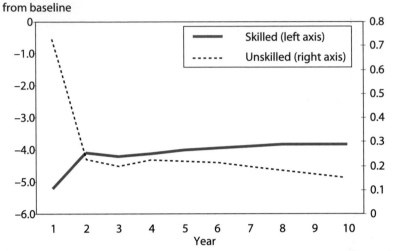

Skilled and Unskilled Wages in Private Formal Sector

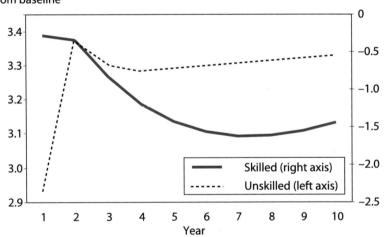

Skilled and Unskilled Employment in Private Formal Sector

Source: Agénor and others 2003b.

broad program of labor market reforms outlined in this chapter, including the size of the effects on the growth and job-creation challenges that MENA faces in the next two decades.

Simulations that address this critical question were conducted of a composite, "realistic" package of policies targeting public sector employment, payroll taxes in the private sector, and the role of labor unions. On the basis of available data and a sense of what is feasible for policy-makers in the region, the simulations assume a 5 percentage point reduction in the payroll tax on unskilled labor, a 5 percent reduction in the number of unskilled workers in the public sector, and a reduction in the bargaining power of trade unions to a neutral level. Although modest in light of the rigidities in MENA's labor markets, these goals are ambitious relative to the record of reforms in the 1990s, when only a few MENA countries managed to reduce public sector employment. In Egypt and Morocco, legislation that aimed to deregulate labor markets has strengthened the power of labor unions.

Although this realistic package of labor market reforms brings some benefits, the effects on output and employment are not large. Over the long term, output increases 0.9 percent and private formal sector employment rises 4.0 percent for unskilled labor and 3.1 percent for skilled labor. Such modest long-term effects have important implications. The challenge is not only to reduce high unemployment but also to create sufficient jobs to absorb new entrants in the labor force. With labor force growth rates exceeding 3 percent a year, employment increases of 3 to 4 percent over a 10-year horizon suggest limitations on the ability of labor market reforms alone to address MENA's employment challenge.

Where policy reforms take place, the simulations indicate that a piecemeal approach to labor market reform is unlikely to bring substantial benefits in terms of output and employment growth. Instead, a comprehensive approach is needed to allow policymakers to exploit complementarities between individual policies. Indeed, the effect of the realistic policy package is approximately equal to the growth rates derived from the individual policy simulations described earlier. Thus, fostering a sustained increase in growth rates and job creation in these countries may require a more comprehensive program of structural reforms (chapter 6). The idea that labor market reform programs must be sufficiently broad (covering a wide range of complementary policies) and deep (of substantial magnitude) to have much of an effect has been emphasized in other contexts of the world (Coe and Snower 1997).

Using Active Labor Market Policies in MENA

From wage and employment subsidies, to training and retraining for the unemployed, to direct job-creation programs and job-search and assistance services, active labor market policies are important interventions used widely in both developing and industrial countries. The policies are designed to create employment opportunities and to manage labor market risks. They have been used to moderate cyclical downturns, to reduce structural imbalances or otherwise improve the functioning of the labor market, to increase productivity, to support disadvantaged or at-risk workers, to support threatened industries or employers, or to achieve some combination of these objectives. Each objective calls for different types of policies and different client populations (table 5.5). Their popularity dates to the global recession in the 1970s, when OECD countries struggled with slow growth and high unemployment.

As globalization and rapid technological change increase the volatility in the labor market, accelerate structural change, and place a premium on the acquisition of productive skills, an effective active labor market policy assumes heightened importance. In MENA, as in other regions that lack functioning national unemployment insurance systems, active labor market programs constitute a major instrument of national employment for tackling labor market dislocations.

Upward Trajectory in the Use of Active Labor Market Policies

All countries in MENA employ active labor market policies, but with varying intensity and success (Tzannatos 2002). The programs have evolved from their historical focus on training and recruiting workers

TABLE 5.5

Tailoring Active Labor Market Programs to Objectives

Objective	Program orientation	Targeting orientation
To moderate cyclical downturns	Direct job creation (such as public works) Wage subsidies Training (subsidies or grants to workers or employers) Self-employment support	Vulnerable groups (with least resiliency) Hard-hit regions and industries
To reduce structural imbalances	Employment services (such as information, search assistance, mobility assistance) Training Wage subsidies	Proximate regions, industries, or occupations
To improve general labor market functioning	Employment services Training (such as apprenticeship, school-to-work transition)	All
To enhance skills and productivity	Training and retraining (including in-service, apprenticeship)	At-risk or disadvantaged worker categories (especially for retraining)
To support disadvantaged or at-risk workers	Employment services (counseling, job search assistance) Training (such as grants, subsidies) Wage subsidies	At-risk or disadvantaged worker categories

Source: Betcherman, Olivas, and Dar 2003.

into the public sector to a focus on the consequences of labor shedding and unemployment. With ongoing plans to privatize public enterprises and efforts to restructure the civil service, active labor market policies will become increasingly relevant for addressing the consequences of labor retrenchment. The high levels of unemployment, its concentration among educated young adults, and the segmentation of labor markets along public–private and national–expatriate lines have created new incentives to expand the range and coverage of active labor market policies, especially those that focus on youths.

Wide Use of Public Works Programs

In addition to providing poor communities with infrastructure, public works programs create temporary jobs for the unemployed and supplement safety nets. Morocco and Tunisia have a long tradition of using these programs, and Algeria and Egypt introduced them in the 1990s following structural adjustment programs (table 5.6). Morocco's 30-year-old Promotion Nationale manages projects located mostly in disadvantaged rural areas, including projects involving reforestation, well-water recapture, dam and road construction, and road paving. During 1990–99, the program created some 40,000 person-years of employment in labor-intensive activities. Tunisia's public works program is an important vehicle for transferring income to the poorer segments of society. During 1987–91, Tunisia's program employed an average of 75,000 workers a year, one-third in urban areas and two-thirds in rural areas (World Bank 2002c).

Increases in Microfinance and Unemployment Lending

Most countries in MENA have microfinance schemes to promote self-employment (see box 5.5 on the Republic of Yemen's experience). These

TABLE 5.6

Job Creation as a Result of Public Works Programs

Country	Program	Workers (percentage of the labor force)
Algeria	Indemnité d'Activités d'Intérêts General, Travaux d'Utilité Publique, and Rural Employment	2.3
Egypt, Arab Rep. of	Public Works	0.4
Morocco	Promotion Nationale	0.6
Tunisia	Chantiers Nationauz/Regionaux	2.7
Yemen, Rep. of	Public Works	0.1

Source: World Bank 2002c.

programs have grown rapidly in recent years, with the number of clients in the region doubling between 1997 and 1999. Microfinance programs offer loans for enterprise investment to individuals just below or above the poverty line, with the goal of reducing the vulnerability of the poor to economic stress. Expectations have been high, and governments throughout the region have taken great interest in these programs (table 5.7). As of 2001, microfinance remained mostly unregulated, but this situation appears to be changing (Brandsma and Hart 2002).

BOX 5.5

Community-Driven Development and Microfinance for the Poor in the Republic of Yemen

The Republic of Yemen has developed a successful approach to community-driven development and financially sustainable microfinance. Small community projects are being implemented in even the most remote areas of the country. These localized development efforts started with the Public Works Project in 1996 and were later strengthened by the establishment of the Social Fund for Development.

The social fund not only finances local demand-driven projects, but also works with members of the community to ensure the success of each project. Care is taken to consult all stakeholders, including the more marginal members of the community. Furthermore, community ownership is ensured by upfront contributions, and the social fund finances the project after confirming that a system of user charges (including cross-subsidies for the poor) is in place to meet operation and maintenance costs. The fund also supports community capacity building to enable communities to better plan and execute development projects.

The fund provides technical assistance, training, and loan funds to support the development of sustainable microfinance entities that follow best-practice approaches. These microfinance intermediaries have also provided savings services to the poor. To avoid Islamic prohibitions against interest-based lending, the fund has developed loan products that build on Islamic banking principles that have proven financially successful.

These activities have been successful throughout the Republic of Yemen. In remote villages, the social fund has worked with communities to restore traditional water-harvesting systems and has increased girls' school enrollment by providing educational facilities. In some communities, the fund has supported new health facilities, and in others it has improved access by supporting road building. One male client has transitioned to a third-generation loan, moving from selling fruits out of a wheelbarrow to owning a small store. One female microfinance client, who had dropped out of school at the age of 10, reports that she was able to return to school many years later because the microfinance program helped to stabilize the family income.

Source: World Bank 2002c.

TABLE 5.7

Microfinance Programs and Unemployment Lending Programs in MENA Countries, 1999

Indicator	Egypt, Arab Rep. of	Jordan	Lebanon	Morocco	Tunisia	West Bank and Gaza	Yemen, Rep. of	Total or average
Number of microfinance programs	15	8	5	7	6	3	4	48
Number of unemployment programs	1	3	11	—	5	5	0	25
Number of active microfinance clients	90,897	17,777	4,438	42,571	3,251	7,264	2,619	168,817
Number of active unemployment clients	40,000	5,320	6,330	—	22,575	1,537	n.a.	75,762
Female microfinance clients (percent)	25	47	95	76	64	100	26	46
Female unemployment clients (percent)	20	25	23	—	20	44	n.a.	21

— Not available.
n.a. Not applicable.
Note: Averages are weighted.
Source: Brandsma and Hart 2002.

A related, rapidly developing program is unemployment lending, which offers small investment capital loans to the unemployed. Unlike microfinance lending, unemployment lending programs are intended to reduce unemployment rather than to provide sustainable financial services for the poor, and the business activities funded are usually new activities. These programs are managed by large governmental or quasi-governmental organizations that subsidize the cost of borrowing.

Both types of programs were initially concentrated in urban areas, and men were the primary beneficiaries. As microfinance institutions achieved scale and became more efficient, they began to expand steadily to rural areas and to women. Women rose from 31 percent of active microfinance clients in 1997 to 46 percent in 1999. Despite this progress, women still account for only about 21 percent of unemployment lending program clients.

Training and Retraining Programs for the Unemployed

As elsewhere around the world, vocational training and retraining programs have become increasingly popular in MENA to address skill shortages among the unemployed and to meet the skill needs of modernizing economies. Training programs have been targeted at the long-term unemployed, people who were laid off in mass retrenchments, and youths (generally school dropouts). Algeria has the largest training system; of its 290,000 training posts, 260,000 of them are in public training centers and 15,000 are in public enterprises. Egypt has some 36,000 students in 120 publicly managed training centers. In the West Bank and Gaza, there are 29 centers outside the Ministry of Education and Ministry of Higher Education with about 24 specializations and 3,000 trainees, but there is little program coordination with the job market. The Republic of Yemen has some 5,000 students in 15 public training centers that focus primarily on industry and commerce.

Evidence of the Limitations of Active Labor Market Policies

Despite the political appeal and contribution to poverty alleviation of active labor market policies, evidence from industrial and developing countries suggests that such policies do little to remedy structural problems in labor markets or to reduce high unemployment in MENA (Abrahart, Kaur, and Tzannatos 2002). Even with spending already high and projected to grow, these programs are likely to cover only a small share of the labor force. Inappropriately designed, such programs may entail significant fiscal costs and negative economic effects. Public works programs, for example, provide current benefits without improving the long-term employability of workers. Participants tend to have a smaller probability of being employed later in a nonassisted job and are likely to earn less. Self-employment assistance programs tend to work for only a small part of the unemployed population and are associated with large deadweight effects (workers would have received assistance without the program) and displacement effects (replacing unsubsidized workers with subsidized workers). Business failure rates in these programs are high, though mentoring and business counseling services help to reduce them.

Training programs tend to be cyclical, with better outcomes when the economy is expanding. International evaluations have shown that closely targeted on-the-job training programs, usually aimed at women and other disadvantaged groups, offer the highest returns. Evaluations of retraining for laid-off workers find limited improvement in reemployment probabilities. The evidence suggests that, if used, the programs should be small in scale and targeted to groups that can benefit most from them. Evaluations of youth training programs find better results for enterprise-based training than for classroom training. Overall, however, the evidence suggests that it is difficult to overcome previous education problems with short-duration training programs.

To be effective, then, active labor market policies need to be carefully designed and targeted. For most countries in MENA, this effort will require impact evaluation studies and continuous review of the program mix to ensure wide coverage, cost-effectiveness, and maximum effect on labor market outcomes. It may mean expanding job-search and assistance programs, among the most successful active labor market policies elsewhere but with limited reach in MENA because of low participation, inadequate funding, or bans on job intermediation services in some countries. Programs may need to be better aligned with the profile and needs of the unemployed. Many programs focus on the educated, who face the highest unemployment rates but who do not constitute a majority of unemployed workers. More resources need to be devoted to poorly educated workers, including women, a problem that will become more acute in the short term as MENA countries become more integrated into global commodity markets (Betcherman, Olivas, and Dar 2003).

Considering the Special Case of Labor-Importing Countries

Much of the analysis of labor market reforms and active labor policies, especially on microfinance, training and retraining, and job-search programs, applies equally to the labor-exporting and labor-importing countries in MENA. Segmentation of labor markets along public–private lines is common to both groups, and both need to reform public sector hiring and wage-setting practices and institutionalized rigidities in the private sector. However, the segmentation of labor markets in the labor-importing countries along national–expatriate lines creates additional complexities for interventions in all areas of policy reform (Girgis 2002, IMF 1997). For example, lowering wages for nationals in the public sector may not bring the reservation wage of young labor market entrants down to the levels in the expatriate-dominated private sector. Similarly, creating flexible hiring and dismissal arrangements to encourage employment of nationals in the private sector may not be sufficient to overcome wage and nonwage differentials between nationals and the expatriate work force.

Labor Force Nationalization Policies Are Gaining Momentum

With an estimated 480,000 unemployed nationals in the Gulf Cooperation Council (GCC) countries, together with 7 million expatriate workers, policymakers have tried to nationalize the labor force through quotas and increased restrictions on work permits for expatriates, as well as the use of subsidies for the hiring of nationals (box 5.6). These efforts have been especially intense in Bahrain, Oman, and Saudi Arabia, where strong pressures on labor markets have led to rising unemployment among nationals. Kuwait, Qatar, and the United Arab Emirates have recently stepped up efforts to nationalize the labor force, and active labor market policies for nationals are likely to gain momentum and become codified into law.

These policy initiatives appear to have produced tangible results (figure 5.17). In Bahrain, Kuwait, Oman, and Saudi Arabia, the share of nationals rose in the past decade from 65 percent to about 80 percent in the public sector and from 25 percent to 32 percent in the private sector. The number of expatriate workers in the public sector fell in both rela-

---

BOX 5.6

Labor Force Nationalization Programs in the Gulf Cooperation Council Countries

Bahrain
Begun in 1998, Bahrain's nationalization program was the earliest formal labor market strategy launched in the GCC area to create employment opportunities for nationals. Today, the program seeks to create 6,000 jobs a year for Bahrainis. Firms have been asked to increase employment of nationals by 5 percent a year until half their labor force is Bahraini, and new firms must have a work force that is 20 percent Bahraini. A human resources development support program, introduced in 1994, offers financial incentives to small and mid-sized firms in the manufacturing sector that employ Bahrainis as at least 30 percent of their work force.

Kuwait
The latest economic plan is targeted to create 10,000 jobs a year for Kuwaitis during the next 5 years and to raise the share of nationals to 25 percent of the labor force. Policies to achieve these objectives include raising the cost of expatriate labor through increased licensing fees, limiting employment of expatriates in certain businesses and activities, and upgrading the skills of nationals. Some of these policies were codified in the new labor law of 2000, which also imposed a 2.5 percent tax on listed companies to finance the provisions of the law.

Oman
The current 5-year plan established labor market policies that aim at creating 17,400 new jobs a year and increasing the proportion of nationals from 36 percent to 42 percent of the labor force. The National Vocational Qualification Program, which was launched by the government in 1995 and is financed by taxes on expatriate workers, is designed to improve the skills of Omani nationals. Oman is the only GCC country that has taken steps to reduce employment in the public sector.

BOX 5.6 (continued)

Qatar

In 1997, the Qatari government issued a directive to private businesses to ensure that nationals make up at least 20 percent of their employees. More recently, the government has taken steps to increase nationalization of the labor force in the oil and gas sector to 50 percent by 2005. With a lower national labor force growth rate and a continuing need for imported labor, nationalization efforts have not been as intense as in other Gulf states.

Saudi Arabia

Using a combination of incentives and targets, Saudi Arabia's sixth development plan aims for the creation of 319,500 jobs for nationals and a 1.5 percent a year reduction in the number of non-Saudi workers. The policy includes financial support for firms committed to training nationals, minimum targets for employment of nationals, and restrictions on the employment of skilled and semiskilled workers. In 1995, private sector establishments with more than 20 employees were required to increase their Saudi work force by no less than 5 percent annually and to bar non-Saudis from certain job categories. In some sectors, the work force must be 75 percent Saudi, and nationals must account for at least 51 percent of the wage bill.

United Arab Emirates

No formal nationalization programs cover the entire federation, but officials have focused on nationalizing particular sectors of the labor force, such as finance, by supporting vocational training and internship programs for nationals. National participation in the financial sector has risen 187 percent since 1997, and policymakers have set a 30 percent nationalization target for this sector. Dubai's Strategic Development Plan aims to increase the share of nationals in the labor force from 7 percent to 10 percent by raising labor force participation and by facilitating the employment of nationals in the private sector.

Source: IMF 1997.

---

tive and absolute terms because of strict replacement policies; any further efforts are likely to erode productivity. Job nationalization in the private sector, where it occurred, appears to have been in response to government pressure—ranging from moral persuasion to more direct policies— to accelerate nationalization of the labor force. In Oman, strict management of expatriate inflows is credited with raising the share of Omanis in the private sector from 86,500, or 15 percent, in 1996 to 137,423, or almost 22 percent, in 1999.

FIGURE 5.17

Replacement of Expatriate Workers by Nationals in the Gulf Cooperation Council, 1990–2000

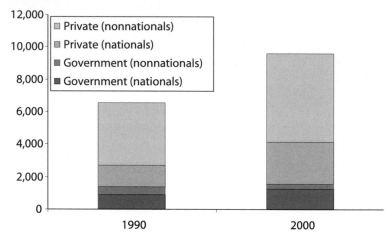

Number of workers
(thousands)

Legend:
- Private (nonnationals)
- Private (nationals)
- Government (nonnationals)
- Government (nationals)

Source: Girgis, Hadad-Zervos, and Coulibaly 2003.

Effectiveness of Policies Is Unclear

It is difficult to separate the effects of labor force nationalization policies from overall economic and policy conditions (Girgis, Hadad-Zervos, and Coulibaly 2003). For example, Omanis increased as a share of private sector employment at a time of strong growth performance and job creation in the private sector, accompanied by active labor market policies. Moreover, there are reasons to believe that certain policies might be counterproductive. Administrative measures, such as mandatory quotas for nationals and restrictions on nonnationals in certain sectors, may increase employment among nationals in the short term, but such restrictions raise costs for private firms, through increased wages and administrative costs, and undermine the staffing flexibility that firms require to stay competitive. Such measures are also administratively burdensome and expensive for governments and firms alike. Moreover, they encourage rent seeking and job diversion. Nationals reporting themselves as self-employed, for example, may merely be sponsoring expatriate workers who run establishments on their behalf.

The experience of Malaysia and Singapore with managing expatriate labor is instructive (Ruppert 1999b). Both countries encouraged immigration at one time because of labor supply shortages and weak demand for nationals in specific skill categories. As the national labor force expanded, both countries adjusted their immigration and labor market policies through a rigid system of permits and restrictions. Subsequent analysis found that the success in managing expatriate labor had more to do with the countries' diversified economies and thriving tradable sectors and less to do with the sometimes draconian labor restrictions. Evidence suggests that such restrictions, despite great efficiency in processing by government officials, led to illegal recruitment, an increase in illegal migration, a thriving industry in forged documents, and a black market in work permits.

Subsidies Are Potentially Effective but Expensive

Several countries are providing or considering subsidies for hiring nationals to promote nationalization of the labor force and to reduce unemployment. Subsidies attempt to bridge the wage gap between the public and private sectors for nationals. They do so by targeting the reservation wage of nationals and the wage gap between nationals and expatriates in the private sector by bringing the expected wage of nationals in private sector firms closer to that of expatriate workers. The advantages of subsidies are especially evident in small countries such as Kuwait, Qatar, and the United Arab Emirates, where both the deadweight loss (where a job would have gone to the same person or another national without the subsidies) and the substitution loss (where the same job would have gone to another national) are potentially low because few nationals work in the private sector (Diwan and Girgis 2002).

However, international evidence suggests that employment and wage subsidies give rise to other problems. Unlike the OECD countries, for example, where the cost to government of the subsidies is defrayed by reduced unemployment benefits and higher taxation, governments in the GCC would have to shoulder the full cost of the subsidy—which may be high, given the wage differentials between nationals and expatriates. The effectiveness of subsidies would be enhanced and the costs to government and the rest of the economy would be lowered if subsidies were combined with fees and taxes to increase the costs of hiring expatriates. But there are other incentive problems associated with subsidies. The take-up rate of subsidies will be high only if employers have the flexibility to lay off workers at the end of the subsidy period. Moreover, take-up tends to be higher in low-wage industries, indicating that firms might use the subsidies to place nationals mostly in low-paying jobs. A general equilibrium perspective reveals other potential costs of subsidies (box 5.7).

BOX 5.7

Subsidies to Private Employment: General Equilibrium Effects

Observers have argued that subsidizing employment in the private sector would reduce unemployment in MENA countries. A simple, partial equilibrium analysis of this policy yields unambiguous results. By lowering the relative cost of skilled labor, a subsidy increases demand for skilled labor, which may be particularly important if wages are fixed. As long as the increase in labor demand does not prompt greater participation in the labor force, unemployment of skilled labor is likely to fall.

However, such a partial equilibrium view can be misleading in at least two respects. First, the increase in subsidies must be financed. If the government reduces another component of expenditure and keeps overall spending constant, the net effect on the budget would be zero. General equilibrium effects could still be significant. If the government chooses to reduce investment spending on infrastructure, then, to the extent that public capital generates a positive externality for private production and investment, the subsidy could end up reducing demand for labor in the longer term.

Alternatively, if the government chooses to increase spending and either to borrow from the rest of the economy and let its fiscal deficit increase or to raise taxes to keep the budget deficit constant, the increase in borrowing can have a large crowding-out effect on private investment. Over time, the fall in investment may restrain the expansion of demand for all categories of labor—including unskilled labor. Thus, the long-run effect of the policy on employment may be either nil or negative.

Source: Agénor and others 2003b.

Similar Considerations Apply to All Active Labor Market Policies

Efficiency and effectiveness concerns constrain the scope for labor-importing countries to adopt active labor market strategies to promote nationalization of the labor force and reduce unemployment. Much as with other active labor market policies, the current policies and those under consideration are not a panacea to the structural problems in labor markets. To the extent that the preferences for expatriate labor are driven by skill mismatches, as is widely reported, targeting the wage differentials or providing subsidies for hiring nationals may not be sufficient to overcome the demand for expatriates. Under these circumstances, imposing quotas may cause more damage to the private sector, and take-up rates for wage and unemployment subsidies would be modest. The potentially high costs of large nationalization schemes warrant more careful attention to design, monitoring, and evaluation of effects. And most important, active labor market policies must be part of a comprehensive framework of reform of the public sector and of institutional sources of labor market inflexibility in the private sector.

Taking Stock of What Has Been Learned

The empirical simulations indicate that the interventions examined would lead to positive labor and macroeconomic effects. In most cases, they would contribute to higher employment, private investment, and output growth in the long run. Reflecting complementarities between policies, the simulations suggest that a comprehensive rather than a piecemeal approach delivers the biggest effect. However, the employment and growth payoffs associated with even the most comprehensive package of interventions are modest considering the magnitude of job creation needed in MENA. The same is true for active labor market policies, which also require careful targeting and monitoring.

Labor market reforms are a necessary component of policy reforms, but they are not sufficient for addressing the scope of the employment challenge facing the region now and over the next two decades. Although certain priorities for reform, such as reducing the role of the public sector in labor markets, are common to all countries in the region, the importance and likely effect of other reforms will vary across countries. Economic and political conditions and a careful understanding of labor market issues in each country must determine the priority areas of reform.

Appendix

Quantifying the Growth and Employment Effects of Labor Market Reforms in Labor-Exporting MENA Countries

This appendix briefly describes the quantitative macroeconomic framework designed by Agénor and others (2003b) for analyzing the effect of labor market reforms on growth and unemployment in labor-exporting MENA countries. The model is based on the Integrated Macroeconomic Model for Poverty Analysis framework developed by

Agénor, Izquierdo, and Fofack (2003) and Agénor and others (2003a). Some of the components of the model (such as the treatment of domestic demand and savings, external trade, and balance of payments) are standard. But the model also offers a detailed treatment of the labor market, explicitly accounting for features such as a large informal urban sector, public sector employment and the "leadership effects" of public sector wages, powerful trade unions, and international migration of labor. It also accounts for other characteristics of labor-exporting MENA countries, such as pay-as-you-go pension systems financed by payroll contributions.

The production and labor market features of the model are summarized in figure A5.1. The point of departure is a distinction between rural and urban production and between informal and formal production (with both private and public production) within the urban sector. Leontief production functions are specified to combine intermediate input and value added measures into production aggregates. Value added is specified as nested sets of constant elasticity of substitution (CES) and Cobb-Douglass (CD) functions. Top-nest CD functions imply decreasing returns to scale in rural and urban informal production. Urban informal production uses only labor, whereas rural value added uses a lower-nest CES function of labor and public capital (land is assumed to be in fixed supply). Public sector production requires both skilled and unskilled labor. Finally, urban value added in the private formal sector combines public and private capital and unskilled and skilled labor in a three-level nested CES function structure that exhibits constant returns to scale. Rural and urban production in the private formal sector is subsequently allocated between exports and domestically marketed goods using CES specifications.

The labor market is segmented into five categories of workers: rural, urban informal, urban unskilled, urban skilled, and overseas workers. The first four categories are employed domestically, whereas the fifth category is working abroad and transferring remittances to the domestic economy. Rural workers are employed solely in the rural sector, and the rural labor force is predetermined in each period by rural–urban migration and an exogenous birth rate. Rural–urban migration is determined partly by the expected urban–rural consumption wage differential, where the expected urban wage accounts for the likelihood of entering the formal urban segment of the labor market (where employment is determined by demand) and partly by lagged persistence effects. The agricultural wage rate is determined by profit maximization.

FIGURE A5.1

A Stylized View of the Labor Market in Labor-Exporting MENA Countries

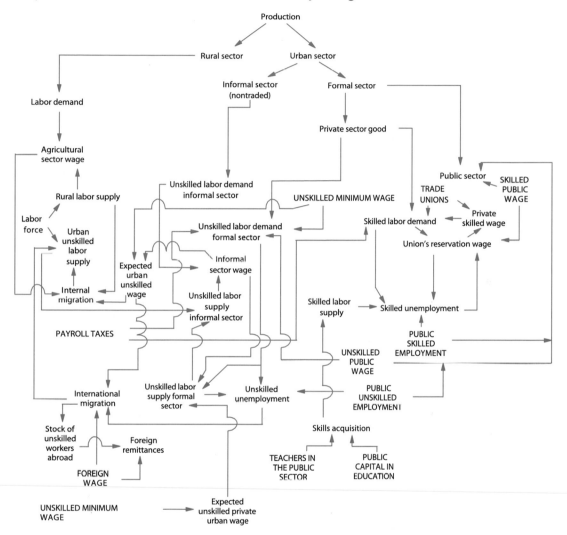

Rural migrants add to the pool of urban informal unskilled labor, whereas overseas migrants, unskilled retirees, individuals with upgraded skills, and individuals joining the formal sector labor force leave the urban informal labor market segment. The wage rate for the urban informal sector is determined by profit maximization, whereas the supply of labor in the informal sector is predetermined in each period by rural and formal sector migration, skills upgrading, overseas migration, retirement, and an exogenous birth rate. The growth rate of formal sector unskilled labor supply is determined by the expected formal–informal sector wage differential, where the expected formal wage rate is derived from the probability of finding employment in the formal sector. Unskilled formal sector employees face an exogenous rate of real minimum wage, and private sector demand for their labor is derived from profit maximization. Public sector unskilled employment is exogenously determined, whereas unemployment is derived residually.

The supply of skilled labor is determined by skills upgrading, retirement, and an exogenous death rate. The number of newly skilled individuals is determined by a CES function that combines the effective number of teachers and the capital invested in education. Private sector skilled wages are derived from wage bargaining, whereas employers set employment levels on the basis of profit maximization. Public sector skilled employment and real wage levels are exogenous, whereas skilled unemployment is derived residually. Overseas migration is determined partly by the expected urban–overseas wage differential, where the overseas wage rate is exogenously determined, and partly by lagged persistence effects. Finally, the number of retirees joining the pension system is a constant share of the number of formal sector unskilled and skilled employees in each period. The real pension benefit rate is indexed to the formal sector price index.

Intermediate and final demand by the agents of the model, including production units, households, and the government, is determined by profit and utility maximization and by fixed shares. Government consumption and investment demands are derived from constant share specifications. The demand for imports of agricultural and formal sector goods is determined by cost-minimization of Armington specifications. Prices clear the markets for agricultural, informal, and formal sector goods.

The model is used to conduct a variety of policy experiments, including a reduction in payroll taxation, cuts in public sector wages and employment, a reduction in trade unions' bargaining power, an increase in employment subsidies, and a composite reform program. Three alternative fiscal closure rules were considered. In the first, there is no offsetting change in revenue, and the government borrows domestically to balance its budget—implying full crowding out of private investment, which is determined residually. In the second and third, the policy is budget neutral, and the government raises sales taxes on the private, formal sector goods or increases income taxes on capitalists and rentiers; there is, therefore, no scope for crowding out.

A broad message of the simulations is that, although labor market reforms may have a significant effect on the composition of employment, a comprehensive program of structural reforms may be essential to exploit policy complementarities and foster growth and job creation in the region.

CHAPTER 6

Foundations of Future Growth and Job Creation

Over the next two decades, the Middle East and North Africa (MENA) faces a challenge of job creation that is unprecedented in the region's modern history. The labor force of the region totaled some 104 million workers in 2000, and it is expected to reach 146 million by 2010 and 185 million by 2020. If the current stock of unemployed workers remains unchanged, the economies of the region will need to create some 80 million new jobs in the next two decades. With an estimated unemployment rate of 15 percent, the more ambitious goal of absorbing unemployed workers, in addition to new entrants, implies a need to create close to 100 million jobs, or a doubling of the current level of employment, in the first two decades of the 21st century. By any measure, MENA faces a monumental challenge, especially with the added requirement that the new jobs be accompanied by higher wages and greater worker productivity in a manner consistent with the expansion of educational attainment in the region.

Traditional Engines of Employment Growth

In the face of high unemployment at present and mounting labor force pressures, could the traditional engines of job creation meet MENA's employment challenge in the future? If MENA countries were to replicate the job-creation record of the 1990s in the present decade, projections indicate that unemployment would rise significantly across the region (figure 6.1). The reasons for this outcome are straightforward.

Option of Public Sector Employment Will Diminish

While the public sector may continue to be a source of employment for a minority of new job seekers, it is highly unlikely (and undesirable) that it will remain a leading source of job creation. Fiscal constraints and low worker productivity imply that any expansion in public sector employ-

FIGURE 6.1

Current and Forecast Unemployment in MENA, Assuming Past Trends

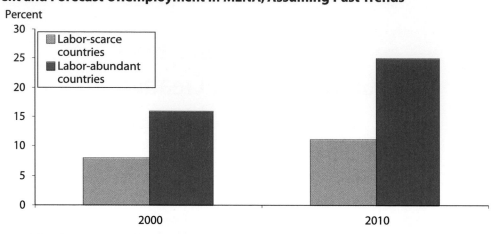

Note: Forecast is based on current unemployment rates, employment growth rates in the 1990s, and projected labor force growth in 2000–10. Labor-abundant countries include Algeria, the Arab Republic of Egypt, the Islamic Republic of Iran, Morocco, and Tunisia. Labor-scarce countries include Bahrain, Kuwait, Oman, and Saudi Arabia.
Source: World Bank staff estimates.

ment will come at an increasing fiscal cost and may not be sufficient to absorb the lines of unemployed and new graduates queuing for government employment. Moreover, the compression of real wages in the public sector in the 1990s suggests that returns to government employment will continue to fall for both new and old workers (chapter 4). Barring an acceleration in employment growth in the formal private sector, the rising numbers of new entrants will be pushed into the informal economy.

The expansion of the informal sector may not be undesirable to the extent that it lowers unemployment and does not entail a loss of social protection for workers. However, given that informal employment is not the first choice and, for many workers, not even the last resort, further informalization of work in the context of low growth and high unemployment may put further pressure on wages and increase job insecurity. Attempting to improve labor market outcomes in both formal and informal sectors by reforming systems of labor regulations, employment protection, and industrial relations is one course of action. Another is targeting the incentives driving job seekers to the public sector, to push workers into the private sector and, through the general equilibrium effects analyzed in the previous chapter, encourage higher employment in the formal sector and lower overall unemployment. But, as observed in chapter 5, not even the most ambitious agenda for reforming labor markets will be sufficient to achieve the employment growth required in MENA over the next few decades to reduce unemployment and absorb new entrants into labor markets.

Future Role of Regional Migration Is Limited

Near-term prospects for alleviating pressures on labor markets—much less eliminating them—through labor migration are equally limited (Fergany 2001). Although regional migration provided an important outlet for workers in the labor-exporting countries during the oil booms of the 1970s and 1980s, the 1990s saw a rapid deceleration in the net inflows of MENA workers to the receiving countries. The negative effects of lower oil revenues and the first Gulf War were reinforced by the replacement of workers from the region with migrants from Asia as well as efforts in the Gulf countries to nationalize the labor force and to replace nonnational workers (table 6.1). Current unemployment rates, together with the projected rapid expansion of the national labor force in receiving countries, provide further incentives to reduce the inflows of all migrant workers. These policies particularly affect expatriate workers from MENA countries, given their high substitutability with the national labor force because of similarities in language, education, and skill composition (Girgis 2002). Under these circumstances, the potential for regional migration to play a significant role in the future is significantly curtailed.

Migration to Europe Is Constrained by Policy

If the dynamics of demography in the sending and receiving countries offer little hope for regional migration, the reverse is true for migration from MENA to Europe (Dhonte, Bhatacharya, and Yousef 2001). Europe's demographic outlook runs opposite to that of MENA (figure 6.2). According to United Nations projections, the working-age population (ages 15–64) in the current 15 European Union (EU) member states will increase by 1 million people a year between 2000 and 2010, while the retirement age population (64 and above) will expand by close to four times

TABLE 6.1

Distribution of the Labor Force in Kuwait, by Arab and Asian Origin

Sector	1989			2000		
	Arab (percent)	Asian (percent)	Total number	Arab (percent)	Asian (percent)	Total number
Technical, managerial, clerical, and government	75	22	180,000	61	34	176,000
Trade, services, agriculture, unclassified	31	69	350,000	19	81	401,000
Production	43	56	253,000	32	68	428,000
Total	45	54	783,000	32	67	1,005,000

Source: Girgis 2002.

as much, or 3.6 million a year. The resulting increase in dependency ratios is expected, among other things, to adversely affect the sustainability of Europe's pension systems. As such, replacement migration on a large scale has been proposed as one of the few means of raising the number of workers relative to retirees and supporting pension systems. And because the demographic structure of the accession countries is similar to that of current EU members, the likelihood is low that migrants from elsewhere in Europe could completely fill the demographic gap.

Although MENA's young population structure and rising working-age cohorts are a potential source of workers (especially given MENA's geographic proximity, its existing networks of migrants, and the large wage gaps between the two regions), the political economy governing Europe's migration policy runs to the contrary (Johansson and Silva-Jauregui 2003). Migration has become a contentious issue in Europe, driven by a host of factors, including labor market conditions and cultural identity. With a large pool of long-term unemployed workers in the current EU members, competition from foreign workers is not viewed positively. Moreover, EU migration policy in the medium term is likely to focus first on accommodating workers from the prospective accession countries, who are likely to provide competition to the already dwindling flows of MENA workers. The Euro–Mediterranean initiative focuses exclusively on trade flows and

FIGURE 6.2

Net Population Increase in the European Union and North Africa, 2000–10

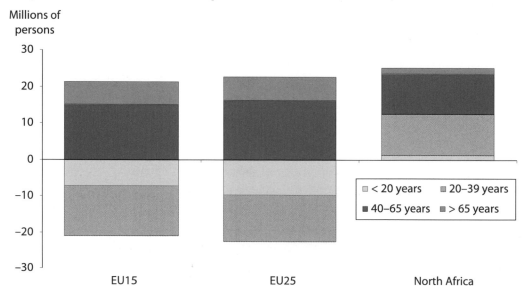

Note: EU15 includes current members of the European Union. EU25 includes applicant accession countries. North Africa includes Algeria, the Arab Republic of Egypt, Morocco, and Tunisia.
Source: United Nations Population Prospects 2002.

provides little institutional scope in support of labor mobility between MENA and Europe (box 6.1). Thus, although there is potential for considerable flows of migrant workers from MENA to Europe, this outcome would require a significant change in EU migration policy and would provide only a partial solution to the employment challenge in MENA.

MENA's Need for New Engines of Job Creation

With the traditional engines of job creation in MENA unable to meet the employment challenge in the 21st century, what options do the

---

BOX 6.1

Is Migration a Substitute for Trade?

Trade is fundamentally a substitute for migration (and vice versa) between poorer and richer countries (Schiff 1996). With relatively free labor mobility, convergence of incomes proceeds faster than with trade alone, and welfare gains are larger and more direct as people move from poorer to richer countries. So the best policy is to promote such greater labor mobility by reducing the policy barriers to labor mobility. But labor mobility is, in practice, far from free, with receiving countries imposing significant and rising restraints for a number of political economy reasons, which are generally far more restrictive than for trade.

Migration can complement trade. Even if migration is generally restricted, it can still be used as an important policy tool and a safety net in richer countries to complement trade policies in poorer countries, especially in a temporary adjustment phase (Diwan and others 2003). In the medium term, it can support trade by allowing a window of trade reforms to proceed in poorer countries (when the employment outcomes may be still fragile); by boosting integration between receiving and sending countries (language, familiarity, proximity, networks, and investment); and by using demographic transition differences. This situation is probably the case for the MENA region today.

At certain adjustment stages, trade and migration may be essential and temporary complements. Trade liberalization may increase unemployment in the short term. Unskilled workers in previously protected sectors may be displaced. And demographic transitions may swell labor out-migration pressures as countries restructure for faster growth. In rich, industrial receiving countries, demographic transitions in the opposite direction (sharply falling population and working-age population, as in Europe and Japan) may gain by accommodating rising in-migration, thereby boosting growth, productivity, and trade.

Source: World Bank 2003f.

economies of the region have? The most promising option is private sector–led growth. Chapter 3 shows that output per laborer could have grown by as much as 3.4 percent a year in the 1990s, rather than 0.7 percent, had the rates of capital accumulation matched those observed in the 1980s, holding total factor productivity (TFP) growth and human capital accumulation fixed. A combination of higher investment and faster TFP growth could have achieved the same higher growth rate. Assuming that such growth performance would have affected wages and employment proportionately, unemployment across the region could have been much lower than that observed. With the tight fiscal and monetary constraints on the public sector, however, this outcome rests on the assumption that much of the needed investment would have to come from the private sector. How could the private sector accomplish this objective? What set of policies and institutions could establish a new development model that would drive the mobilization of resources for future job creation and growth?

Foundations of New Development Policies

This report and the accompanying volumes on trade and investment (World Bank 2003f) and governance (World Bank 2003a) argue that, to accelerate job creation and growth, MENA must address a set of long-standing policy and institutional challenges to complete three fundamental, interrelated realignments within its economies:

1. *From public sector to private sector dominated*, by reducing the barriers to private activity while creating regulatory frameworks that ensure that private and social interests coincide

2. *From closed to more open*, by facilitating integration into global commodity and factor markets while establishing safeguards for financial stability and social protection

3. *From oil dominated and volatile to more diversified and stable*, by making fundamental changes in institutions managing oil resources and their intermediation to economic agents.

The growth and employment effects of an integrated package of policy realignments that improves the business and investment climate for the private sector and fosters integration with the world economy is potentially very large, as the companion reports demonstrate. The World Bank trade study (2003f) estimates that, on the basis of experience of comparable countries, output per worker could increase by some 2 to 3 percent a year. The World Bank governance study (2003a), using similar international evidence, suggests that improving the institutions of accountability and public administration could boost output growth per capita by 0.8 percent and 1.3 percent a year. A conservative lower bound estimate of the sum of these projected effects, taking into account the overlap in the channels through which the policy changes operate, would be output growth per worker of 2.5 to 3.5 percent a year.

Reinvigoration of the Private Sector

Since the late 1980s, most MENA countries have tried, with varying intensity and success, to expand private sector activity. At the same time, the importance of the public sector has declined, as seen in steps taken to privatize and reduce subsidies to state-owned enterprises (SOEs), because of constraints arising from lower oil revenues and fiscal consolidation. But governments still represent a large share of value added in MENA, about one-third of gross domestic product (GDP) on average, more than comparator middle-income countries in Latin America and East Asia. Although state ownership of hydrocarbon resources in MENA distorts these numbers, the share of the public sector is high even in the more diversified economies such as the Arab Republic of Egypt and Tunisia. Strategic service sectors, such as banking, telecommunications, and transportation, remain under public ownership in most countries in the region. As a result, the contribution of the private sector to value added increased only marginally in the 1990s (figure 6.3). The same pattern has characterized the share of the private sector in total investment, which was not large enough to compensate for the decline in public investment (chapter 3).

These disappointing trends reflect not only macroeconomic policy outcomes, but also weaknesses in the business environment that discourage entrepreneurship and firm creation (Assaf and Benhassine 2003). New firms, particularly small and medium-size enterprises, face significant barriers to entry, both in time and cost of administrative approvals. For new firms in MENA, the costs of complying with regulations represent an average of 74 percent of per capita gross national income (GNI)—well above the 22 percent in Eastern Europe and 57 percent in East Asia (figure 6.4). New firms also face significant difficulties securing start-up and operating capital with public banks. In many MENA countries, public banks dominate the banking system and favor state enterprises, larger industrial firms, and offshore enterprises. Judicial systems are also a constraint. Regulations do not facilitate the restructuring of still viable businesses, and nonviable firms are not permitted to close operations expeditiously, thereby raising the social and economic costs of bankruptcy. In addition to these regionwide patterns, recent surveys reveal country-specific patterns in the business and investment climate (box 6.2).

FIGURE 6.3

Private Sector Contribution to Gross Domestic Product in MENA Countries

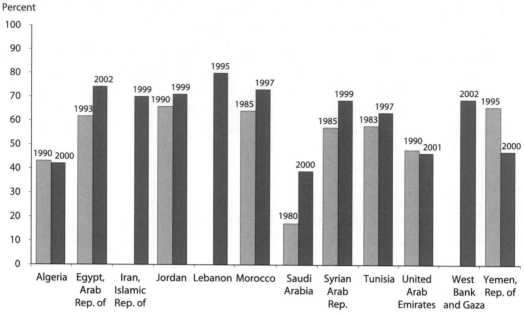

Percent

Source: Assaf and Benhassine 2003.

FIGURE 6.4

Firm Entry Costs, by Region

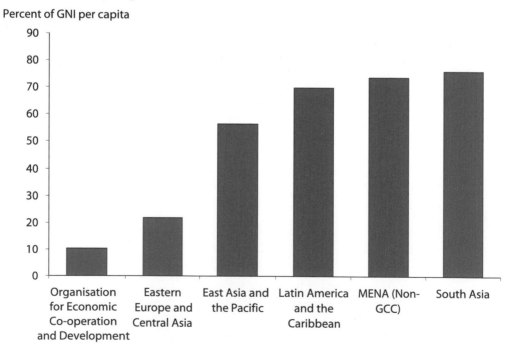

Percent of GNI per capita

Note: GCC = Gulf Cooperation Council; GNI = gross national income.
Source: World Bank 2003g.

BOX 6.2

Aspects of the Investment Climate in Algeria, the Arab Republic of Egypt, the Republic of Yemen, and the Gulf Cooperation Council

Despite the widely acknowledged importance of the private sector in MENA, precise information about its composition, activities, and constraints is generally lacking. Firm-level surveys have been carried out in some countries, including Algeria, Egypt, and the Republic of Yemen. These surveys permit closer examinations of the business and investment climate. The results point to unique aspects of the investment climate in the individual countries as well as to similarities across countries:

- *Old versus new firms in Algeria.* Old firms complain proportionally more than new firms about unfair competition and the informal sector. Old firms complain less, however, about corruption and access to credit.

- *Small versus large firms in Egypt.* Small firms complain more than large firms about the difficulties of accessing credit, exporting goods, and dealing with the tax administration. Small firms also complain more about corruption and the time needed to resolve disputes in court.

- *Northern versus southern firms in the Republic of Yemen.* Firms in the traditionally laissez-faire northern part of the country face greater impediments to doing business than firms in the formerly socialist south, particularly with regard to trade regulations, the legal system, and licensing.

- *National versus foreign firms in the Gulf Cooperation Council.* Foreign firms in general face higher tax rates than national firms. In some countries, foreign firms are subject to investment restrictions in certain sectors and to limits on their ownership of companies.

Sources: Assaf and Benhassine 2003; Banerji and McLiesh 2002; Fawzy 1999.

MENA compares poorly with East Asia and the Organisation for Economic Co-operation and Development in the complexity of filing a legal claim and in the time needed to initiate and complete such a claim—more than 300 days on average (figure 6.5). Even where the legal process is defined, the unpredictability of enforcement creates problems for entrepreneurs. Nearly half of surveyed firms in the region expressed concern over the unpredictability of the legal system (World Bank 2003g). Businesses also suffer from weaknesses in infrastructure; the financial system; and the administration of licensing, regulations, taxes, and import duties. Almost half of private businesses complain that infra-

FIGURE 6.5

Contract Enforcement Duration, by Region

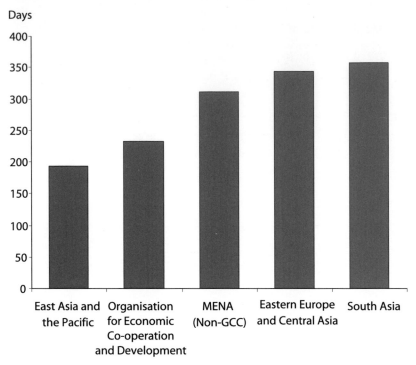

Source: World Bank 2003g.

structure is a moderate to major obstacle to their activities. Weaknesses in telecommunications and transport, two significantly underdeveloped backbone services, greatly impede business activity and investment. Weak public institutions also impose many costs on business, particularly with regard to delays and costs associated with clearing customs.

Necessity for Integration into the World Economy

MENA remains one of the least-integrated regions, having failed to take advantage of the expansion in world trade and foreign direct investment (FDI) in the past two decades. Since the mid-1980s, global trade has expanded more than output, to the advantage of middle-income countries in Latin America and East Asia. In MENA, despite large hydrocarbon exports, trade declined from about 100 percent of GDP in the mid-1970s to 60 percent in the mid-1980s, and it has stagnated since (World Bank 2003f). Excluding oil, trade declined from 53 percent of GDP in the early 1980s to 43 percent in 2000. These negative trends were accompanied by (a) high and increasing product concentration; (b) loss of export dynamism in nonfuel exports, as the region exported fewer products that grew significantly faster than world trade in the 1990s; and (c) little participation in global production sharing, with the region exporting primarily finished goods with low value added and importing parts and components for an inefficient, inward-looking manufacturing base (figure 6.6).

Integration with global private capital flows has also been sluggish, in sharp contrast to the experience of comparable country groupings (figure 6.7). Excluding the Gulf countries, MENA received about US$2.2 billion in net inflows of FDI in 2000, or slightly more than 1 percent of the US$158 billion that flowed to developing countries worldwide. These inflows averaged less than half a percentage point of GDP for most of 1985–2000. Egypt accounted for half the MENA total (US$1.2 billion), and Jordan (US$750 million) and Tunisia (US$560 million) for about a quarter each. The remaining countries received small amounts, and some, such as the Republic of Yemen, had significant outflows.

FIGURE 6.6

Trends in Trade Integration
(exports plus imports as a percentage of gross domestic product)

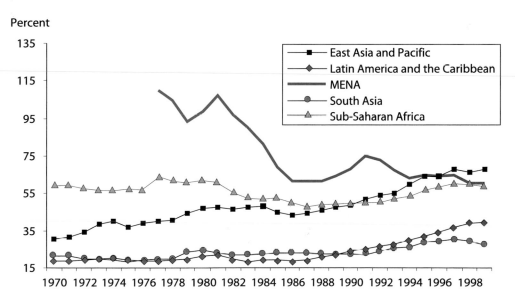

Sources: World Bank 2002a, 2002e.

FIGURE 6.7

Share of Foreign Direct Investment Inflows into MENA

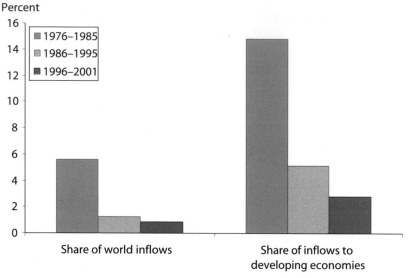

Source: UNCTAD 2002.

MENA's weak integration with world markets reflects unfavorable incentives, compounded by large behind-the-border constraints. Exchange rates in the region have been persistently overvalued, by as much as 22 percent on average during 1985–2000 (Nabli and Véganzonès-Varoudakis 2002). Trade regimes in MENA are among the most protective in the world. Most favored nation tariffs remain high, with an average weighted tariff of 17 percent for the region, and nontariff barriers are widespread, including slow administration of customs and standards. According to the World Bank, trading costs on imports, excluding taxes and duties, average 11 percent of the value of trade, adding another layer of protection (World Bank 2003f). Transport, logistics, and communications costs are high across most of the region, adding a third layer. These transaction costs, combined with the weaknesses in the business climate and constraints on the participation of foreign capital in some key sectors, such as banking and finance, have discouraged FDI.

Improved Management of Oil Resources

To develop more stable and diversified economies, many countries in the region need to improve the management of oil resources and to broaden the productive base of economic activities. Although oil resources finance expansions in physical and human capital and subsidies of goods and services, they also make countries vulnerable to volatility in international oil markets and pro-cyclical fiscal policy. And as is well documented in the literature, large oil rents lead to an appreciation in the real exchange rate, which is a drag on the external competitiveness of other traded goods and services. Diversifying productive activities is especially urgent for countries such as the Syrian Arab Republic and the Republic of Yemen, whose known oil reserves may be depleted in the not-too-distant future. More generally, diversification is a growing priority because per capita exports of hydrocarbon products have been declining across the region during the past two decades as a result of falling real prices, rising domestic demand for energy, and rapid population growth. With the continued decline in per capita oil rents, it will be increasingly important for governments to ensure the efficiency of public expenditures (figure 6.8).

Better Governance Needed to Complete the Three Transitions

Achieving the three transitions requires fundamental changes in the role of government in some areas of policymaking and considerable enhancement of its effectiveness in others. A broad governance agenda is a central requirement of reform efforts that target an improved business and investment climate, deeper trade integration, and greater economic diversification (World Bank 2003a).

The governance component of MENA's reform agenda goes beyond the traditional focus on government intervention in the economy through public sector employment and SOEs. As the recent experience

FIGURE 6.8

Per Capita Oil Exports in MENA Countries, 1980–2000

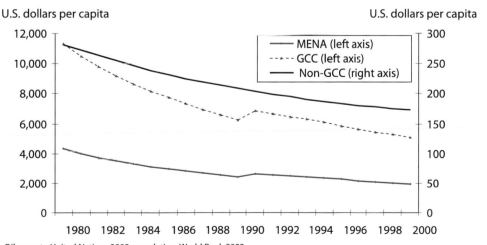

Sources: Oil exports: United Nations 2002; population: World Bank 2002e.

of transition economies in Eastern and Central Europe demonstrates, it requires changes in government capacity and incentives to initiate and sustain the policies and institutions that address the region's development goals—in this case, rapid growth and job creation. Governance is also more than the policies themselves, incorporating inclusiveness and accountability in the processes through which policies are conceptualized and implemented.

The governance gap in the region, with weaker governance than would be predicted by income, makes the governance agenda all the more critical to MENA's development future (figure 6.9). The quality of bureaucratic performance and delivery of public services is weaker than in other countries with similar per capita income levels and significantly below that of the better performing countries in East Asia, Eastern Europe, and Latin America. While institutional quality tends to improve with per capita income, the relationship between the two is weak in MENA. The hypothesis advanced in the literature is that achieving high per capita income has not required good governance because per capita incomes are strongly correlated with reliance on oil (World Bank 2003a). Although oil and other rents may in the past have allowed MENA to advance its development agenda despite—and perhaps at the price of—the

FIGURE 6.9

Per Capita GDP in MENA and the Rest of the World

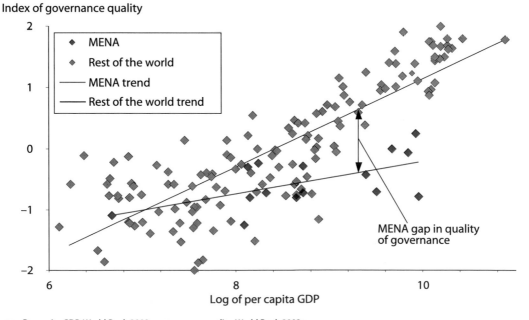

Sources: Per capita GDP: World Bank 2002e; governance quality: World Bank 2003a.

governance gap, better governance will be essential for completing the three transitions in the future.

Better governance means better bureaucratic performance and greater predictability, thus reducing risks and transaction costs that discourage private investment. The priority of accelerating MENA's integration into the global economy makes improving the administration of regulations affecting international trade and investment flows particularly important. Better governance will enhance the effective delivery of public goods and services, including the reliability of infrastructure services such as ports, telecommunications, energy, and water. More generally, as the region advances toward private sector–led growth and globally oriented, stable economies, demands for public services will become more complex, requiring further improvements in service delivery and governance structures. Accountability and inclusiveness will serve as a guide for the efforts of governments to improve governance in areas of importance for the transitions and will provide mechanisms for amending, correcting, and refining policies, if not always guaranteeing better policy outcomes.

Road to Completing the Transitions

While all MENA countries need to complete the three fundamental transitions, how they do so will depend on each country's specific initial conditions. Priorities and sequencing of policy changes will vary by resource endowments, reform progress to date, and quality of institutions of governance. Political economy factors are integral to the design and implementation of development programs (chapter 7). The remainder of this chapter analyzes groups of countries that broadly share initial conditions and, hence, policy agendas.

Initial Conditions and Country Groupings

Oil resources and labor market pressures are prime determinants of the constraints and priorities in completing the transitions. Large oil resources under government control can delay the transition to private sector–led growth. Hydrocarbon exports facilitate imports by easing fiscal and balance of payments constraints, but over the long term, oil exports may impede the development of other tradables through their effect on resource allocation and the real exchange rate.

Similarly, the relative abundance of labor will also influence the priorities and constraints. Labor market pressures place a high premium on initiatives that promote employment, including policies to encourage the growth of small and medium-size enterprises. These pressures also condition the sequencing of reforms that could result in job destruction, through restructuring at home and competition from abroad. International evidence suggests that market orientation and international openness can lead to higher growth and employment even in the short term if coupled with policies to promote private investment and manage the effects of job destruction.

Countries in the region can thus be classified according to their labor and oil endowments: countries that are resource poor but labor abundant, countries that are both labor and resource abundant, and countries that are resource rich but labor scarce (table 6.2). Of the 16 countries examined here, 10 are oil exporters with about 58 percent of the population, and 2 others are important producers of hydrocarbon products, with an additional 27 percent of the population. Some countries are difficult to classify. Egypt has significant hydrocarbon resources but has become a small net importer of oil products in recent years. Syria and the Republic of Yemen also have oil resources but may become oil importers in the next decade.

Governance is another key factor to take into account. Countries with weaker governance may be more constrained in the speed of transition. More specifically, countries with public institutions of weaker quality may have to focus more on developing internal systems of accountability, including a review of existing legislation on the interaction of government and the business community and institutional arrangements for implementation. All countries in the region need to focus more on developing feedback mechanisms between clients and public service providers and between regulatory agencies and consumers, providing more choice to consumers through competitive service providers and strengthening mechanisms of checks and balances in government.

TABLE 6.2

Country Groupings Based on Resource Endowments in MENA

Grouping	Resource-rich countries	Resource-poor countries
Labor-abundant countries	Algeria (30.2), Islamic Rep. of Iran (66.4), Syrian Arab Rep. (16.6), and Rep. of Yemen (18.0)	Djibouti (0.7), Arab Rep. of Egypt (67.8), Jordan (5.0), Lebanon (3.5), Morocco (29.1), and Tunisia (9.5)
Labor-scarce countries	Bahrain (0.7), Kuwait (2.2), Oman (2.6), Qatar (0.6), Saudi Arabia (22.1), and United Arab Emirates (2.8)	n.a.

n.a. Not applicable.
Note: Population in millions in 2000 is shown in parentheses. Labor-abundant or labor-exporting countries are those with net inflows of workers remittances; labor-importing countries are those with net outflows. Broadly, resource-rich countries are those with large positive net oil exports. Iraq, Libya, and the West Bank and Gaza are not included because of lack of data.
Source: United Nations Population Prospects 2002.

There are also significant differences among MENA countries in their previous success in transitioning toward an open, market-driven economy. Countries that made significant progress during the 1990s in realigning their economies will face different challenges from those faced by countries that are still in the early stages of transition. In the initial stages of the transition, rapid progress can be achieved through more policy-intensive programs. For example, prices can be liberalized and trade tariffs can be reduced with little institutional reform. Additional progress, however, will be less policy based, requiring substantial strengthening of institutions, including upgrading and reinforcing investment promotion and customs institutions.

Transition in Resource-Poor Countries

An effective development program based on market orientation and integration into the global economy requires a strong supply and investment response from the private sector, both domestic and foreign, with technological and productivity gains in the more market-driven and internationally open economic sectors. Also important are minimizing and managing potential output and employment losses in sectors unable to compete under the new incentive structures. To achieve these objectives, international experience suggests that countries should meet several preconditions: macroeconomic stabilization, flexible exchange rates in line with fundamentals, and a business and investment friendly climate that is regulated effectively to promote competition. Most of the diversified economies in the region have broadly fulfilled the first two preconditions. But the third remains a challenge, undermining the beneficial effect of the trade agreements signed with the EU and other partners.

Egypt, Jordan, Morocco, and Tunisia strengthened their macroeconomic frameworks during the 1990s by bringing aggregate demand to sustainable levels and by reducing instability in prices and exchange rates. Stability in key macroeconomic variables will ensure that changes in relative prices induced by the domestic and external reform packages will not be distorted by macroeconomic instability. In Egypt, for example, public debt as a share of GDP has risen significantly in recent years, suggesting that, though the fiscal deficit can still be financed, sustainability will require some adjustment. And Lebanon, with a high debt stock of 175 percent of GDP, faces the more difficult challenge of reducing fiscal and external balances to sustainable levels.

Exchange rate management is more challenging for the resource-poor countries. International experience indicates that successful trade reform packages are preceded by a real depreciation of the currency, which dampens excess demand for imports (Agénor and Montiel 2001).

With the exception of Lebanon, the resource-poor countries have brought real exchange rates broadly in line with fundamentals. Two issues that the authorities in each country should consider are how trade reform will affect fundamentals and whether further real depreciation is warranted. More generally, authorities will also have to consider whether existing exchange rate systems are flexible enough to help manage the uncertainties associated with the effects of trade reform. Egypt and Tunisia have relatively flexible systems, and both are introducing further reforms to improve management and increase flexibility. Jordan and Morocco may require additional flexibility in exchange rates. In Lebanon, macroeconomic reforms are needed before the country can reap any benefits from trade reforms.

Creating a business and investment friendly climate has proved more difficult in all the resource-poor economies. These economies need to strengthen the mechanisms of interaction between business and government in areas where the government acts as regulator or service provider. Countries need to improve the efficiency of customs administration, domestic taxation, and business licensing. Morocco has put in place a strong customs administration, significantly reducing delays and costs for businesses. Jordan also has a relatively efficient customs administration. In Egypt and Tunisia, however, the situation is different and requires urgent action. The application of standards and inspections is another significant impediment to imports, and it increases the anti-export bias, especially in Egypt, where most businesses view these processes as the greatest constraints to trade.

Most countries need to enhance competition by reforming regulatory regimes to promote private participation in all economic sectors. Furthermore, they need to strengthen regulatory capacity by drawing on international best practice to ensure competition and the safety and integrity of the financial systems. Liberalization of telecommunications services has been successful in Morocco. It has led to better access, higher quality, and lower cost to consumers and has provided a boost to growth and employment (Mustafa 2002). The other resource-poor countries have also made progress, but they are at different stages of liberalization and regulatory change. Morocco and Jordan lead in regulatory reform of the electricity sector, promoting private participation in the unbundled segments of the sector. Egypt and Tunisia have not yet adequately separated regulatory and operational functions to assure new investors that future policy developments will be competitively neutral. Regulatory reform of air transport is at an early stage, with inefficient national carriers and airports continuing to provide services under restricted competition.

Reform and development of financial services, particularly the banking system, are another important concern. Regulatory reform requires enhancing competition by promoting private banking and financial institutions while establishing prudential and supervisory standards to ensure stability. International experience suggests that opening the sector to foreign banks is particularly beneficial, both for strong price competition and for spillover effects, such as training and financial innovation. Morocco and Tunisia are the most advanced of the diversified economies in terms of financial sector reform, with a significant share of banking assets in private and foreign banks. Lebanon's banking system has a dominant private sector presence as well. However, public banks with weak lending portfolios dominate Egypt's banking system.

Another focus of regulatory reform efforts and improved services is on small and medium-size enterprises (Lall 2002). One aspect of this reform will be to reduce barriers to entry, including the costs and delays associated with licensing. All countries in this group are setting up programs to promote small and medium-size enterprises. Egypt, for example, is creating a pilot one-stop shop for investors in selected governorates. Another key area of improvement in the business environment is contract enforcement and protection of property rights. This area requires faster case resolution, increased certainty through training and greater transparency, and an independent judiciary. In four of the five countries in this group, investors consider the executive power to be too powerful, leading them to fear political interference in judicial decisions.

Transition in Resource-Rich, Labor-Abundant Countries

The oil-rich countries have a more complicated task ahead in making the transition to market-oriented economies. Vast oil rents have permitted the creation of large public sector enterprises, which are protected by trade barriers and supported by extensive subsidies. These rents have led to overvalued exchange rates, while the volatility of oil prices has been transmitted to the rest of the economy through pro-cyclical fiscal policies. Thus, although preconditions for the oil-rich and labor-abundant countries such as Algeria, the Islamic Republic of Iran, and Syria are generally in line with those in the resource-poor group, they require policy reforms that are deeper in intensity and wider in scope. The business climate in Algeria, the Islamic Republic of Iran, and Syria would benefit strongly from deregulation and from the introduction of competition into backbone services provided by inefficient public enterprises. For example, electricity transmission losses in Algeria and the Islamic Republic of Iran are among the highest in MENA.

Similarly, the financial sector remains in the hands of the public sector, which controls up to 95 percent of banking system assets. Many state-owned banks have large portfolios of nonperforming loans that undermine the balance sheets of the banks, thus requiring periodic recapitalization and limiting the availability of credit to private firms. In Algeria, for example, successive buybacks of bad public enterprise debt during 1993–97 amounted to about 30 percent of GDP. Bank balance sheets have been cleaned up several times since then, at significant additional costs. Because the operations of the private sector in oil-exporting countries are even more regulated than they are in the resource-poor countries, attracting FDI will require significant improvements in the business environment. For example, the resource-rich and labor-abundant countries need to eliminate price controls and regulations to allow the price signals from domestic and external liberalization to take effect.

The presence of large oil rents provides both reform opportunities and challenges. Oil revenues reduce short-term concerns with revenue loss from trade reform, while reductions in domestic energy subsidies can provide substantial savings to the budget. The resource-rich countries need to better manage short-term oil price volatility and long-term oil resources. Explicit fiscal rules are needed for saving and for drawing down resources from a temporary stabilization fund to insulate government spending from oil booms or busts (Davis and others 2001). Algeria and the Islamic Republic of Iran have already instituted stabilization funds.

Transition in Resource-Rich, Labor-Scarce Countries

When oil rents are very large relative to the size of the population or the economy, improved management extends beyond the objective of stabilizing government spending to considerations of saving these resources for intergenerational equity. Kuwait has maintained a fund for future generations since the 1970s, demonstrating the benefits as well as the policy and institutional requirements for these vehicles. For example, the accumulation of a large stock of wealth in foreign assets requires strong systems of financial management and accountability.

Although the presence of oil rents gives rise to similar challenges for all the resource-rich countries, the business climate agenda in the resource-rich and labor-scarce countries is somewhat different. These countries have more dynamic service sectors, with substantial recent openings in some countries to foreign and domestic private investment in water, power, and telecommunications. Independent power projects are being enhanced in Abu Dhabi, Dubai, Oman, and elsewhere. Water sectors are also being opened to foreign and domestic investment.

Corporatization and privatization measures are being advanced, along with pricing reforms. Regulatory improvements are being introduced in the financial sector, and high standards of technical excellence, which match global standards, are being established in infrastructure services.

The public enterprise sector remains extensive, however, with most large, non-oil industries in public hands and heavily reliant on direct and indirect subsidies, including low-cost loans. Recent labor nationalization policies adopted by Gulf Cooperation Council (GCC) countries, if not carefully targeted, may impede economic diversification and expansion of the private sector (chapter 5).

The GCC countries have embarked on deeper reforms to accelerate their integration with the global economy. They have established a US$335 billion customs union, which will allow them to forge a larger common market with lower trade barriers to the rest of the world. The goal is to facilitate intragroup trade, collective negotiations with the World Trade Organization, and increased foreign investment. The agreement covers establishment of a monetary union and a common currency by 2010 in order to deepen integration and reduce the transaction costs and uncertainty of bilateral exchange rates.

Sequencing of Reforms and Adjustment of Costs

Once significant progress has been made on the preconditions, countries must decide on the sequencing of reforms. The debate on the speed of implementation is intense. A gradualist approach spreads the costs of reform over time, permits the creation of adequate capacity and learning for further implementation, and facilitates the building of support for the reforms among beneficiaries. A more intensive approach enhances credibility and reduces uncertainty and opportunities for capture. A balance must be struck between the benefits and costs of adopting either approach. In cases such as the investment and business climate, especially in the context of the labor market reforms outlined in chapter 5, most MENA countries need to proceed rapidly because of the well-established complementarities between product and labor market policies (box 6.3).

In other cases, such as trade reform, the tradeoffs faced by the country groups and even within groups may diverge, giving rise to separate optimal trajectories of implementation.

Although the medium-term benefits of trade reform are well established, the short-term adjustment costs are cause for concern in MENA countries (box 6.4). International experience suggests that adjustment costs in countries that have implemented trade reform programs have generally been small, with interindustry shifts minimizing the dislocation of employment and with the duration of unemployment in most industries short (World Bank 2003f). Research has also demonstrated that labor turnover in many industries exceeds displacement from trade liberalization. Still, trade reform can cause large output and employment losses when adjustment in specific industries, such as agriculture, is slow

BOX 6.3

Cross-Market and Interactive Effects of Product and Labor Market Policies

Over the past two decades, Organisation for Co-operation and Development countries have initiated labor market reforms to encourage employment and product market reforms to address the negative effects of anticompetitive regulations on productivity and consumer welfare. Recent empirical analysis has looked at how these regulatory reforms influence employment, job security, and wage inequality and how labor market policies and institutions influence innovation and industry structure. In these studies, the degree of product market liberalization is measured along three dimensions. *The level of state control* relates to the size and scope of the public sector, including the level of control of public entities by legislative bodies and the degree of price controls. *Barriers to entrepreneurship* refer to the complexity of licensing, burdens for start-ups, and legal barriers to competition. Finally, product markets are affected by *explicit barriers to trade and foreign investment*, including ownership barriers, tariffs, and discriminatory provisions.

These studies conclude that regulatory reform in product markets can boost employment, whereas labor market reforms can enhance innovation and output growth. Entry restrictions lead to inefficiencies in production as they reduce output, shelter inefficient firms from competition, limit enterprise creation, and reduce the potential for technology spillovers. These effects operate through many channels. Lack of competition in certain markets increases the rents captured in wage premiums by insiders, thereby depressing labor demand in favor of capital. Output levels are lower in monopolistic markets than in competitive markets, hence leading to lower demand for all inputs including labor. These effects combine to reduce and distort labor demand, thus putting upward pressures on wages in certain industries and reducing enterprise creation and survival. Although anticompetitive measures are often instituted to protect employment in certain sectors, the resulting inefficiencies are likely to spill over to the entire economy and reduce output and employment.

Source: Nicoletti and Scarpetta 2003.

because of labor market rigidities. Evidence from Morocco and Tunisia in the late 1980s suggests that net job losses from trade liberalization were small (figure 6.10). After more than a decade of trade policy reforms (including in the context of implementing EU association agreements), most of the resource-poor countries would gain little from a gradualist approach to trade reform.

In the resource-rich and labor-abundant countries, however, trade liberalization should proceed at a slower rate. Algeria, the Islamic Republic of Iran, and Syria are significantly more closed than other MENA country groups and are underperforming in terms of trade-to-

BOX 6.4

Effect of Globalization on the Labor Market

Globalization provides opportunities for economic growth, employment, and rising incomes. Research has found that developing countries that were "globalizers"—those that opened up their economies to trade after 1980—experienced 5 percent annual per capita growth in the 1990s compared with –1 percent a year for others. What is the effect of economic openness on employment and wages? How does it alter the distribution of income? Who wins and who loses?

Employment

Economic openness brings about structural changes that increase the rates of job destruction and job creation, thereby increasing volatility and turnover in labor markets. To the extent that liberalization affects formerly protected sectors, job destruction can be significant. On the other hand, by stimulating improvements in productivity and output, liberalization of trade and investment can create jobs as well. As markets open up, restructuring often first leads to the destruction of jobs before new ones are created—so that, in the short run, unemployment rates may rise. Over time, however, unemployment tends to decline. On a cross-sectional basis, countries that are open have lower unemployment rates than those that are not.

Wages

Wage growth between 1980 and 2000 for globalizers was twice that of less-globalized developing countries. However, according to data from 70 countries, the wage effects of trade and FDI seem to be different. The impact of trade liberalization on wages, negative in the short run, gradually improves, becoming positive after 3 years on average. On the other hand, FDI provides a significant initial boost to wages, but this effect diminishes over time, disappearing after 5 years on average. The wage effect of globalization thus depends on the mix of trade and investment.

Distribution of Wages

Many studies conclude that liberalizing trade and investment increases returns to education. As a consequence, wage differentials between skilled and unskilled workers widen. Much of this analysis has been undertaken in high-income countries; however, this effect has also been observed in a number of developing countries. The fact that these changes have occurred while the supply of skilled workers has been growing in most countries (both industrial and developing) suggests that the demand for skilled labor has been increasing even faster.

Sources: Dollar and Kraay 2001; Rama 2001; World Bank 2002b.

FIGURE 6.10

Trends in Employment and Trade in Morocco, 1980–99

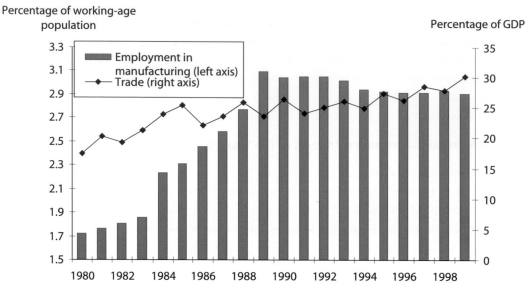

Note: Exports include goods and services.
Sources: Employment data: UNIDO 2002; exports and working-age population data: World Bank 2002e.

GDP ratios. A slow pace of reform is consistent with weaknesses in the administration of customs and other trade regulations, which also require time to be brought up to speed (World Bank 2003d). Even more important, public sector enterprises still employ a large share of the labor force in these countries and require time to adjust to internal and external competition to avoid large labor dislocations. Algeria's experience suggests that fiscal retrenchment and trade reform could lead to significant job losses that have the potential to set back reform. An estimated half a million workers lost their jobs in Algeria in 1991–98 as a result of a partial restructuring of inefficient public enterprises, which led to a partial reversal of the liberalization program (World Bank 2003f). As a result, the World Bank proposes a transition in these countries that could last up to 10 years compared with 3 to 4 years in the resource-poor countries.

Although a favorable business environment and good macroeconomic policies are critical for ensuring an overall positive employment effect from trade liberalization, there may be a case for insulating specific sectors or even firms that could suffer large losses. In resource-poor countries, the sectors most likely to suffer losses are the capital-intensive manufacturing sector, the public sector, and agriculture. In addition, some highly protected sectors that are labor intensive, in particular apparel and footwear, fear competition from low-cost producers. Granting more time for these sectors and firms may be justified in light of rigidities that could cause widespread labor dislocations. Such dislocations are not easily neutralized by expansion elsewhere and could, thereby, undermine political support for the program. More time may also be needed to ensure that the improved business environment is having its effect and that the private sector is growing and job creation is accelerating to absorb displaced workers.

Strengthening of Governance Aspects of the Transition

The governance aspects of implementing the necessary policy and institutional actions are challenging. They are covered extensively in the companion report on governance (figure 6.11). The required reforms focus on putting into place systems of accountability and enhancing the separation of powers, with the executive shedding responsibilities to the judiciary and legislative branches as well as to independent regulators. Strengthening accountability requires greater voice for citizens, particularly stakeholders, in each area of reform. Internal administrative quality could be enhanced through mechanisms to improve the efficiency of the bureaucracy and the use of public money. More generally, the sustainability of all mechanisms for reform depends on building a stronger institutional environment for external accountability by promoting an independent press and greater reliance on free and fair elections.

Role of Human Capital in the Transition

MENA's transition to more market-driven and globally oriented economies requires continuing progress in widening and deepening the stock of human capital and, more critically, changes in the qualitative outputs of the region's educational systems (UNDP 2003). Higher employment and worker productivity during the transition will be driven by greater educational attainment in general and especially by the availability of skills compatible with the needs of the private sector and the global economy. The demand for existing skills affects both labor relocation from the public sector and the pace of new hiring in the private sector. At the global level, innovations in information and communication technologies have transformed how goods and services are produced and what products are produced (Golladay and others 1998). Information and communication technologies are the foundation of the new "knowledge economy" and are associated with the employment of more skilled workers (box 6.5).

FIGURE 6.11

A Program to Enhance Governance

Inclusiveness

Enhancement measures

■ Mandate universal suffrage for all elected posts.
■ Reduce discrimination in laws and regulations.
■ Broaden government consultative mechanisms.
■ Encourage broad-based civil-society organizations.
■ Monitor whether public service agency staff treat citizens equitably.
■ Redress past exclusions.

Program to enhance governance

Internal accountability

External accountability

National checks and balances

■ Increase oversight authority and capability of parliaments over the executive.
■ Ensure greater independence of the judiciary.
■ Improve professional capacity of parliaments and the judiciary.
■ Empower other independent oversight agencies, and mandate reviews by them.

National actions

■ Mandate greater freedom of information and public disclosure of government operations.
■ Invite external oversight to ensure open, fair, regular elections.
■ Invite public debate on policies by representative civil-society groups.
■ Generate, monitor, and disseminate data on governance quality.
■ Encourage independent and responsible media.

Administrative measures

■ Improve performance orientation, including monitoring of government budgets.
■ Reform the civil service to enhance its service orientation and professional competence.
■ Strengthen the resources and capacity of local agencies to design, adapt, and deliver public services.
■ Ensure independence of regulatory agencies.
■ Foster an ethic of service to the public in the civil service.

Local actions

■ Introduce feedback mechanisms, from clients to providers, and publish results.
■ Increase competition among public service agencies—and with private providers.
■ Move toward increased devolution to elected local authorities.
■ Create opportunities for involvement of community empowerment associations.

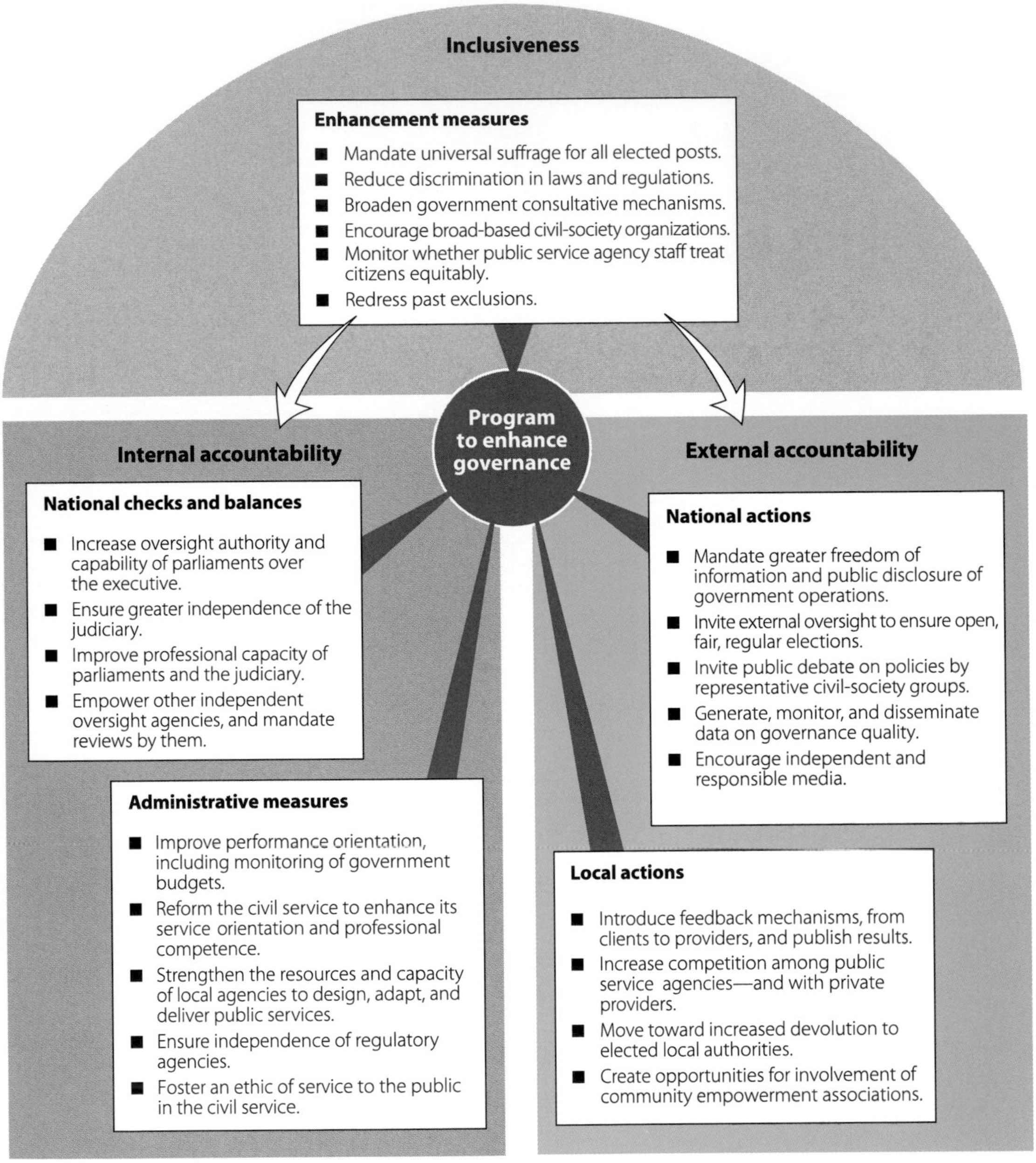

Source: World Bank 2003f.

Maintaining and Expanding Access to Education

MENA countries now report nearly universal enrollment at the primary level and large shares of youths completing secondary school (figure 6.12). Despite these gains, many young people remain outside the educational system. Dropout and illiteracy rates are high in some countries,

---

BOX 6.5

Effect of Technological Change on the Labor Market

Technological innovations, specifically information and communication technologies (ICTs), offer employment benefits as well as risks. One major concern is that the diffusion of technological change has been uneven, with a "digital divide" separating rich and poor countries. Technological change also affects aggregate employment by eliminating and creating jobs. The ultimate effect depends on the relative weight of these two forces.

The general conclusion, drawn largely from industrial countries, is that technological change is necessary for long-run employment growth. And research suggests that employment gains in services have been largest in countries that had the greatest investments in ICTs. Technological change clearly alters the composition of employment through job creation and destruction. Since the adoption of ICTs is associated with the employment of more skilled workers, shifts in labor demand to higher-skilled workers will increase returns to education, as observed to some extent in Tunisia. According to international experience, however, technological change is more responsible than globalization for the widening skill differentials in many countries.

Source: World Bank 2002b.

---

blocking access to life-long learning opportunities for many. The goal of universal basic education and literacy is important for MENA. A vast literature documents the social benefits of basic education, including lower fertility rates, reduced infant mortality rates, better nutrition, longer life expectancies, and improvements in many other social indicators. From a labor market perspective, a lack of basic education in a large segment of the work force may retard productivity gains and reduce international competitiveness.

Basic skills, however, should not be thought of as an end goal of educational development and reforms. Rapid technological change worldwide has raised the general level of skills required to be competitive in global markets. Even in traditional activities, the ability of firms to compete increasingly depends on their ability to incorporate new technologies. Thus, MENA must continue to expand the availability of higher education and specialized training programs.

Building on Past Success

MENA's sequenced expansion of schooling levels has raised mean schooling levels by strengthening the position of secondary education and by reducing the share of students with only primary schooling or no

FIGURE 6.12

School Enrollment Rates in MENA Countries, Most Recent Year

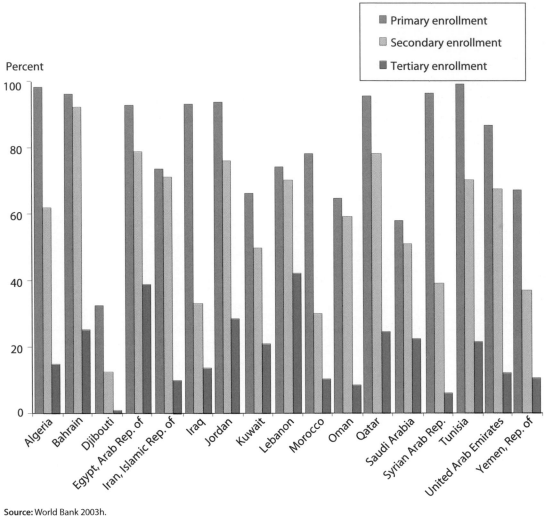

Source: World Bank 2003h.

formal education. Higher education has grown as well, but not at the expense of building a solid base of people educated at the secondary level. This strategy has promoted a degree of equity in education and income not evidenced in many other regions. Furthermore, as MENA governments increase investments in higher education and specialized training, these schools will have a large and growing base of qualified individuals pursuing postsecondary education.

In terms of education, MENA is now in a position similar to that of East Asia in the early 1980s, with a broad base of primary and secondary graduates (figure 6.13). East Asia raised mean schooling levels by investing in secondary education, reducing dropout rates, and sequencing later investments in higher education. In contrast, many Latin American countries in the same time period invested heavily in higher education without ensuring a solid base of secondary school students. The result has been greater income and educational inequality in Latin America (De Ferranti and others 2003).

MENA countries should maintain their investments in primary and secondary schooling while beginning to increase allocations to higher education. The financial costs of this strategy will be eased over time by the expected declines in the growth rates among the young population (ages 0–14), allowing states to invest in higher education, to reduce attrition at the secondary level, and to boost the overall quality of education. The effects of declining growth rates among school-age students, however, should not be overstated as they may be partially countered by a rising demand for education at both basic and higher levels. A larger role for the private sector in education will become increasingly necessary.

Improving Educational Quality and Addressing the Skill Mismatch

Apart from expanding access to education and deepening the skill base in the economy, MENA countries must address concerns about the quality of educational outputs and skill mismatches as they affect labor market

FIGURE 6.13

Education Pyramids

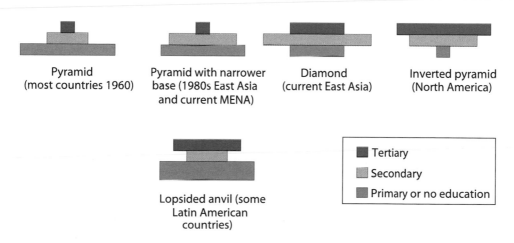

Pyramid (most countries 1960)

Pyramid with narrower base (1980s East Asia and current MENA)

Diamond (current East Asia)

Inverted pyramid (North America)

Lopsided anvil (some Latin American countries)

Tertiary
Secondary
Primary or no education

Source: De Ferranti and others 2003.

imbalances today and the requirements of the transition in the future (Galal 2002). Evidence from the transition economies of Eastern and Central Europe and the former Soviet Union indicates that the stock of human capital acquired under central planning became less relevant in the new market economy. On the eve of restructuring, the transition economies were considered to be endowed with high levels of human capital. But with the launch of reforms in ownership, technology, and trade, demand for certain skills increased, thereby rendering previous types of training obsolete and creating significant mismatches between the human capital demanded by new enterprises and that available in the work force (World Bank 2002d).

In MENA, evidence on skill mismatches comes from surveys of firms and comparisons of the profiles of education in the labor force and the unemployed (figures 6.14 and 6.15). In both the labor-abundant and labor-importing countries, entrepreneurs regularly cite the lack of skills as an important constraint to hiring, in some cases suggesting that it outweighs concerns with labor market regulations (Assaf and Benhassine 2003). The educational systems in MENA have been geared largely toward meeting the requirements of employment in the public sector, with few links to the private sector. In most countries in the region, workers with little or no education and those with postsecondary education constitute a small share of the unemployed. Most of the unemployed workers either are semiskilled or have intermediate or secondary educations, a sign of the undervaluation of their training in the economy. But even for the most educated workers, analysis of returns to education in chapter 4 suggests that the private sector rewards their education less than the public sector.

Great numbers of students are acquiring more education, but it is not always translated into higher employment and wages (AFESD 2002). Tackling these mismatches is largely a matter of improving the underlying quality of education. MENA education and training curricula continue to rely on rote learning and nonparticipatory teaching methods. An improvement in the quality of educational systems in the region will require a shifting of the focus on quantitative outputs toward knowledge application and problem solving.

A recent comparison of exam questions on the French baccalaureate examination in mathematics and biology with similar exam questions in several MENA countries revealed that the MENA tests were devoted to recognition and repetition of definitions and theorems and the performance of other routine procedures, whereas the baccalaureate exams assessed the ability to solve, predict, verify, generalize, and apply mathematical principals to real-world problems (table 6.3). A similar conclusion can be drawn from the results of the Trends in International

FIGURE 6.14

Distribution of Labor Force in Tunisia, by Educational Attainment, 2001

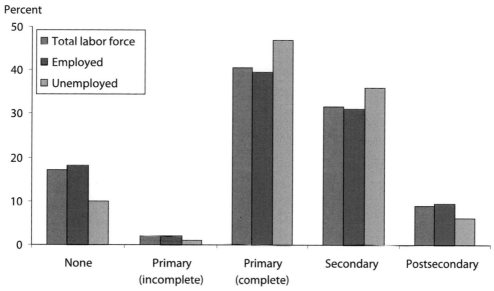

Source: INS 2001.

FIGURE 6.15

Distribution of Labor Force in Egypt, by Educational Attainment, 1998

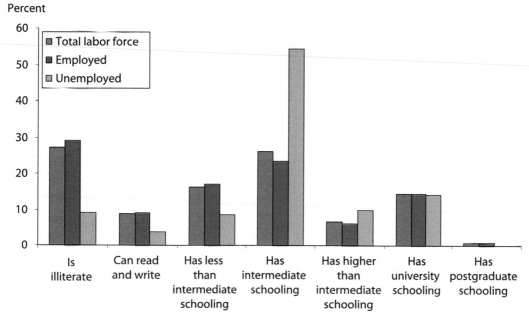

Source: Arab Republic of Egypt, CAPMAS 1998.

Mathematics and Science Study test (TIMSS), a standardized test that has been used in more than 40 countries to measure knowledge application. MENA students generally score lower on the TIMSS than the average score for developing regions (Berryman 1997).

The qualitative deficiencies in MENA educational systems have many causes. The rigid, centralized management of education and vocational training has resulted in inflexible educational and training systems that operate in isolation from their economic environment (Billeh 2002, Heyneman 1997). There are few performance indicators for schooling and, thus, little measurement of school quality. Only Egypt, Jordan, and Oman have attempted to assess the performance of their students relative to national learning standards. Without information on quality, incentives for educational reform have been limited. Teacher promotion in most of the region is based on seniority and not on performance. Examinations at the end of each education cycle serve as more of an elimination device (for access to a higher level) than as a tool for measuring skills. Except in a few countries, private educational institutions remain outside the recognized formal education sector.

TABLE 6.3

Student Performance Expectations in France and MENA

Mathematics examinations	
France	MENA
No	Representing
Using equipment	No
Performing routine procedures	Performing routine procedures
Performing more complex procedures	Performing more complex procedures
Solving	No
Predicting	No
Verifying	No
Generalizing	No
Describing and discussing	No
Justifying and proving	Justifying and proving
Biology examinations	
France	MENA
No	Demonstrating knowledge of simple information
Demonstrating knowledge of complex information	No
Demonstrating knowledge of thematic information	No
Deducing scientific principles	No
Using scientific principles to explain	Using scientific principles to explain
Constructing and using models	No
Designing investigations	No
Interpreting investigational data	No

Source: Berryman 1997.

Although education plays a primary role in a country's ability to seize the opportunities offered by the global economy, the success of educational reform depends very much on the national context, which determines whether the new skills developed in the educational system are used effectively in productive activities. If competitive, relevant skills are demanded and rewarded in the economy, there will be increased demands on the educational sector to respond. But reforming education will not be sustainable if there are few incentives in place for its productive use.

MENA's lack of openness to trade has also prevented educational advancement in the region from having a larger growth payoff. Empirical studies of the relationships among openness, human capital, and TFP have found that outward-oriented economies experience higher growth through higher TFP as a result of the positive effect of openness and through a higher impact of human capital on growth (Miller and Upadhyay 2000). Specific mechanisms associated with trade liberalization provide incentives for maximizing the private rate of return to education through growth-enhancing activities. A lack of openness, therefore, does not allow a country to benefit fully from its investments in human capital.

Facing the Challenges Ahead

The economic transformation that started in the 1990s is far from complete, and the employment challenge has grown. The potential payoff from completing the transitions outlined in this chapter is enormous, especially the effects on job creation, investment, and growth. An improved business and investment environment and greater macroeconomic stability would provide the foundation for the expansion of the private sector and the integration of MENA into the world economy. The effects on employment and efficiency would be reinforced by the emergence of dynamic export sectors and larger flows of FDI. All these changes will require reform of MENA educational systems. More fundamentally, the transformation of MENA's economies along the contours described in this chapter will require addressing the governance gap in the region to promote inclusiveness and accountability.

Few of these recommendations are new to the citizens or governments of the region. Indeed, the imperative for new development policies to complete the transitions needed for job creation and growth has been widely acknowledged by policymakers and debated in public arenas since the beginning of stabilization and structural adjustment programs in the 1980s. MENA countries are also aware that the incomplete progress with the reform agenda has been fully reflected in the poor labor market and growth outcomes in the 1990s. A renewed commitment to accelerating MENA's transition must begin with an understanding of the reasons for the slow and protracted pace of reform programs. The final chapter of this report explores the political economy behind MENA's resistance to reform and the path to securing the needed transitions in the future.

CHAPTER 7

Toward a New Social Contract

The economic difficulties faced by the Middle East and North Africa (MENA) in the past two decades have focused attention on the social contract, especially among those too young to remember the era of rapid economic growth before the 1980s. States and societies are confronting the reality that the post–World War II social contract is no longer sustainable. With mounting economic and political pressures, states have tried to balance reforming the status quo and respecting the pillars supporting state–society relations. The limitations of this approach are visible in the deteriorating conditions in MENA's labor markets. More importantly, this approach fails to address the underlying causes of the high unemployment rates: an outdated development model that is increasingly incapable of meeting the challenge of rapid labor force growth.

MENA Needs a Vision of the Future of Its Labor Markets

Addressing the challenge of job creation in the MENA region requires the transformation of societies and economic structures (Al-Hamad 2000). The problems to be overcome are enormous; their complexity is daunting. Yet the costs of inaction and the benefits of dynamic labor markets underscore the imperative of acting quickly and decisively. In no small measure, MENA's economic future will be determined by the fate of its labor markets. If current trends continue, rising unemployment and low productivity will undermine economic performance and the well-being of workers. If labor market outcomes improve, however, MENA's growth will accelerate, raising the living standards of populations across the region.

The need for a comprehensive approach to reform does not diminish the value of incrementalism in advancing reform agendas. Nor does it underestimate the importance of sequencing reforms in ways that maximize prospects for success. It does, however, shape the view of what is

needed to restore economic opportunity and secure the well-being of
MENA's workers and their families. MENA requires a broad-based
transformation of its political economies to strengthen the core drivers
of economic growth and to create viable prospects for job creation on the
massive scale needed to absorb the tens of millions of men and women
entering the work force over the coming two decades.

Securing these gains is more likely if today's policy reforms are guided
by a clear vision of how tomorrow's labor markets should be organized.
The desired outcome is not an unregulated labor market that exposes
workers to harsh working conditions, employment volatility, and income
insecurity. Nor is it a labor market in which growth is achieved through
a race to the bottom, accompanied by declining living standards for
workers and worsening income inequality. New development policies are
needed that support a race to the top and that ensure that workers participate in the benefits of economic growth (Posusney 2003).

If states no longer serve as employers of first resort, they can be more
engaged as partners in creating and sustaining opportunities for employment. A vigorous state role in improving social services—especially
health, education, and social security—is essential to establishing the
conditions that will permit workers to thrive and economies to grow at
competitive rates. State support will be needed to transform existing institutions of labor representation into a true system of collective bargaining. New state capacities are required for the effective administration of fiscal mechanisms for funding social programs aimed at
overcoming dysfunctions in labor markets and at protecting workers
during economic transition.

Indeed, the challenge of comprehensive reform is foremost a challenge of governance. Efforts to reform MENA's economies hinge on the
credibility of government and the capacity of state institutions to manage a complex, long-term process of change. MENA governments are
handicapped by the limits of institutional structures that were organized
to support redistributive and interventionist policies and by the difficulties such institutions face in adapting to new tasks, new policy demands,
and new regulatory environments. Governments need the institutional
and regulatory instruments to manage the difficult process of economic
transition under conditions of economic volatility and social vulnerability. Furthermore, such instruments are necessary to establish and maintain conditions that promote socially equitable strategies of market-oriented economic growth.

Governance reforms are essential as well to permit MENA governments to credibly articulate and realize a new vision of state–society relations. The tasks associated with this aim demand a degree of government initiative, creativity, and competence that must be cultivated

aggressively throughout the region. To move forward, governments themselves must link economic performance to the quality of governance. They must create rule-of-law mechanisms to ensure their own accountability and transparency in budgeting and fiscal policy. These mechanisms will enable citizens to scrutinize government performance and hold officials accountable for their actions. No less important, governments need to improve the quality and quantity of data on which effective policymaking depends, building more effective infrastructures for data collection and analysis.

Governance demands extend well beyond building new bureaucratic capacities. Governments must also create conditions in which coalitions that support socially equitable growth strategies can emerge, not only from the top down, but also from the bottom up. They must take the lead in changing expectations about the public sector as a primary employer and must actively support the private sector as an engine of job creation. This effort includes strengthening collective bargaining frameworks and extending the benefits of formal employment to a larger share of workers, even as labor markets become more flexible.

Successful Reform Requires a New Social Contract

Reform of the MENA social contract is crucial for the future of the region's labor markets. The redistributive–interventionist social contract jeopardizes the well-being of workers (Yousef 2001). It shifts economic activity to the informal sector and leaves too many workers unprotected. It constrains investment and growth, undermining the capacity of governments to deliver on their commitments to economic and social justice. Under conditions of high unemployment, resistance to reform deepens among those whom the social contract protects. Formal sector workers exhibit a strong preference for income security, even at the expense of declining real wages and productivity and even as the protections offered by the social contract are being eroded by the demands for sustaining it.

MENA's redistributive–interventionist social contract offers a minority of workers security of employment, but at the expense of declining wages and standards of living. It sustains redistributive policies that mitigate inequality but are underfunded, poorly administered, and increasingly ineffective. The social contract is important in preserving programs that benefit the working poor, but safety nets are stretched beyond their capacity. The existing social contract is deeply embedded in MENA political economies. It intensifies labor market distortions and exacerbates economic insecurity for many even as it raises the social and political costs of reform. The combination of a deeply embedded redistributive social contract, declining state revenues, and the worst projected employment gap in the world confronts MENA governments.

MENA cannot sustain the current social contract. The rigid, exclusionary, and inefficient aspects of the social contract need to be restructured. Yet reforms will not be credible unless they take into account the social needs of workers and ensure that economic outcomes are socially acceptable among MENA's citizens more broadly. Such reform requires a renewed political commitment to widely valued social policies—a new social contract that links reform to the principles of poverty reduction, income equality, and income security that have guided MENA's political economies for almost 50 years. Absent such links, reforms are unlikely to achieve legitimacy among the majority of MENA's population, whose support is essential for its success (box 7.1).

A new social contract will have long-term benefits for MENA. It will balance the need for labor market flexibility with the rights of workers

---

BOX 7.1

Elements of a New Social Contract: Lessons from World Bank Research

World Bank research indicates that the following elements should be included in the new social contract:

- Markets should be promoted as engines of future economic transformation and should be regulated to deliver socially acceptable outcomes.

- States should support the creation of institutions that deliver better governance processes and outcomes, including processes that make them accountable and inclusive.

- Labor regulations should guarantee fairness while preserving flexibility and incentives for performance.

- Educational reform should be guided by projected labor market needs, skill acquisition, and lifetime learning.

- Conditions for effective collective bargaining should be created, and unions should be empowered to serve as capable partners in collective bargaining.

- Redistribution, finely targeted, remains an important element of social policy to reduce income inequality.

Sources: Aidt and Tzannatos 2002; Barr 1994; World Bank 1995b.

and help to prevent social dislocation and conflicts by offering a positive role to labor in the transition to and coordination of more flexible systems of production. It will extend the benefits of formal employment to a larger share of workers in the private sector. Furthermore, it will create mechanisms for supporting workers as they respond to changes in the structure of employment associated with privatization and the shift to more open economies with different skill requirements and greater dependence on new information technologies. The recent passage of new labor codes in several MENA countries highlights both the challenges and the payoffs from inclusive processes of labor market reforms that seek to balance employer and employee rights (box 7.2).

What Needs to Be Done Is Widely Acknowledged

While MENA's circumstances are distinctive in their severity, they are not unique. Over the past two decades many countries have faced labor market crises and responded to the political challenges with reforms. Around the world, governments have reduced the scope of state intervention in markets, reorganized regulatory frameworks, and undertaken wide-ranging economic restructuring, including the large-scale privatization of state-owned enterprises, while trying to preserve important aspects of social welfare as well as wage and employment protections (Harik 1992).

In postsocialist states of Eastern and Central Europe, these transitions were facilitated by the urgency of establishing new systems of economic and political governance (World Bank 2002d). Elsewhere, policymakers have advanced economic reforms within stable polities (Anderson 1999, Schmitter and Schneider 2003). In several Latin American countries, for example, politicians and reformers effectively navigated complex political environments containing entrenched, often competing interests (Schamis 1999, Silva 1993). Despite the presence of supporters of the status quo, governments built effective reform coalitions and successfully re-regulated economies around market-based principles. MENA countries have also undertaken selective reforms, with positive, if limited, effects on economic performance.

The challenges confronting MENA governments do not arise from a lack of information about what needs to be done. Pathways to reform are much better mapped today than they were only two decades ago, including the need to tailor reforms to country-specific conditions and to link them to socially desirable outcomes. Past decades have produced extensive knowledge about what works in development strategies and policy reform, as well as what does not.

BOX 7.2

Path to Reforming Labor Markets in MENA

The Arab Republic of Egypt and Morocco recently joined Jordan and Tunisia in introducing important reforms to labor market regulations. The reforms grew out of protracted processes that began in the 1990s—even earlier in some cases—and involved delicate negotiations among government, business, and labor. The laws seek to usher in a new era of labor relations, which embodies a balance between greater flexibility in hiring, firing, and wage setting for businesses and enhanced recognition of trade union rights for workers. The inclusion of all stakeholders was considered critical to advancing the reform agenda. Yet, despite the long incubation and consultations, the new codes do not necessarily enjoy widespread acceptance among all affected constituencies.

Some business owners have expressed reservations. Moroccan textile factory owners fear that the shorter workweek and higher minimum wage will make them uncompetitive in international markets. Entrepreneurs there and in Tunisia have also complained that mandated severance payments are higher than before, although it is now easier to lay off permanent workers and business owners are increasingly using temporary workers to avoid severance payments. In Egypt, where enforcement of workers' protections has been particularly weak outside the public sector, business owners fear the threat of legal strikes while their de facto hiring and firing prerogatives have not really improved.

Many workers are also unenthusiastic. Egypt, Jordan, and Tunisia, with a history of government interference in union leadership selection, permit only one union confederation. Union leaders must both satisfy governments and achieve legitimacy among the membership base, although corporatism has restricted the ability of workers to remove unresponsive leaders. Jordan's union confederation leaders, seeing little advantage to workers in the proposed code revisions, walked out of the negotiations, and the new law was enacted over their objections. In Egypt and Tunisia, senior unionists endorsed the new codes, but dissidents charged them with failing to consult local leaders and the rank and file. Even in Morocco, the only country with a competitive union environment, some workers have complained that unionists are co-opted by owners, affiliated party leaders, or the government.

Further steps are needed to promote acceptance of the letter and the spirit of the new laws. Restrictions on trade union activity need to be relaxed as part of broad efforts to encourage political reform. Top-down management of unions should be reversed unless it reflects workers' preferences rather than governments' efforts at control. Empowering unions may slow labor market reforms, as has happened in some Latin American countries, but it is the only way to ensure that workers take ownership of reforms.

Source: Posusney 2003.

Reforms Have Been Too Limited and Too Slow

Despite this knowledge and the urgency of reform, MENA's track record has been poor. Although some countries have made limited progress on select aspects of economic reform, none has comprehensively restructured the framework in which the reforms are embedded. Employment and wage guarantees remain. Regulatory environments continue to push job creation toward the informal sector, hence excluding workers from the benefits of the social contract. Progress toward privatization has been uneven, with governments continuing to favor reform of public enterprises over privatization.

No less troubling, by the mid-1990s the pace of reform had slowed. Improvements in economic performance in the early 1990s—the result of economic stabilization programs and some other limited reforms—weakened the determination of governments to forge ahead with policy shifts that carried higher political risks. Instead, a number of governments pulled back, preferring to focus on less-sensitive issues, such as monetary and exchange rate policy, while overlooking the climate for domestic and foreign investment and preferring to expand participation in bilateral and multilateral trade agreements while neglecting measures to promote export-oriented sectors of the economy.

These selective reforms have had positive effects, including expanded opportunities for employment in the private sector. But they have not generated sufficient growth to ease the economic and political challenges of public sector and labor market restructuring. Sequencing reforms to postpone the difficult task of reorganizing the social contract until economies rebounded has proved ineffective. By the second half of the 1990s, MENA's overall economic performance was weak, as reflected by anemic growth, rising unemployment, and an inability to absorb the rising number of workers. The gap between labor supply and demand expanded across the region.

Overcoming the Obstacles to Reform Is Critical

Why, despite economic stagnation, the exhaustion of selective reform strategies, and a worsening employment crisis, have MENA governments been reluctant to change course? This reluctance is often explained as the rational response of incumbent leaders to circumstances in which the costs of reform are immediate, while its benefits are both delayed and, to some extent, uncertain. Yet aversion to political risk is at best a partial explanation for the trajectory of economic reform in MENA.

Certainly, periods of economic transition entail adjustment costs that are not evenly distributed across social groups. Political caution and attention to the effects of reform on workers and the poor are warranted. It is also true that the MENA social contract has created powerful social actors with a vested interest in sustaining it. But there are also political, economic, and social costs associated with maintaining a nonviable status quo. In MENA, these costs are becoming more severe, confirming the belief that slow and selective reform lacks credibility and exacerbates social polarization.

Inadequate responses to sustained economic stagnation have become a serious drain on the political resources of MENA governments, and those who benefit from the status quo find their positions increasingly insecure. The erosion of living standards for other segments of the population intensifies popular disaffection, even as new communications technologies make citizens more aware of the gaps between their economic conditions and those in other parts of the world. Addressing the employment challenge and restoring economic growth would generate significant, lasting political gains for MENA governments.

Soft Budget Constraints and Political Challengers Have Impeded Reform

Two factors, in particular, help explain the weak commitment to comprehensive reform: soft budget constraints and the links between economic and political reform (Chaudhry 1997; Smith 2004; Vandewalle 2003). Revenues generated outside the domestic economy and flowing directly to the state through foreign aid, oil exports, and strategic rents cushioned the impact of economic stagnation and permitted governments to adopt limited reforms, while postponing difficult decisions about structural adjustment and reorganization of the social contract (figures 7.1 and 7.2). Second and more important, shifts in the relationship between economic and political reform and in how governments managed this relationship shaped the organization and limits of economic reform in MENA during the 1990s.

During the initial phases of economic reform in the 1980s, MENA governments accepted an instrumental connection between economic and political reform. Governments recognized the existing social contract as a constraint on their capacity to reduce state intervention in the economy, to shrink the public sector, and to reorganize state–labor relations. Unable to sustain their redistributive commitments, governments in Algeria, Egypt, Jordan, Morocco, and Tunisia initiated experiments in political reform to secure popular support for market-oriented economic

FIGURE 7.1

Oil Exports, 1990s

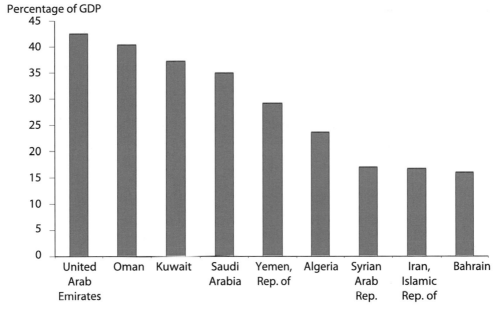

Source: World Bank 2002e.

FIGURE 7.2

Net Remittances as a Share of Gross Domestic Product

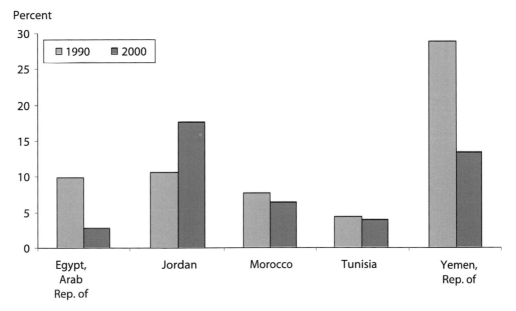

Source: World Bank 2002e.

reforms. These reforms involved reductions in consumer subsidies and other austerity measures to reduce state expenditure on programs associated with the interventionist–redistributive social contract (Layachi 1998; Zoubair 1999).

The experiments included increased opportunities for participation by opposition political parties, expansion of civil liberties and freedom of the press, increased participation in political life by civil-society groups and international nongovernmental organizations (NGOs), and efforts to strengthen the rule of law, to reduce corruption, and to secure the confidence of domestic and foreign investors. These openings expanded possibilities for citizens to engage in debate about the economic future of the region (Ayubi 1995; Norton 1994, 1996).

However, political openings, partial and fragile, produced consequences that undermined their sustainability (Heydemann 2002; Salamé 1994). Extended periods of political compression before the 1980s weakened the prospects for the emergence of new actors as the political space expanded. The exclusion of opposition movements from political life over time gave way to increasingly radical and often clandestine modes of organization and mobilization (Esposito and Voll 1996). Some of these militant groups attracted significant popular support during the 1980s and early 1990s, thereby challenging the capacity of governments to contain and manage the scope of political change (Bayat 2000).

Governments Have Decoupled Economic and Political Reform

The challenge of radical movements led MENA governments to change course. Reluctant reformers from the outset, by the early 1990s they adopted policies that weakened the link between economic restructuring and political change. Economic reform and political reform became loosely coupled—or were decoupled entirely—as governments responded to the appeal of opposition movements and, in some cases, the violence of extremist groups by reviving strategies of political control and by reinvigorating the national security concerns that had impeded the reform of governance in MENA (Bellin 2004).

Whereas in the 1980s MENA governments viewed political reform as a precondition for economic reform, by the mid-1990s they saw economic performance as a precondition for political reform (Brynen, Korany, and Noble 1995; Niblock and Murphy 1993). Where economic stagnation previously had provided a compelling rationale for political reform, it now justified the reassertion of political control. Pursuing economic and political reform simultaneously was seen as a threat to political stability.

As a result, top-down management of reform by decree replaced earlier efforts to generate support for economic reform by opening the political arena (Pool 1993). Engagement with reform remained selective and limited. Efforts to advance structural adjustment programs coincided with the erosion of political inclusiveness and accountability. This erosion was evident in the imposition of new constraints on civil society and NGOs, restrictions on the press, and other measures to control mobilization and autonomous collective action.

This shift had important implications for the structure and effect of economic reform programs. Reform by decree was an adequate mechanism for advancing policy objectives that required change in bureaucratic practices and regulatory procedures and the modification of state economic policies. Although the gains achieved through reform by decree were not trivial, this approach has narrow limits. It has little ability to achieve reforms that hinge on the compliance and participation of social groups whose well-being might be adversely affected by reforms.

Moreover, reform by decree reproduces state-centered approaches to the management of economic and social policy, sustaining interventionist and paternalistic patterns of state–society relations. In compressing the political space, MENA governments reduced the range of policy instruments available for managing the politics of economic policy reform. They not only curtailed opportunities for shaping public preferences on questions of social and economic policy, but also undermined government flexibility and sustained the governance gap in the region.

The combination of reform by decree and compression of political space constrained the development of precisely the forms of state capacity that are needed to sustain the long-term transition toward market-oriented political economies in MENA (O'Donnell, Schmitter, and Whitehead 1986). Transparency, the deepening of rule of law, and above all the accountability of economic policymaking all suffered (Brown 1997). Not least, possibilities for establishing a consensus around a redefined vision of state–labor relations and a renewed social contract became more remote.

Today, Economic and Political Reforms Must Be Linked

Soft budget constraints and the challenge of opposition groups shaped the structure and limits of reform processes in MENA during the 1980s and 1990s. Both factors created incentives for selective, top-down strategies that rested on weak linkages among economic reform, governance reform, and a broader commitment to political change (box 7.3). These strategies have run their course. They weaken the capacity of governments to address severe employment imbalances, to resolve labor market dysfunctions, and to advance a new vision of the MENA social contract as the basis for more productive relations among labor, the state, and the private sector.

Conditions on the ground have changed in recent years. With fewer opportunities for labor migration, less regional circulation of oil revenues, reduced foreign aid, and intense competition for foreign investment, the era of soft budget constraints is ending (Moore and Salloukh 2003, Zanoyan 1995). Increasingly, MENA governments will depend on domestic sources of revenue to sustain desirable social policies. Without an institutional and regulatory setting that supports both economic growth and responsible fiscal policies, domestic revenues will fall short and redistributive policies will become unsustainable.

BOX 7.3

Economic Foundations of Political Liberalization

The study of regime transitions has long been concerned with the tradeoffs between government-provided social welfare and political liberalization. Two events a decade apart prompted a more concentrated focus on the economic conditions leading to political liberalization: the debt crisis in Latin America in the 1980s and the collapse of state socialism in Eastern Europe and the former Soviet Union in the early 1990s. A consensus has emerged suggesting that economic crises deny governments the resources needed to secure the support of their constituencies (Haggard and Kaufman 1995). MENA, too, offers examples of partial political liberalization following periods of declining oil revenues and fiscal retrenchment. Yet the record of political liberalization in the region remains weak.

A recurrent theme in the "rentier state" literature is that economic benefits and political liberalization are substitutes in the production of political support, at least in the short run, meaning that there is a basic tradeoff between the costs of restructuring the social contract and the costs of repression (Ross 2001). Governments that restrict participation can maintain their legitimacy for only so long by providing public benefits. When forced to undertake substantial reforms, however, these governments cannot maintain legitimacy unless they extend the political franchise to previously excluded segments of society. Economic crises undermine the authoritarian bargains struck between leaders and their supporters. More generally, poor economic performance diminishes the bargaining power of autocrats and increases the strength of the opposition.

BOX 7.3 (continued)

Recent empirical evidence supports the simultaneity of economic and political liberalization under conditions of general economic stress, particularly in response to declining natural resource exports, foreign aid, remittances, or nontax revenues. Of particular relevance to MENA is the finding, from the experience of nondemocratic countries during 1985–2001, that demographic transitions, entailing labor force growth and lower dependency ratios, are associated over time with lower government welfare expenditures, lower public sector wages, and greater political liberalization.

Demographic Transitions and Public Sector Wages

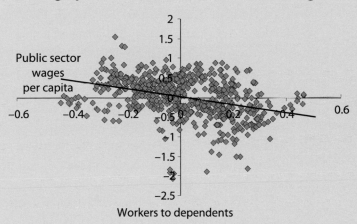

Workers to dependents

Source: Partial residual plots from a panel regression model.

Demographic Transitions and Political Liberalization

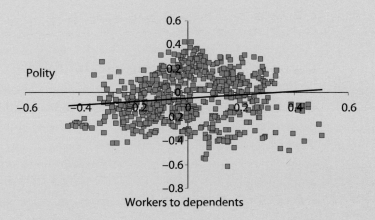

Workers to dependents

Note: Polity is a measure of political liberalization.
Source: Partial residual plots from a panel regression model.

Source: Desai, Olofsgård, and Yousef 2003.

MENA's political context has also changed over the past decade. Governments are now in a position to renew the processes of political reform that have been on hold for more than a decade. At the same time, MENA publics remain interested in electoral reform, good governance, and integration of responsible opposition parties in the political mainstream. In this setting, opportunities exist to revitalize commitments to political reform, to accommodate popular interest in choice, to strengthen the credibility of governments, and to create the political context for a comprehensive approach to reform (AbuKhalil 2003, Tessler 2002).

Under these conditions, resistance to economic reforms is at odds with the strong preference of MENA governments for political stability and social peace (Richards 2001). Although the broader political and economic factors that have shaped reform strategies in MENA over the past 15 years can help to explain the weak commitment to reform under these conditions, it is no longer clear that the factors that once impeded comprehensive reform are as constraining to policymaking today as they once were. Reforms are no longer a greater source of political risk than the problems that they are intended to address.

To move the reform process beyond its current limits, governments will need to revive national conversations about reforming the labor market, restructuring redistributive programs, and redefining the terms of the social contract. With the existence of large middle classes in MENA societies, the revival of political life—once again a prerequisite for economic growth—is certainly possible (Easterly 2000; figure 7.3). A selective, top-down approach to economic reform that sidesteps the need for political change to secure the legitimacy of reform and the credibility of government commitments is no longer adequate (Henry and Springborg 2001).

Support from External Partners Is Critical

As the region steps up to unlock the promise of a better future, external partners, as vigorous proponents of reform, have an important role to play in supporting MENA's transition. Although Europe is MENA's most important trade partner, other partners also need to support faster and deeper integration of MENA into the world economy by facilitating the accession of more MENA countries to the World Trade Organization, encouraging more intraregional trade and investment, and lifting economic sanctions. A more liberal policy toward agricultural exports and labor migration from MENA would reinforce the foundations of a strong Euro–Mediterranean partnership (Diwan and others 2003).

FIGURE 7.3

Share of the Middle Class

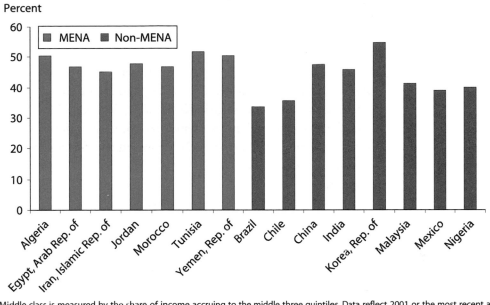

Percent

Note: Middle class is measured by the share of income accruing to the middle three quintiles. Data reflect 2001 or the most recent available year.
Sources: Household survey data for MENA countries, World Bank 2002e for all others.

Although external financial and economic support would be welcome, MENA's prosperity depends heavily on establishing regional security and stability (Khalidi 2004). There is strong evidence that violence and conflict have severely impeded the pace of reform and of trade and investment integration, at times rivaling the detrimental influence of poor domestic policies. Persistent conflict has also had large neighborhood effects throughout the region, spilling from conflict-ridden countries to neighboring countries. Greater commitment is required on the part of MENA governments to contain internal sources of instability. And the international community needs to rethink its response to the devastating effect of conflict in the region. Multilateral efforts are urgently needed to resolve the Israeli–Palestinian conflict and to return Iraq to a state of normalcy.

Main Responsibility Rests with MENA

Almost a decade ago, MENA governments were asked to "Claim the Future" and take the steps needed to secure the economic well-being of their citizens (World Bank 1995a). Since that earlier study, some progress has been made, but far more remains to be done. Images of well-educated but unemployed youths now define MENA for much of the world. Because of earlier inaction, MENA's leaders now face more difficult choices and a more urgent need to act. The old social contract no longer provides a viable starting point for reform. A new social contract is needed, one that integrates market-based strategies of growth, inclusiveness, and accountability with long-standing commitments to social equity.

Statistical Appendix

TABLE A.1

Total Labor Force Participation, Ages 15–64

(percent)

Country	1950	1960	1970	1980	1990	2000	2010	2020
MENA	**57.1**	**56.2**	**54.4**	**54.5**	**54.6**	**57.1**	**61.1**	**63.7**
Non-GCC	**57.5**	**56.6**	**54.6**	**54.3**	**54.3**	**56.6**	**60.9**	**63.8**
Algeria	55.6	52.8	48.7	49.1	50.0	55.7	62.6	67.7
Egypt, Arab Rep. of	58.2	58.3	56.9	56.4	56.9	59.0	62.6	64.4
Iran, Islamic Rep. of	57.8	56.5	53.9	52.9	52.9	54.7	62.3	68.6
Iraq	55.2	53.0	50.6	48.7	46.0	48.2	50.5	52.3
Jordan	50.9	50.4	50.9	47.7	48.4	55.3	59.3	62.1
Lebanon	48.7	49.0	49.3	48.8	50.7	55.7	59.2	61.1
Libya	56.8	55.0	55.1	57.4	54.0	53.1	56.2	56.4
Morocco	62.3	61.4	59.8	61.0	61.7	63.2	64.9	65.7
Syrian Arab Rep.	56.8	55.5	54.5	52.9	52.3	54.8	59.2	61.6
Tunisia	56.1	56.1	54.5	59.5	58.5	61.2	64.3	65.6
West Bank and Gaza	37.0	37.9	38.8	37.0	38.0	41.4	44.4	45.9
Yemen, Rep. of	59.1	58.4	56.9	55.9	57.0	57.5	58.2	59.3
GCC[a]	**49.7**	**49.5**	**50.3**	**56.4**	**57.7**	**61.4**	**62.3**	**63.3**
Bahrain	50.5	50.3	50.8	61.4	66.7	68.3	68.4	68.7
Kuwait	60.5	65.2	58.9	61.9	67.1	73.4	73.7	70.9
Oman	49.6	46.4	44.7	51.3	56.5	60.2	61.8	62.2
Qatar	32.5	40.6	44.5	43.1	42.7	76.5	74.4	74.1
Saudi Arabia	49.2	48.8	49.1	53.6	58.0	57.1	58.9	61.3
United Arab Emirates	49.1	49.0	66.6	76.3	49.4	75.2	72.7	70.8

Note: Averages are weighted.
[a] Includes nonnationals.
Source: 1950–2010: ILO 2003b; 2020: staff estimates.

TABLE A.2

Male Labor Force Participation, Ages 15–64

(percent)

Country	1950	1960	1970	1980	1990	2000	2010	2020
MENA	**92.3**	**89.9**	**85.8**	**83.3**	**81.3**	**80.7**	**81.3**	**82.5**
Non-GCC	**92.2**	**89.8**	**85.6**	**82.9**	**81.4**	**80.1**	**81.2**	**82.7**
Algeria	91.8	88.6	83.6	80.5	79.5	79.6	80.7	82.4
Egypt, Arab Rep. of	92.7	90.4	86.2	83.5	82.5	81.1	82.1	83.1
Iran, Islamic Rep. of	94.8	92.4	87.0	83.8	82.2	79.1	81.3	84.8
Iraq	92.2	88.3	83.7	80.1	76.1	76.0	76.2	76.9
Jordan	87.1	85.3	85.0	78.6	75.9	79.7	80.7	81.6
Lebanon	86.3	85.3	80.4	78.0	77.6	80.8	81.6	82.7
Libya	91.3	88.2	86.5	85.6	82.3	77.9	79.2	79.1
Morocco	93.0	90.5	86.4	84.7	83.4	82.6	82.7	83.2
Syrian Arab Rep.	88.5	87.0	85.0	82.5	80.4	79.7	82.0	83.6
Tunisia	90.9	89.9	85.4	84.7	82.8	82.7	83.5	84.7
West Bank and Gaza	66.5	67.6	69.2	66.2	67.4	71.7	73.0	73.1
Yemen, Rep. of	90.6	89.0	86.4	84.2	84.3	83.0	82.4	83.1
GCC[a]	**93.3**	**92.0**	**88.6**	**86.9**	**81.2**	**84.9**	**82.4**	**81.2**
Bahrain	86.9	86.1	84.8	87.4	89.7	88.7	86.7	86.2
Kuwait	90.0	90.9	88.4	86.8	85.7	87.5	86.2	83.0
Oman	94.8	91.4	87.3	87.8	85.4	83.8	82.2	79.6
Qatar	62.3	64.8	57.5	56.1	45.8	91.3	88.3	86.0
Saudi Arabia	93.9	92.8	89.6	86.4	86.0	83.1	80.4	80.1
United Arab Emirates	91.1	90.6	92.7	94.8	56.4	90.8	88.4	87.2

Note: Averages are weighted.
[a] Includes nonnationals.
Source: 1950–2010: ILO 2003b; 2020: staff estimates.

TABLE A.3

Female Labor Force Participation, Ages 15–64
(percent)

Country	1950	1960	1970	1980	1990	2000	2010	2020
MENA	**21.2**	**22.0**	**22.7**	**24.6**	**26.3**	**32.3**	**39.9**	**44.2**
Non-GCC	**22.1**	**22.9**	**23.7**	**25.6**	**26.8**	**32.8**	**40.4**	**44.5**
Algeria	16.5	17.0	17.6	19.3	20.1	31.2	44.0	52.7
Egypt, Arab. Rep. of	24.5	26.1	27.2	29.3	31.5	37.2	43.3	45.9
Iran, Islamic Rep. of	19.4	19.7	19.7	20.6	22.2	30.0	43.0	52.0
Iraq	16.6	16.5	16.4	16.2	15.0	19.4	24.0	27.0
Jordan	12.8	13.7	14.5	14.7	17.9	27.9	36.0	41.1
Lebanon	10.0	12.6	18.1	21.4	26.4	32.3	37.6	39.7
Libya	20.8	20.5	18.9	23.3	21.3	26.1	32.0	32.8
Morocco	31.6	32.4	34.5	38.1	40.4	43.8	46.9	47.9
Syrian Arab Rep.	23.0	23.1	23.3	23.5	24.6	29.7	36.0	39.1
Tunisia	21.1	22.0	25.3	34.5	34.4	39.6	44.7	46.1
West Bank and Gaza	6.0	6.2	6.5	6.5	6.6	9.9	14.2	17.3
Yemen, Rep. of	27.0	27.4	28.1	28.5	29.7	31.4	33.4	34.9
GCC[a]	**3.0**	**3.8**	**5.8**	**11.3**	**20.1**	**27.1**	**35.4**	**41.1**
Bahrain	3.7	4.8	5.7	18.1	29.8	36.6	41.6	44.8
Kuwait	5.9	8.2	12.2	21.2	38.6	48.3	52.7	52.2
Oman	2.9	4.4	5.9	7.5	13.5	20.5	31.9	39.4
Qatar	2.6	5.5	8.2	14.5	34.0	43.4	48.3	55.2
Saudi Arabia	2.9	3.4	5.0	9.7	16.4	23.9	33.0	39.7
United Arab Emirates	2.6	5.7	9.0	16.5	30.7	36.8	39.9	42.3

Note: Averages are weighted.
[a] Includes nonnationals.
Source: 1950–2010: ILO 2003b; 2020: staff estimates.

TABLE A.4

Total Labor Force
(millions)

Country	1950	1960	1970	1980	1990	2000	2010	2020
MENA	**25.50**	**30.60**	**37.73**	**51.58**	**72.83**	**104.40**	**146.37**	**185.25**
Non-GCC	**24.40**	**29.21**	**35.67**	**47.30**	**64.99**	**92.79**	**130.49**	**164.58**
Algeria	2.70	2.99	3.18	4.56	6.75	10.23	14.92	18.80
Egypt	7.29	8.80	10.90	13.52	17.41	23.68	32.23	39.96
Iran	5.43	6.38	8.05	10.81	15.53	21.94	32.46	40.55
Iraq	1.47	1.87	2.41	3.24	4.23	6.17	8.85	12.13
Jordan	0.12	0.23	0.42	0.50	0.79	1.62	2.35	3.13
Lebanon	0.41	0.49	0.62	0.71	0.82	1.22	1.62	1.88
Libya	0.31	0.39	0.57	0.89	1.25	1.77	2.34	2.77
Morocco	2.94	3.76	4.42	6.23	8.59	11.55	14.67	17.21
Syria	1.07	1.30	1.71	2.29	3.29	5.18	7.72	10.17
Tunisia	1.10	1.24	1.40	2.09	2.76	3.73	4.78	5.34
West Bank and Gaza	0.18	0.21	0.22	0.27	0.41	0.66	1.05	1.59
Yemen	1.37	1.55	1.76	2.18	3.16	5.03	7.51	11.05
GCC[a]	**1.10**	**1.38**	**2.07**	**4.28**	**7.84**	**11.61**	**15.88**	**20.67**
Bahrain	0.03	0.04	0.06	0.13	0.22	0.31	0.40	0.48
Kuwait	0.06	0.11	0.24	0.50	0.89	1.19	1.64	1.91
Oman	0.12	0.13	0.17	0.32	0.56	0.95	1.29	1.69
Qatar	0.00	0.01	0.03	0.07	0.14	0.32	0.36	0.40
Saudi Arabia	0.86	1.06	1.48	2.72	5.33	7.31	10.33	14.25
United Arab Emirates	0.02	0.02	0.09	0.54	0.71	1.52	1.85	1.95

[a] Includes nonnationals.

Source: Based on UN 2002 estimates of the working age population (15-64) and labor participation rates in appendix table A.1.

TABLE A.5

Male Labor Force
(millions)

Country	1950	1960	1970	1980	1990	2000	2010	2020
MENA	**20.82**	**24.67**	**29.87**	**40.12**	**55.82**	**75.54**	**99.52**	**122.27**
Non-GCC	**19.76**	**23.34**	**27.91**	**36.18**	**49.03**	**66.01**	**87.49**	**107.58**
Algeria	2.31	2.51	2.57	3.65	5.41	7.40	9.75	11.56
Egypt	5.75	6.83	8.30	10.00	12.55	16.15	21.01	25.67
Iran	4.53	5.28	6.61	8.74	12.34	15.98	21.31	25.35
Iraq	1.25	1.58	2.03	2.71	3.55	4.95	6.78	9.04
Jordan	0.11	0.20	0.36	0.43	0.65	1.24	1.67	2.13
Lebanon	0.37	0.43	0.51	0.55	0.60	0.86	1.09	1.27
Libya	0.26	0.32	0.48	0.73	1.02	1.35	1.69	1.98
Morocco	2.19	2.76	3.11	4.25	5.74	7.54	9.40	10.98
Syria	0.86	1.03	1.35	1.78	2.52	3.78	5.39	6.98
Tunisia	0.89	1.00	1.06	1.48	1.94	2.53	3.13	3.48
West Bank and Gaza	0.17	0.20	0.20	0.25	0.37	0.59	0.89	1.29
Yemen	1.06	1.19	1.32	1.61	2.34	3.68	5.38	7.84
GCC[a]	**1.06**	**1.33**	**1.96**	**3.94**	**6.79**	**9.52**	**12.03**	**14.69**
Bahrain	0.03	0.04	0.06	0.12	0.18	0.25	0.31	0.35
Kuwait	0.05	0.11	0.22	0.43	0.69	0.91	1.20	1.35
Oman	0.12	0.13	0.15	0.30	0.51	0.83	1.02	1.23
Qatar	0.00	0.01	0.03	0.06	0.11	0.26	0.28	0.28
Saudi Arabia	0.84	1.02	1.41	2.51	4.72	5.97	7.70	9.95
United Arab Emirates	0.02	0.02	0.09	0.52	0.59	1.31	1.52	1.53

[a] Includes nonnationals.
Source: Based on UN 2002 estimates of the working age population (15-64) and labor participation rates in appendix table A.2.

TABLE A.6

Female Labor Force

(millions)

Country	1950	1960	1970	1980	1990	2000	2010	2020
MENA	**4.68**	**5.93**	**7.86**	**11.47**	**17.01**	**28.86**	**46.85**	**62.99**
Non-GCC	**4.65**	**5.88**	**7.75**	**11.12**	**15.95**	**26.78**	**43.00**	**57.00**
Algeria	0.39	0.48	0.61	0.92	1.34	2.84	5.17	7.23
Egypt	1.55	1.97	2.59	3.53	4.86	7.54	11.22	14.30
Iran	0.90	1.09	1.44	2.06	3.19	5.96	11.15	15.20
Iraq	0.22	0.29	0.38	0.53	0.68	1.22	2.07	3.09
Jordan	0.01	0.03	0.06	0.07	0.14	0.39	0.68	1.00
Lebanon	0.04	0.06	0.11	0.16	0.22	0.37	0.52	0.61
Libya	0.06	0.07	0.09	0.16	0.23	0.42	0.65	0.79
Morocco	0.75	0.99	1.31	1.98	2.85	4.02	5.27	6.23
Syria	0.21	0.27	0.36	0.51	0.78	1.40	2.33	3.19
Tunisia	0.20	0.24	0.33	0.61	0.81	1.21	1.65	1.86
West Bank and Gaza	0.01	0.02	0.02	0.02	0.03	0.08	0.16	0.29
Yemen	0.31	0.36	0.44	0.57	0.82	1.36	2.13	3.21
GCC[a]	**0.03**	**0.05**	**0.11**	**0.35**	**1.05**	**2.09**	**3.85**	**5.98**
Bahrain	0.00	0.00	0.00	0.01	0.04	0.07	0.10	0.13
Kuwait	0.00	0.00	0.02	0.06	0.20	0.28	0.44	0.55
Oman	0.00	0.01	0.01	0.02	0.05	0.12	0.27	0.46
Qatar	0.00	0.00	0.00	0.01	0.03	0.06	0.08	0.11
Saudi Arabia	0.03	0.04	0.07	0.21	0.61	1.35	2.63	4.29
United Arab Emirates	0.00	0.00	0.00	0.03	0.12	0.22	0.33	0.42

[a] Includes nonnationals.
Source: Based on UN 2002 estimates of the working age population (15-64) and labor participation rates in appendix table A.3.

TABLE A.7

Total Labor Force Growth

(annual percent change)

Country	1950–1960	1960–1970	1970–1980	1980–1990	1990–2000	2000–2010	2010–2020
MENA	**1.82**	**2.10**	**3.13**	**3.45**	**3.60**	**3.38**	**2.36**
Non-GCC	**1.80**	**2.00**	**2.82**	**3.18**	**3.56**	**3.41**	**2.32**
Algeria	1.01	0.62	3.62	3.91	4.16	3.77	2.31
Egypt	1.88	2.13	2.16	2.53	3.08	3.08	2.15
Iran	1.60	2.33	2.95	3.63	3.45	3.92	2.23
Iraq	2.41	2.56	2.95	2.65	3.78	3.61	3.15
Jordan	6.63	5.91	1.82	4.44	7.23	3.70	2.87
Lebanon	1.70	2.43	1.32	1.48	3.95	2.80	1.50
Libya	2.24	3.84	4.44	3.34	3.47	2.83	1.68
Morocco	2.45	1.62	3.44	3.21	2.96	2.39	1.59
Syria	1.91	2.74	2.93	3.63	4.53	3.99	2.76
Tunisia	1.23	1.19	4.01	2.79	3.02	2.47	1.11
West Bank and Gaza	1.53	0.25	1.99	4.20	4.83	4.64	4.09
Yemen	1.24	1.28	2.12	3.71	4.66	4.00	3.87
GCC[a]	**2.32**	**4.01**	**7.29**	**6.05**	**3.92**	**3.13**	**2.64**
Bahrain	2.67	3.15	8.43	4.71	3.75	2.56	1.73
Kuwait	6.91	7.55	7.19	5.90	2.85	3.24	1.48
Oman	0.68	2.18	6.56	5.67	5.27	3.08	2.69
Qatar	10.34	10.15	7.86	7.61	8.11	1.29	0.92
Saudi Arabia	2.09	3.32	6.12	6.71	3.17	3.45	3.21
United Arab Emirates	2.11	14.05	17.58	2.60	7.69	1.91	0.55

Note: Averages are weighted.
[a] Includes nonnationals.
Source: Appendix table A.4.

TABLE A.8

Male Labor Force Growth

(annual percent change)

Country	1950–1960	1960–1970	1970–1980	1980–1990	1990–2000	2000–2010	2010–2020
MENA	**1.69**	**1.91**	**2.95**	**3.30**	**3.02**	**2.76**	**2.06**
Non-GCC	**1.66**	**1.79**	**2.59**	**3.04**	**2.97**	**2.82**	**2.07**
Algeria	0.80	0.25	3.49	3.94	3.13	2.76	1.71
Egypt	1.74	1.95	1.86	2.28	2.52	2.63	2.00
Iran	1.53	2.24	2.80	3.45	2.58	2.88	1.73
Iraq	2.35	2.49	2.89	2.69	3.32	3.15	2.88
Jordan	6.52	5.85	1.69	4.13	6.43	3.00	2.45
Lebanon	1.38	1.80	0.76	0.86	3.57	2.47	1.46
Libya	2.20	4.12	4.14	3.34	2.81	2.27	1.58
Morocco	2.31	1.17	3.14	3.00	2.72	2.21	1.55
Syria	1.80	2.66	2.78	3.47	4.07	3.55	2.59
Tunisia	1.12	0.64	3.30	2.72	2.62	2.14	1.06
West Bank and Gaza	1.52	0.23	1.95	4.21	4.48	4.18	3.75
Yemen	1.14	1.05	2.00	3.70	4.53	3.81	3.77
GCC[a]	**2.24**	**3.84**	**7.00**	**5.45**	**3.38**	**2.34**	**2.00**
Bahrain	2.57	3.09	7.76	4.00	3.26	2.09	1.35
Kuwait	6.86	7.11	6.64	4.70	2.73	2.84	1.15
Oman	0.46	1.97	6.58	5.34	4.92	2.09	1.84
Qatar	10.19	10.21	7.25	6.32	8.58	0.66	0.11
Saudi Arabia	2.03	3.17	5.81	6.30	2.35	2.55	2.56
United Arab Emirates	1.77	14.20	17.48	1.26	8.02	1.48	0.07

Note: Averages are weighted.
[a] Includes nonnationals.
Source: Appendix table A.5.

TABLE A.9

Female Labor Force Growth

(annual percent change)

Country	1950–1960	1960–1970	1970–1980	1980–1990	1990–2000	2000–2010	2010–2020
MENA	**2.37**	**2.82**	**3.77**	**3.94**	**5.29**	**4.84**	**2.96**
Non-GCC	**2.35**	**2.77**	**3.61**	**3.61**	**5.18**	**4.74**	**2.82**
Algeria	2.19	2.35	4.14	3.79	7.49	6.00	3.36
Egypt	2.42	2.75	3.06	3.21	4.39	3.98	2.42
Iran	1.98	2.75	3.58	4.35	6.25	6.26	3.10
Iraq	2.80	2.94	3.23	2.45	5.92	5.26	4.01
Jordan	7.37	6.28	2.62	6.07	10.32	5.65	3.82
Lebanon	4.12	5.92	3.46	3.34	4.92	3.55	1.58
Libya	2.44	2.43	5.87	3.33	5.98	4.47	1.96
Morocco	2.85	2.76	4.12	3.64	3.43	2.72	1.67
Syria	2.32	3.02	3.49	4.18	5.91	5.08	3.15
Tunisia	1.70	3.18	5.97	2.95	3.92	3.15	1.19
West Bank and Gaza	1.62	0.49	2.42	4.16	8.00	7.58	5.77
Yemen	1.56	1.98	2.50	3.73	4.99	4.51	4.11
GCC[a]	**4.57**	**7.74**	**11.38**	**11.14**	**6.86**	**6.12**	**4.42**
Bahrain	5.34	4.53	16.74	9.12	5.79	4.15	2.80
Kuwait	8.18	14.79	11.96	11.52	3.24	4.45	2.32
Oman	6.22	5.53	6.18	9.35	8.08	8.06	5.38
Qatar	13.46	8.98	15.46	14.72	6.15	3.83	3.30
Saudi Arabia	3.68	6.77	10.77	10.61	7.97	6.68	4.92
United Arab Emirates	10.46	11.03	19.57	14.59	5.90	4.20	2.53

Note: Averages are weighted.
[a] Includes nonnationals.
Source: Appendix table A.6.

Bibliography

The word *processed* describes informally reproduced works that may not be commonly available through libraries.

Abdel-Fadil, Mahmoud. 2002. "A Survey of the Basic Features and Problems of the Informal Small and Micro-Enterprises in the Arab Region." Paper prepared for Forum Euro–Mediterranéen des Instituts Economiques (FEMISE). Processed.

Abrahart, Alan, Iqbal Kaur, and Zafiris Tzannatos. 2002. "Government Employment and Active Labor Market Policies in MENA in a Comparative International Context." In H. Handoussa and Z. Tzannatos, eds., *Employment Creation and Social Protection in the Middle East and North Africa.* Cairo: American University in Cairo Press.

AbuKhalil, As'ad. 2003. "States and Their Roles in Middle Eastern Economies." Washington, D.C., World Bank. Processed.

Adams, Richard. 2003a. "Rural Labor Markets in the Middle East and North Africa." Washington, D.C., World Bank. Processed.

———. 2003b. "Trends in Urban and Rural Poverty and Inequality in the Middle East and North Africa, 1980–2000." Washington, D.C., World Bank. Processed.

Adams, Richard, and John Page. 2001. "Holding the Line: Poverty Reduction in the Middle East and North Africa, 1970–2000." Paper presented at the Annual Conference of the Economic Research Forum for the Arab Countries, Iran and Turkey, Manama, October 25–27.

ADB (Asian Development Bank). 2001. *Key Indicators 2001.* Manila.

AFESD (Arab Fund for Economic and Social Development). 2002. "Investment in Human Capital and Labour Markets in the Arab Countries." Paper presented at the Seminar on Labour Markets and Unemployment in the Arab Countries, Abu Dhabi, November 2–3.

Agénor, Pierre-Richard, and Karim El Aynaoui. 2003. "Labor Market Policies and Unemployment in Morocco: A Quantitative Analysis." Policy Research Working Paper 3091. World Bank, Washington, D.C.

Agénor, Pierre-Richard, and Peter J. Montiel. 2001. "Sequencing and Speed of Reforms." World Bank Institute Course Material on Development Macroeconomics. World Bank, Washington, D.C.

Agénor, Pierre-Richard, Alejandro Izquierdo, and Hippolyte Fofack. 2003. "IMMPA: A Quantitative Macroeconomic Framework for the Analysis of Poverty Reduction Strategies." World Bank, Washington, D.C.

Agénor, Pierre-Richard, Reynaldo Fernandes, Eduardo Haddad, and Dominique van der Mensbrugghe. 2003a. "Analyzing the Impact of Adjustment Policies on the Poor: An IMMPA for Brazil." World Bank, Washington, D.C.

Agénor, Pierre-Richard, Mustapha K. Nabli, Tarik M. Yousef, and Henning T. Jensen. 2003b. "Labor Market Reforms, Growth, and Unemployment in Labor-Exporting MENA Countries." World Bank, Washington, D.C. Processed.

Aidt, Toke, and Zafiris Tzannatos. 2002. *Unions and Collective Bargaining: Economic Effects in a Global Environment.* Washington, D.C.: World Bank.

Al-Hamad, Abdlatif. 2000. "The Dilemmas of Development in the Arab World." Paper presented at Arab World 2000: Transformations and Challenges, Center for Contemporary Arab Studies, Georgetown University, Washington, D.C., March 30–31.

Ali, Ali G. A., and Ibrahim A. Elbadawi. 2002. "Poverty and the Labor Market in the Arab World: The Role of Inequality and Growth." In H. Handoussa and Z. Tzannatos, eds., *Employment Creation and Social Protection in the Middle East and North Africa.* Cairo: American University in Cairo Press.

Al-Qudsi, Sulayman. 1998. "The Demand for Children in Arab Countries: Evidence from Panel and Count Data Models." *Journal of Population Economics* 11(3): 435–52.

Anderson, Lisa. 1986. *The State and Social Transformation in Tunisia and Libya, 1830–1980.* Princeton: Princeton University Press.

———, ed. 1999. *Transitions to Democracy.* New York: Columbia University Press.

Arab Republic of Egypt, CAPMAS (Central Agency for Population Mobilization and Statistics). 1986. *Egypt Labor Force Sample Survey* (LFSS). Cairo.

———. 1988. *Egypt Labor Force Sample Survey* (LFSS). Cairo.

———. 1998. *Egypt Labor Market Survey* (ELMS). Cairo.

Assaad, Ragui. 1996. "Do Workers Pay for Social Protection? An Analysis of Wage Differentials in the Egyptian Private Sector." Working Paper 9610. Economic Research Forum, Cairo.

———. 1997. "The Effects of Public Sector Hiring and Compensation Policies on the Egyptian Labor Market." *World Bank Economic Review* 11(1): 85–118.

———. 2002a. "Informalization and De-Feminization: Explaining the Unusual Pattern in Egypt." Paper presented at the Conference on Rethinking Labor Market Informalization: Precarious Jobs, Poverty, and Social Protection, Cornell University, Ithaca, N.Y., October 18–19.

———. 2002b. "The Transformation of the Egyptian Labor Market: 1988–98." In Ragui Assaad, ed., *The Egyptian Labor Market in an Era of Reform.* Cairo: American University in Cairo Press.

Assaad, Ragui, and Melanie Arntz. 2002. "Constrained Geographical Mobility and Gendered Labor Market Outcomes under Structural Adjustment: Evidence from Egypt." Humphrey Institute of Public Affairs Working Paper. Minneapolis, Minn. Processed.

Assaad, Ragui, and Fatma El-Hamidi. 2001. "Is All Work the Same? A Comparison of the Determinants of Female Participation and Hours of Work in Various Employment States in Egypt." In E. Mine Cinar, ed., *The Economics of Women and Work in the Middle East and North Africa*. Amsterdam: JAI Press.

—————. 2002. "Female Labor Supply in Egypt: Participation and Hours of Work." In I. Sirageldin, ed., *Human Capital: Population Economics in the Middle East*. Cairo: American University in Cairo Press.

Assaf, Nabila, and Najy Benhassine. 2003. "Private Sector Employment and the Investment Climate in the MENA Region: Outlook and Recent Trends." World Bank. Processed.

Ayubi, Nazih. 1995. *Over-stating the Arab State*. London: I. B. Tauris.

Banerji, Arup, and Caralee McLiesh. 2002. "Governance and the Investment Climate in Yemen." Working Paper 28 (September). World Bank, Washington, D.C.

Barr, Nicholas, ed. 1994. *Labor Markets and Social Policy in Central and Eastern Europe: The Transition and Beyond*. New York: Oxford University Press.

Barro, Robert J., and Jong-Wha Lee. 2000. "International Data on Educational Attainment: Updates and Implications." Center for International Development (CID) Working Paper 42 (April). Harvard University, Boston.

Bayat, Asef. 2000. "Social Movements, Activism, and Social Development in the Middle East." Civil Society and Social Movements Programme Paper 3 (November). United Nations, New York.

Beblawi, Hazem, and Giacomo Luciani, eds. 1987. *The Rentier State*. London: Croom Helm.

Behrman, Jere R., Suzanne Duryea, and Miguel Székely. 1999. "Decomposing Fertility Differences across World Regions and over Time: Is Improved Health More Important than Women's Schooling?" Working Paper 406. Inter-American Development Bank, Washington, D.C.

Beinin, Joel. 2003. "Labor, the State, and the Social Contract in Non-Oil Exporting Countries of the Middle East and North Africa." World Bank, Washington, D.C. Processed.

Bellin, Eva. 2004. "The Robustness of Authoritarianism in the Middle East: Exceptionalism in Comparative Perspective." *Comparative Politics* 36(2): 139–57.

Berryman, Sue. 1997. "Preparing for the Global Economy: Focus on Quality." Human Resources and Social Development Division, Middle East and North Africa Region. World Bank, Washington, D.C.

Betcherman, Gordon, Amy Luinstra, and Makoto Ogawa. 2001. "Labor Market Regulation: International Experience in Promoting Employment and Social Protection." Social Protection Discussion Paper 128. World Bank, Washington, D.C.

Betcherman, Gordon, Karina Olivas, and Amit Dar. 2003. "Impacts of Active Labor Market Programs: New Evidence from Evaluations with Particular Attention to Developing and Transition Countries." Social Protection Unit Working Paper. World Bank, Washington, D.C. Processed.

Bianchi, Robert. 1989. *Unruly Corporatism: Associational Life in Twentieth-Century Egypt.* New York: Oxford University Press.

Billeh, Victor. 2002. "Matching Education to Demand for Labor in the MENA Region." In Heba Handoussa and Zafiris Tzannatos, eds., *Employment Creation and Social Protection in the Middle East and North Africa.* Cairo: American University in Cairo Press.

Birks, J. S., and S. A. Sinclair. 1980. *International Migration and Development in the Arab Region.* Geneva: International Labour Organisation.

Bloom, David E., and Jeffrey G. Williamson. 1998. "Demographic Transitions and Economic Miracles in Emerging Asia." *World Bank Economic Review* 12(3): 419–55.

Bongaarts, John, and Rodolfo A. Bulatao. 1999. "Completing the Demographic Transition." Working Paper 125. Population Council, New York.

Brandsma, Judith, and Laurence Hart. 2002. *Making Microfinance Work Better in the Middle East and North Africa.* Washington, D.C.: World Bank.

Brown, Nathan J. 1997. *The Rule of Law in the Arab World: Courts in Egypt and the Gulf.* New York: Cambridge University Press.

Brynen, Rex, Bahgat Korany, and Paul Noble, eds. 1995. *Political Liberalization and Democratization in the Arab World*. Boulder, Colo.: Lynne Rienner.

CAWTAR (Center of Arab Women for Training and Research). 2001. *Arab Women's Development Report*. Tunis, Tunisia.

Central Statistical Organization. 1999. *Yemen National Poverty Phenomenon Survey* (NPPS). Sana'a, Republic of Yemen.

Charmes, Jacques. 1999. "Informal Sector, Poverty, and Gender: A Review of Empirical Evidence." Background paper for the *World Development Report 2001*. World Bank, Washington, D.C. Processed.

Chaudhry, Kiren A. 1997. *The Price of Wealth: Economics and Institutions in the Middle East*. Ithaca, N.Y.: Cornell University Press.

Coe, David T., and Dennis J. Snower. 1997. "Policy Complementarities: The Case for Fundamental Labor Market Reform." International Monetary Fund Staff Paper 44 (March): 1–35.

Collier, Ruth B., and David Collier. 1991. *Shaping the Political Arena: Critical Junctures, the Labor Movement, and Regime Dynamics in Latin America*. Princeton, N.J.: Princeton University Press.

Corden, W. M. 1984. "Booming Sector and Dutch Disease Economics: Survey and Consolidation." *Oxford Economic Papers* 36(3): 359–80.

Courbage, Youssef. 1999. *New Demographic Scenarios in the Mediterranean Region*. Paris: Institut National d'Études Démographiques.

Cowan, Laing G. 1958. *The Economic Development of Morocco*. Santa Monica, Calif.: Rand.

Dasgupta, Dipak, Jennifer Keller, and Thirumalai G. Srinivasan. 2002. "Reform and Elusive Growth in the Middle East: What Has Happened in the 1990s?" MENA Working Paper 25. World Bank, Washington, D.C.

Davis, Jeffrey, Rolando Ossowski, James Daniel, and Steven Barnett. 2001. "Stabilization and Savings Funds for Nonrenewable Resources." Occasional Paper 205. International Monetary Fund, Washington, D.C.

De Ferranti, David, Guillermo E. Perry, Indermit Gill, José Luis Guasch, William F. Maloney, Carolina Sánchez-Páramo, and Norbert Schady. 2003. *Closing the Gap in Education and Technology*. Washington, D.C.: World Bank.

Desai, Raj, Anders Olofsgård, and Tarik M. Yousef. 2003. "The Cost of Legitimacy: Welfare and Political Liberalization in Authoritarian Regimes." World Bank, Washington, D.C. Processed.

Dhonte, Pierre, Rina Bhatacharya, and Tarik M. Yousef. 2001. "The New Demography of the Middle East: Implications for Growth, Employment, and Housing." In Zubair Iqbal, ed., *Macroeconomic Issues and Policies in the Middle East and North Africa*. Washington, D.C.: International Monetary Fund.

Diwan, Ishac, and Maurice Girgis. 2002. "Labor Force and Development in Saudi Arabia." Prepared for the symposium on the Future Vision for the Saudi Economy, Riyadh, October 19–23.

Diwan, Ishac, Mustapha K. Nabli, Adama Coulibaly, and Sara Johansson. 2003. "Economic Reforms and People Mobility for a More Effective EU-MED Partnership." In C. Mallat, ed., *Union Européenne et Moyen Orient, Etat des Lieux*. Beirut: Presses de Université Saint-Joseph.

Djibouti Bureau of Statistics. 1996. *Enquete Djiboutienne Aupres des Menages* (EDAM). Djibouti.

Dollar, David, and Aart Kraay. 2001. "Trade, Growth and Poverty." Working Paper 2615. World Bank, Washington, D.C.

Dömeland, Dörte, and Indermit S. Gill. 2002. "Labor Market Reform in Latin America during the 1990s." In Indermit S. Gill, Claudio E. Montenegro, and Dörte Dömeland, eds., *Crafting Labor Policy: Techniques and Lessons from Latin America*. Washington, D.C.: World Bank.

Duryea, Suzanne, and Miguel Székely. 1998. "Labor Markets in Latin America: A Supply-Side Story." Working Paper 374 (September). Inter-American Development Bank, Washington, D.C.

Dyer, Paul, and Tarik M. Yousef. 2003. "The Fertility Transition in MENA: Causes and Consequences, 1950–2000." World Bank, Washington, D.C. Processed.

Easterly, William. 2000. "The Middle Class Consensus and Economic Development." Working Paper 2346. World Bank, Washington, D.C.

ECLAC (Economic Commission for Latin America and the Caribbean). 2001. ECLAC Database. Santiago.

Egypt, Arab Republic of. Various years. *Annuaire Statistique de l'Egypte*. Cairo.

Elbadawi, Ibrahim A. 2002. "Reviving Growth in the Arab World." Working Paper 206. Arab Planning Institute, Safat, Kuwait.

El-Hamidi, Fatma. 2002. "The Impact of Minimum Wages on Wage Inequality and Employment in the Formal and Informal Sector in Costa Rica." In R. B. Freeman, ed., *Inequality around the World*. New York: McMillan Press.

El-Mikawy, Noha, and Marsha P. Posusney. 2002. "Labor Representation in the Age of Globalization: Trends and Issues in Non-Oil-Based Arab Economies." In Heba Handoussa and Zafiris Tzannatos, eds., *Employment Creation and Social Protection in the Middle East and North Africa*. Cairo: American University in Cairo Press.

ESCWA (Economic and Social Commission for Western Asia). 1994. *Statistical Abstract of the ESCWA Region*, 14th ed. Beirut: United Nations.

———. 2001. "Economic Diversification in the Arab World." United Nations, Beirut.

———. 2002. "Survey of Economic and Social Developments in the ESCWA Region, 2000–2001." United Nations, Beirut.

Esposito, John L., and John O. Voll. 1996. *Islam and Democracy*. New York: Oxford University Press.

Fargues, Philippe. 2003. "Women in Arab Countries: Challenging the Patriarchal System?" Population and Societies Working Paper 387. Institut National d'Études Démographiques, Paris.

Fawzy, Samiha. 1999. "The Business Environment in Egypt." In Samiha Fawzy and Ahmed Galal, eds., *Partners for Development: New Roles for Government and Private Sector in the Middle East and North Africa*. Washington, D.C.: World Bank.

————. 2002. "Investment Policies and Unemployment in Egypt." Working Paper 68. Egyptian Center for Economic Studies, Cairo.

Fergany, Nader. 2001. "Aspects of Labor Migration and Unemployment in the Arab Region." Almishkat Center for Research, Cairo.

Forteza, Alvaro, and Martín Rama. 2001. "Labor Market Rigidity and the Success of Economic Reforms across More than 100 Countries." Policy Research Working Paper 2521 (January). World Bank, Washington, D.C.

Freeman, Richard B. 1993. "Labor Market Institutions and Policies: Help or Hindrance to Economic Adjustment?" Proceedings of the World Bank Annual Conference on Development Economics, 1992. Supplement to the *World Bank Economic Review* and the *World Bank Research Observer*.

Galal, Ahmed. 2002. "The Paradox of Education and Unemployment in Egypt." Paper presented at the Egyptian Center for Economic Studies Conference on Employment and Unemployment, Cairo, January 13–14.

Gill, Indermit S., Claudio E. Montenegro, and Dörte Dömeland, eds. 2002. *Crafting Labor Policy: Techniques and Lessons from Latin America*. Washington, D.C.: World Bank.

Girgis, Maurice. 2002. "National versus Migrant Workers in the GCC: Coping with Change." In Heba Handoussa and Zafiris Tzannatos, eds., *Employment Creation and Social Protection in the Middle East and North Africa*. Cairo: American University in Cairo Press.

Girgis, Maurice, Faris Hadad-Zervos, and Adama Coulibaly. 2003. "A Strategy for Sustainable Employment for GCC Nationals." World Bank, Washington, D.C. Processed.

Golladay, Frederick L., Sue E. Berryman, Jon Avins, and Laurence Wolff. 1998. "A Human Capital Strategy for Competing in World Markets." In Nemat Shafik, ed., *Prospects for Middle Eastern and North African Economies: From Boom to Bust and Back?* New York: St. Martin's Press.

Grunwald, Kurt, and Joachim O. Ronall. 1960. *Industrialization in the Middle East*. New York: Council for Middle Eastern Affairs Press.

Haggard, Stephan, and Robert R. Kaufman. 1995. *The Political Economy of Democratic Transitions*. Princeton, N.J.: Princeton University Press.

Handoussa, Heba, and Gillian Potter. 1992. "Egypt's Informal Sector: Engine of Growth?" Paper presented at Middle East Studies Association (MESA) Conference, Portland, Oregon, October 28–31.

Harik, Iliya. 1992. "Privatization: The Issue, the Prospects, and the Fears." In Iliya Harik and Denis J. Sullivan, eds., *Privatization and Liberalization in the Middle East*. Bloomington, Ind.: Indiana University Press.

Harik, Iliya, and Denis J. Sullivan. 1992. *Privatization and Liberalization in the Middle East*. Bloomington, Ind.: Indiana University Press.

Henry, Clement M., and Robert Springborg. 2001. *Globalization and the Politics of Development in the Middle East*. Cambridge, U.K.: Cambridge University Press.

Heydemann, Steven. 2002. "Why Is the Middle East Still Authoritarian? Social Pacts and Prospects for Democratization in the Middle East." Georgetown University, Washington, D.C. Processed.

Heyneman, Stephen. 1997. "The Quality of Education in the Middle East and North Africa." *International Journal of Educational Development* 17(4): 449–66.

ILO (International Labour Organisation). 1996. *Economically Active Population, 1950–2010*, 4th ed. Geneva.

———. 2002. "Key Indicators of the Labor Market 2001–2002, Including First Update." Geneva.

———. 2003a. *Global Employment Trends*. Geneva.

———. 2003b. LABORSTA Database. Geneva.

IMF (International Monetary Fund). 1997. "Financial Systems and Labor Markets in the Gulf Cooperation Council Countries." Middle Eastern Department. Washington, D.C.

———. 2003. *International Financial Statistics* (IFS). Washington, D.C.

INS (Institut National de la Statistique). 1997. *Tunisian Annual Employment Survey* (AES). Tunis.

———. 2001. *Tunisian Annual Employment Survey* (AES). Tunis.

International Food Policy Research Institute. 1997. *Egypt Integrated Household Survey* (EIHS). Washington, D.C.

International Labour Office. 1960. *Labour Survey of North Africa*. Geneva.

Issawi, Charles. 1982. *An Economic History of the Middle East and North Africa*. New York: Columbia University Press.

Joekes, Susan. 1995. *Trade-Related Employment for Women in Industry and Services in Developing Countries*. Geneva: United Nations Research Institute for Social Development.

Johansson, Sara, and Carlos Silva-Jauregui. 2003. "Migration and Trade: Problems or Solutions for Unemployment in MENA?" World Bank, Washington, D.C. Processed.

Johansson, Sara, Carlos Silva-Jauregui, and Tarik M. Yousef. 2003. "Is Economic Volatility in the Middle East Really High? A Revised View." World Bank, Washington, D.C. Processed.

Jordan Department of Statistics. 1997. *Jordan Household Income and Expenditure Survey* (JHIES). Amman.

———. 2001. *Annual Report of Employment and Unemployment Survey* (AREUS). 2001. Amman.

Karshenas, Massoud, and Valentine Moghadam. 2002. "Female Labor Force Participation and Economic Adjustment in the MENA Region." In E. Mine Cinar, ed., *The Economics of Women and Work in the Middle East and North Africa*. Amsterdam: JAI Press.

Kawar, Mary. 2000. "Gender and Generation in Household Labor Supply in Jordan." MEAwards Working Paper 43. Population Council, Cairo.

Kerr, Malcolm. H. 1971. *The Arab Cold War: Gamal 'Abd al-Nasir and His Rivals*. New York: Oxford University Press.

Khalidi, Rashid. 2004. "Reform and Democracy in the Arab World: Historical Insights." Columbia University. Processed.

Kuwait. 2001. *Kuwait Population Census*. Kuwait City.

Lall, Sanjaya. 2002. "Strengthening Small and Medium Enterprises for International Competitiveness." In Samiha Fawzy, ed., *Globalization and Firm Competitiveness in the Middle East and North Africa*. Washington, D.C.: World Bank.

Layachi, Azzedine, ed. 1998. *Economic Crisis and Political Change in North Africa*. London: Praeger.

Lebanon Ministry of Social Affairs. 1996. *Population and Housing Survey*. Beirut.

Maloney, William F. 1999. "Does Informality Imply Segmentation in Urban Labor Markets? Evidence from Sectoral Transitions in Mexico." *World Bank Economic Review* 13(2): 275–302.

Miles, Rebecca. 2002. "Employment and Unemployment in Jordan: The Importance of the Gender System." *World Development* 30(3): 413–27.

Miller, Stephen M., and Mukti P. Upadhyay. 2000. "The Effects of Openness, Trade Orientation, and Human Capital on Total Factor Productivity." *Journal of Development Economics* 63(2): 399–423.

Moghadam, Valentine. 2002. "Enhancing Women's Economic Participation in the MENA Region." In Heba Handoussa and Zafiris Tzannatos, eds., *Employment Creation and Social Protection in the Middle East and North Africa*. Cairo: American University in Cairo Press.

Moore, Pete, and Bassel F. Salloukh. 2003. "Fiscal Crisis and State–Society Relations in the Arab World: Jordan, Kuwait, and Syria in Comparative Perspective." Paper presented at the Fourth Mediterranean Social and Political Research Meeting, Florence, Italy, March 19–23.

Morocco. 1991. *Morocco Living Standard Survey* (MLSS). Rabat.

———. 1999. *Living Standard Measurement Survey* (LSMS). Rabat.

Mustafa, Mohammad. 2002. "Benchmarking Regulators: Making Telecom Regulators More Effective in the Middle East." World Bank Group Private Sector and Infrastructure Network, Washington, D.C. Processed.

Nabli, Mustapha K., and Jennifer Keller. 2002. "The Macroeconomics of Labor Market Outcomes in MENA over the 1990s: How Growth Has Failed to Keep Pace with a Burgeoning Labor Market." World Bank, Washington, D.C. Processed.

Nabli, Mustapha K., and Marie-Ange Véganzonès-Varoudakis. 2002. "Exchange Rate Regime and Competitiveness of Manufactured Exports." Working Paper 27 (August). World Bank, Washington, D.C.

———. 2003. "Reforms and Growth in MENA Countries: New Empirical Evidence." World Bank, Washington, D.C. Processed.

Niblock, Tim, and Emma Murphy. 1993. *Economic and Political Liberalization in the Middle East*. London: British Academic Press.

Nicoletti, Giuseppe, and Stefano Scarpetta. 2003. "Regulation, Productivity, and Growth: OECD Evidence." Policy Research Working Paper 2944. World Bank, Washington, D.C.

Norton, Augustus Richard. 1994. *Civil Society in the Middle East*, Vol. 1. New York: Brill.

———. 1996. *Civil Society in the Middle East*, Vol. 2. New York: Brill.

O'Donnell, Guillermo, Philippe C. Schmitter, and Laurence Whitehead, eds. 1986. *Transitions from Authoritarian Rule: Prospects for Democracy*. Baltimore, Md.: Johns Hopkins University Press.

OEFRE (Institut für Öffentliches Recht). 2003. International Constitutional Law Database. Available online at http://www.oefre.unibe.ch/law/icl/home.html.

O'Higgins, Niall. 2003. "Trends in the Youth Labour Market in Developing and Transition Countries." Paper prepared for the World Bank Youth Employment Workshop, Washington, D.C., June 2.

Olmsted, Jennifer. 2003. "Reexamining the Fertility Puzzle in MENA." In E. A. Doumato and M. P. Posusney, eds., *Women and Globalization in the Arab Middle East: Gender Economy and Society*. Boulder, Colo.: Lynne Rienner.

Omran, Abdel-Rahim. 1980. *Population in the Arab World: Problems and Prospects*. New York: United Nations Fund for Population Activities.

ONS (Office National des Statistiques). 1990. *Situation de l'emploi*. Algiers: Government of Algeria.

Ozler, Sule. 2000. "Export-Orientation and Female Share of Employment: Evidence from Turkey." *World Development* 28(7): 1239–48.

Page, John. 1998. "From Boom to Bust—and Back? The Crisis of Economic Growth in the Middle East and North Africa." In Nemat Shafik, ed., *Prospects for Middle Eastern and North African Economies: From Boom to Bust and Back?* London and New York: Macmillan and St. Martin's Press.

Palestinian Central Bureau of Statistics. 1999. *West Bank and Gaza Labor Force Survey* (LFS). Ramallah.

Pool, David. 1993. "The Links between Economic and Political Liberalization." In Tim Niblock and Emma Murphy, eds., *Economic and Political Liberalization in the Middle East*. London: British Academic Press.

Posusney, Marsha P. 1997. *Labor and the State in Egypt: Workers, Unions, and Economic Restructuring*. New York: Columbia University Press.

———. 2003. "Globalization and Labor Protection in Oil-Poor Arab Countries: Racing to the Bottom?" *Global Social Policy* 3(3): 267–97.

Pritchett, Lant. 1994. "Desired Fertility and the Impact of Population Policies." *Population and Development Review* 20(1): 1–55.

Przeworski, Adam, and John Sprague. 1986. *Paper Stones: A History of Electoral Socialism*. Chicago: University of Chicago Press.

Radwan, Samir. 2002. "Employment and Unemployment in Egypt: Conventional Problems, Unconventional Remedies." Working Paper 70. Egyptian Center for Economic Studies, Cairo.

Rama, Martín. 1999. "Public Sector Downsizing: An Introduction." *World Bank Economic Review* 13(1): 1–22.

———. 2001. "Globalization, Inequality, and Labor Market Policies." Paper prepared for the European on-line Annual World Bank Conference in Development and Economics, Washington, D.C.

Rama, Martín, and Raquel Artecona. 2000. "A Database of Labor Market Indicators across Countries." World Bank, Washington, D.C.

Rashad, Hoda, and Zeinab Khadr. 2002. "New Challenges in the Demography of the Arab Region." In Ismail Sirageldin, ed., *Human Capital: Population Economics in the Middle East*. Cairo: American University in Cairo Press.

Richards, Alan. 2001. "The Political Economy of Economic Reform in the Middle East: The Challenge to Governance." Paper prepared for "The Future of Middle East Security," RAND, Santa Monica, Calif.

Richards, Alan, and John Waterbury. 1998. *A Political Economy of the Middle East*, 2nd ed. Boulder, Colo.: Westview Press.

Ross, Michael L. 2001. "Does Oil Hinder Democracy?" *World Politics* 53(3): 325–61.

Roudi-Fahimi, Farzaneh. 2001. "Fertility Policies in the Middle East and North Africa." Paper presented at the Second Mediterranean Social and Political Research Meeting, Florence, Italy, March 21–25.

———. 2002. "Iran's Family Planning Program: Responding to a Nation's Needs." MENA Policy Brief. Population Reference Bureau, Washington, D.C.

Rueschemeyer, Dietrich, Evelyne Huber Stephens, and John D. Stephens. 1992. *Capitalist Development and Democracy*. Chicago: University of Chicago Press.

Ruppert, Elizabeth, 1999a. "The Algerian Retrenchment System: A Financial and Economic Evaluation." *World Bank Economic Review* 13(1): 155–83.

———. 1999b. "Managing Foreign Labor in Singapore and Malaysia: Are There Lessons for GCC Countries?" Working Paper 2053. World Bank, Washington, D.C.

Ruppert Bulmer, Elizabeth. 2000. "Labor Market Trends in Jordan and the Links to Growth." World Bank, Washington, D.C. Processed.

————. 2002. "The Public Sector as Dominant Employer in MENA." World Bank, Washington, D.C. Processed.

————. 2003. "The Impact of Israeli Border Policy on the Palestinian Labor Market." *Economic Development and Cultural Change* 51(3): 657–76.

Sachs, Jeffrey D., and Andrew M. Warner. 1997. "Sources of Slow Growth in African Economies." *Journal of African Economies* 6(3): 335–76.

Said, Mona. 2001. "Public Sector Employment and Labor Markets in Arab Countries: Recent Developments and Policy Implications." In Djavad Salehi-Eshfahani, ed., *Labor and Human Capital in the Middle East*. Reading, U.K.: Ithaca Press.

————. 2002. "A Decade of Rising Wage Inequality? Gender, Occupation, and Public–Private Issues in the Egyptian Wage Structure: 1988–98." In Ragui Assaad, ed., *The Egyptian Labor Market in an Era of Reform*. Cairo: American University in Cairo Press.

Salamé, Ghassan, ed. 1987. *Foundations of the Arab State*. London: Croom Helm.

————. 1994. *Democracy without Democrats? The Renewal of Politics in the Muslim World*. London: I. B. Tauris.

Schamis, Hector E. 1999. "Distributional Coalitions and the Politics of Economic Reform in Latin America." *World Politics* 51(1): 236–68.

Schiavo-Campo, Salvatore, Giulio de Tommaso, and Amitabha Mukherjee. 2003. "An International Statistical Survey of Government Employment and Wages." Policy Research Working Paper 1806. World Bank, Washington, D.C.

Schiff, Maurice W. 1996. "South–North Migration and Trade: A Survey." Policy Research Working Paper 1696. World Bank, Washington, D.C.

Schmitter, Philippe C., and Carsten Q. Schneider. 2003. "The Liberalization of Autocracy and the Consolidation of Democracy: Exploring a Cross-Regional Time-Series Data Set." Paper presented at the Annual Meeting of the American Political Science Association, Philadelphia, August 28–31.

Shaban, Radwan A., Ragui Assaad, and Sulayman Al-Qudsi. 2001. "Employment Experience in the Middle East and North Africa." In Djavad Salehi-Eshfahani, ed., *Labor and Human Capital in the Middle East*. Reading, U.K.: Ithaca Press.

Silva, Eduardo. 1993. "Capitalist Coalitions, the State, and Neoliberal Economic Restructuring in Chile, 1973–1988." *World Politics* 45(4): 526–59.

Singerman, Diane, and Barbara Ibrahim. 2001. "The Cost of Marriage in Egypt: A Hidden Variable in the New Arab Demography." In Nicholas S. Hopkins, ed., *The New Arab Family*. Cairo: American University in Cairo Press.

Smith, Benjamin. 2004. "Oil Wealth and Regime Survival in the Developing World, 1960–1999." *American Journal of Political Science* 48(2), April 2004.

Standing, Guy. 1999. "Global Feminization through Flexible Labor: A Theme Revisited." *World Development* 27(3): 583–602.

Stanton Russell, Sharon. 1992. "International Migration and Political Turmoil in the Middle East." *Population and Development Review* 18(4): 719–27.

Statistical Center of Iran. 2000. *Household Expenditure and Income Survey (HEIS)*. Tehran.

Tessler, Mark. 2002. "Islam and Democracy in the Middle East: The Impact of Religious Orientations on Attitudes toward Democracy in Four Arab Countries." *Comparative Politics* 34(2): 337–54.

Thompson, Elizabeth. 2000. "The Climax and Crisis of the Colonial Welfare State in Syria and Lebanon during World War II." In Steven Heydemann, ed., *War, Institutions, and Social Change in the Middle East*. Berkeley, Calif.: University of California Press.

Tzannatos, Zafiris. 2002. "Social Protection in the Middle East and North Africa: A Review." In Heba Handoussa and Zafiris Tzannatos, eds., *Employment Creation and Social Protection in the Middle East and North Africa*. Cairo: American University in Cairo Press.

UNCTAD (United Nations Conference on Trade and Development). 2002. UNCTAD FDI Database. United Nations, New York.

UNDP (United Nations Development Programme). 2002. *Arab Human Development Report*. New York: United Nations.

————. 2003. *Arab Human Development Report*. New York: United Nations.

UNIDO (United Nations Industrial Development Organization). 2002. UNIDO Database. United Nations, New York.

United Nations. 1949. "Final Report of the United Nations Economic Survey Mission for the Middle East." United Nations, Lake Success, New York.

————. 1993. *The Sex and Age Distribution of the World Populations*. New York: United Nations.

————. 2002. COMTRADE Database. New York.

————. 2003. "Fertility, Contraception and Population Policies." United Nations, New York.

United Nations Population Prospects. 2002. *World Population Projections to 2150*. New York: United Nations.

————. 2003. *World Population Prospects: The 2002 Revision*. New York: United Nations.

Vandewalle, Dirk. 2003. "Social Contracts, Institutional Development, and Economic Growth and Reform in Middle East Oil Exporters." World Bank, Washington, D.C. Processed.

Vitalis, Robert, and Steven Heydemann. 2000. "War, Keynesianism, and Colonialism: Explaining State–Market Relations in the Postwar Middle East." In Steven Heydemann, ed., *War, Institutions, and Social Change in the Middle East*. Berkeley, Calif.: University of California Press.

Wahba, Jackline. 2002. "Formal Testing of Informalization of Labor in Egypt." World Bank, Washington, D.C. Processed.

Wahba, Jackline, and May Mokhtar. 2002. "Informalization of Labor in Egypt." In Ragui Assaad, ed., *The Labor Market in a Reforming Economy: Egypt in the 1990s*. Cairo: American University in Cairo Press.

Waldner, David. 1999. *State Building and Late Development*. Ithaca, N.Y.: Cornell University Press.

Waterbury, John. 1998. "The State and Economic Transition in the Middle East and North Africa." In Nemat Shafiq, ed., *Prospects for Middle Eastern and North African Economies: From Boom to Bust and Back?* London: MacMillan.

Williamson, Jeffrey G., and Tarik M. Yousef. 2003. "Demographic Transitions and Economic Performance in the Middle East and North Africa." In Ismail Sirageld, ed., *Human Capital: Population Economics in the Middle East*. Cairo: American University in Cairo Press.

World Bank. 1952. *The Economic Development of Iraq: Report of a Mission Organized by the International Bank for Reconstruction and Development at the Request of the Government of Iraq*. Baltimore, Md.: Johns Hopkins University Press.

———. 1955. *The Economic Development of Syria*. Baltimore, Md.: Johns Hopkins University Press.

———. 1995a. *Claiming the Future: Choosing Prosperity in the Middle East and North Africa*. Washington, D.C.

———. 1995b. *Will Arab Workers Prosper or Be Left Out in the Twenty-First Century?* Regional Perspectives on World Development Report. Washington, D.C.

———. 1995c. *World Development Report 1995: Workers in an Integrating World*. Washington, D.C.

———. 2002a. *Global Development Finance*. Washington, D.C.

———. 2002b. *Globalization, Growth and Poverty: Building an Inclusive World Economy*. Washington, D.C.: World Bank and Oxford University Press.

———. 2002c. *Reducing Vulnerability and Increasing Opportunity: Social Protection in the Middle East and North Africa*. Washington, D.C.

———. 2002d. *Transition: The First Ten Years: Analysis and Lessons for Eastern Europe and the Former Soviet Union*. Washington, D.C.

———. 2002e. *World Development Indicators*. Washington, D.C.

———. 2003a. *Better Governance for Development in the Middle East and North Africa: Enhancing Inclusiveness and Accountability*. Washington, D.C.

———. 2003b. Doing Business Database. Washington, D.C.

———. 2003c. *Gender and Development in the Middle East and North Africa: Women in the Public Sphere*. Washington, D.C.

———. 2003d. "Iran—Medium Term Framework for Transition: Converting Oil Wealth into Development." MNSED Report 25848 (April). Washington, D.C.

———. 2003e. "Republic of Tunisia Employment Strategy." Middle East and North Africa Social and Human Development, World Bank, Washington, D.C.

———. 2003f. *Trade, Investment, and Development in the Middle East and North Africa—Engaging with the World*. Washington, D.C.

———. 2003g. *World Business Environment Survey*. Washington, D.C.

———. 2003h. *World Development Indicators*. Washington, D.C.

Yousef, Tarik M. 2001. "Demography, the Social Contract, and Intergenerational Relations in the Middle East and North Africa." Paper presented at the Second Mediterranean Social and Political Research Meeting, Florence, Italy, March 21–25.

————. 2002. "Egypt's Growth Performance under Economic Liberal-
ism: A Reassessment with New GDP Estimates, 1886–1945." *Review
of Income and Wealth* 48(4): 561–80.

Zanoyan, Vahan. 1995. "After the Oil Boom: The Holiday Ends in the
Gulf." *Foreign Affairs* 74(6): 2–7.

Zoubir, Yahia H., ed. 1999. *North Africa in Transition: State, Society, and
Economic Transformation in the 1990s.* London: Praeger.

Index

253